# ASIA BOND MONITOR
## NOVEMBER 2022

ASIAN DEVELOPMENT BANK

ADB

© 2022 Asian Development Bank
6 ADB Avenue, Mandaluyong City, 1550 Metro Manila, Philippines
Tel +63 2 8632 4444; Fax +63 2 8636 2444
www.adb.org

Some rights reserved. Published in 2022.

ISBN 978-92-9269-859-1 (print); 978-92-9269-860-7 (electronic); 978-92-9269-861-4 (ebook)
ISSN 2219-1518 (print), 2219-1526 (electronic)
Publication Stock No. TCS220523-2
DOI: http://dx.doi.org/10.22617/TCS220523-2

The views expressed in this publication are those of the authors and do not necessarily reflect the views and policies of the Asian Development Bank (ADB) or its Board of Governors or the governments they represent.

ADB does not guarantee the accuracy of the data included in this publication and accepts no responsibility for any consequence of their use. The mention of specific companies or products of manufacturers does not imply that they are endorsed or recommended by ADB in preference to others of a similar nature that are not mentioned.

By making any designation of or reference to a particular territory or geographic area, or by using the term "country" in this document, ADB does not intend to make any judgments as to the legal or other status of any territory or area.

Corrigenda to ADB publications may be found at http://www.adb.org/publications/corrigenda.

Note:
ADB recognizes "China" as the People's Republic of China; "Hong Kong" and "Hongkong" as Hong Kong, China; "Korea" as the Republic of Korea; "Siam" as Thailand; "Vietnam" as Viet Nam; "Russia" as the Russian Federation; "Hanoi" as Ha Noi; and "Saigon" as Ho Chi Minh City.

Cover design by Erickson Mercado.

# Contents

## Emerging East Asian Local Currency Bond Markets: A Regional Update

# Emerging East Asian Local Currency Bond Markets: A Regional Update

# Executive Summary

## Recent Developments in Emerging East Asian Financial Conditions

Emerging East Asia witnessed the accelerating deterioration of financial conditions and rising bond yields between 31 August and 4 November, largely driven by aggressive monetary tightening in major advanced economies.[1] Nearly all major emerging East Asian central banks continued to pursue monetary tightening to combat persistent domestic inflation and the impact of tightening by the United States (US) Federal Reserve.

During the review period from 31 August to 4 November, regional currencies depreciated against the US dollar by a gross-domestic-product-weighted average of 4.2%, equities declined by a market-weighted-average of 7.5%, and risk premiums, as proxied by credit spreads, widened by a gross-domestic-product-weighted average of 28 basis points. Deteriorating financial conditions were much more pronounced during the review period than during any prior months in 2022. The accelerated deterioration in financial conditions followed the release of higher-than-expected August inflation data in the US, which led to market expectations that the Federal Reserve would persist with its aggressive monetary tightening. The Federal Reserve raised its policy rate by 75 basis points in November, and implied that interest rates may rise higher than previously expected.

Aggressive monetary tightening in the US and negative market sentiment also led to portfolio outflows from the region. Regional equity markets recorded aggregate net outflows of USD5.6 billion during the review period. The largest net outflows were observed in the People's Republic of China (PRC), amounting to USD7.8 billion, amid a negative economic outlook due to uncertainties related to pandemic containment measures. Portfolio outflows were also noted in most regional bond markets in September as accelerated US monetary tightening not only subdued investment sentiment toward risky assets but also made yields on regional bonds relatively less attractive.

The risk outlook for regional financial conditions remained tilted to the downside. In the short-term, the region faces a bleak economic outlook and uncertainties over a larger-than-expected slowdown in the PRC, continued global inflationary pressure, aggressive monetary tightening both globally and domestically, and greater-than-expected fallout from the Russian invasion of Ukraine. Over the medium term, during the transition of some regional economies to net-zero emissions, emerging East Asia's financial sector will be challenged by asset vulnerability, especially in high-emitting sectors that could experience higher cash flow uncertainties, increased financing costs, and stranded asset issues.

## Recent Developments in Local Currency Bond Markets in Emerging East Asia

Amid headwinds to the global and regional outlooks, the expansion of emerging East Asia's local currency (LCY) bond market moderated to 2.3% quarter-on-quarter (q-o-q) and 12.5% year-on-year (y-o-y) in the third quarter (Q3) of 2022 from 3.1% q-o-q and 14.0% y-o-y in the second quarter (Q2). The amount of LCY bonds outstanding in emerging East Asia reached USD22.0 trillion at the end of September. Issuance of LCY bonds totaled USD2.2 trillion during Q3 2022, contracting 1.1% q-o-q and rising 5.4% y-o-y, compared with issuance growth of 13.6% q-o-q and 12.1% y-o-y in Q2 2022.

Government bonds continued to dominate emerging East Asia's LCY bond market. At the end of September, outstanding government bonds reached USD14.0 trillion and accounted for 63.6% of the regional bond market's size. During Q3 2022, issuance of government bonds totaled USD1.4 trillion on a contraction of 4.5% q-o-q, as some governments had already fulfilled most of their

---

[1] Emerging East Asia is defined to include member states of the Association of Southeast Asian Nations (ASEAN) plus the People's Republic of China; Hong Kong, China; and the Republic of Korea.

annual financing requirements. Regional corporate bond issuance totaled USD0.8 trillion on growth of 5.7% q-o-q, which was largely driven by Chinese companies (7.2% growth in issuance) taking advantage of monetary easing measures designed to stimulate economic recovery. Corporate bond issuance in member economies of the Association of Southeast Asian Nations (ASEAN) contracted 2.0% q-o-q in Q3 2022 on rising interest rates and a bleak economic outlook.

The dimming economic outlook and monetary tightening in both regional and global markets weighed on ASEAN+3's sustainable bond market in Q3 2022.[2] Sustainable bonds outstanding in ASEAN+3 economies reached USD521.6 billion at the end of September on moderating growth of 1.7% q-o-q versus 5.0% q-o-q in Q2 2022. The region's sustainable bond issuance totaled USD49.8 billion in Q3 2022 on a contraction of 25.3% q-o-q, reversing the 2.6% q-o-q growth posted in Q2 2022. ASEAN+3's sustainable bond market witnessed improved diversification in terms of market profile and bond types. The region's sustainable bond market has significant potential for increased issuance from the public sector, more long-term bonds, and more bonds issued in local currencies.

## Special Topics on Financial Markets

The November 2022 issue of the *Asia Bond Monitor* presents two special sections.

### Special Section 1: Local Currency Bond Market Development and Exchange Rate Volatility

Recent accelerated monetary tightening in the US has led to currency depreciations and capital outflows in emerging markets, highlighting their vulnerability to global shocks. Several studies have linked LCY bond market development and financial stability by addressing financial market structural issues such as the "double mismatch" problem. The research highlighted in this special section provides empirical evidence that, after controlling for economic fundamentals, emerging economies benefit from lower exchange rate volatility during periods of market turmoil when they have a larger LCY bond market, a greater share of LCY bonds in the overall bond market, and relatively more long-term bonds. Emerging

economies should therefore consider designing policies to develop their LCY bond markets to promote financial stability and resiliency in the face of external shocks.

### Special Section 2: Does Regional Trade Integration Automatically Foster Regional Financial Integration? The Case of Regional Comprehensive Economic Partnership

The Regional Comprehensive Economic Partnership (RCEP) free trade agreement among 15 economies in Asia and the Pacific came into effect on 1 January 2022. New empirical analysis explores whether growing regional trade integration within the trading bloc, where 50% of all current trade is intra-RCEP, has also led to greater regional financial integration. The evidence clearly shows that the financial markets of RCEP economies have not yet become more closely integrated with each other. This suggests that financial integration requires institutional efforts such as the ASEAN+3 Bond Market Initiative to standardize regional market practices and enhance financial collaboration.

---

[2]  ASEAN+3 is defined to include member states of the Association of Southeast Asian Nations (ASEAN) plus the People's Republic of China; Hong Kong, China; Japan; and the Republic of Korea.

# Global and Regional Market Developments

**Bond yields rose and financial conditions deteriorated in emerging East Asia on accelerating monetary tightening.**

Government bond yields rose across emerging East Asia during the review period from 31 August to 4 November, largely due to higher bond yields in advanced economies and continued monetary tightening globally. To address financial and price stability concerns, almost all major regional central banks hiked interest rates during the review period, which, in combination with a bleak economic outlook, weighed on domestic financial conditions in the region. During the review period, emerging East Asia's major currencies depreciated against the United States (US) dollar by a gross-domestic-product (GDP)-weighted average of 4.2%, equity markets retreated by a market-weighted average of 7.5%, and risk premiums widened by a GDP-weighted average of 28 basis points (bps) (**Table A**).[1]

Government bond yields in the US and major European markets surged between 31 August and 4 November. The 2-year government bond yield in the US and Germany rose by 117 bps and 93 bps, respectively, following policy rate hikes by their respective central banks (**Table B**). The 10-year government bond yield rose 97 bps and 75 bps in the US and Germany, respectively, on higher policy rates and persistent inflation. In the United Kingdom, 10-year bond yields surged by 74 bps following the 23 September announcement of a series of tax cuts, which led to market panic over concern that government indebtedness would sharply increase. This was further exacerbated when bond price declines triggered margin calls among pension funds, forcing additional bond sales. The Bank of England was forced to initiate a temporary bond-buying program on 28 September. The Bank of England later raised by 75 bps its policy rate on 3 November.

### Table A: Changes in Financial Conditions in Major Advanced Economies and Select Emerging East Asian Markets

| | 2-Year Government Bond (bps) | 10-Year Government Bond (bps) | 5-Year Credit Default Swap Spread (bps) | Equity Index (%) | FX Rate (%) |
|---|---|---|---|---|---|
| **Major Advanced Economies** | | | | | |
| United States | 117 | 97 | – | (4.7) | – |
| United Kingdom | 5 | 74 | 5 | 0.7 | (2.1) |
| Japan | 4 | 3 | 13 | (2.5) | (5.2) |
| Germany | 93 | 75 | 8 | 4.9 | (1.0) |
| **Select Emerging East Asian Markets** | | | | | |
| China, People's Rep. of | 2 | 6 | 28 | (4.1) | (4.1) |
| Hong Kong, China | 140 | 100 | – | (19.0) | (0.005) |
| Indonesia | 123 | 34 | 14 | (1.9) | (5.7) |
| Korea, Rep. of | 48 | 48 | 41 | (5.0) | (5.7) |
| Malaysia | 31 | 40 | 20 | (4.9) | (5.7) |
| Philippines | 132 | 136 | 17 | (6.0) | (4.1) |
| Singapore | 38 | 51 | – | (2.8) | (0.7) |
| Thailand | 20 | 67 | 25 | (0.8) | (2.9) |
| Viet Nam | 172 | 139 | 18 | (22.1) | (5.7) |

( ) = negative, – = not available, bps = basis points, FX = foreign exchange.
Notes:
1. Data reflect changes between 31 August 2022 and 4 November 2022.
2. A positive (negative) value for the FX rate indicates the appreciation (depreciation) of the local currency against the United States dollar.
Source: *AsianBondsOnline* computations based on Bloomberg LP data.

---

[1] Emerging East Asia is defined to include member states of the Association of Southeast Asian Nations (ASEAN) plus the People's Republic of China; Hong Kong, China; and the Republic of Korea.

**Table B: Changes in Monetary Stances in Major Advanced Economies and Select Emerging East Asian Markets**

| Economy | Policy Rate 5-Nov-2021 (%) | Rate Change (%) | | | | | | | | | | | | | Policy Rate 4-Nov-2022 (%) | Change in Policy Rates (basis points) |
|---|---|---|---|---|---|---|---|---|---|---|---|---|---|---|---|---|
| | | Nov-2021 | Dec-2021 | Jan-2022 | Feb-2022 | Mar-2022 | Apr-2022 | May-2022 | Jun-2022 | Jul-2022 | Aug-2022 | Sep-2022 | Oct-2022 | Nov-2022 | | |
| United States | 0.25 | | | | | ↑0.25 | | ↑0.50 | ↑0.75 | ↑0.75 | | ↑0.75 | | ↑0.75 | 4.00 | ↑375 |
| Euro Area | (0.50) | | | | | | | | | ↑0.50 | | ↑0.75 | | ↑0.75 | 1.50 | ↑200 |
| United Kingdom | 0.10 | | ↑0.15 | | ↑0.25 | ↑0.25 | | ↑0.25 | ↑0.25 | | ↑0.50 | ↑0.50 | | ↑0.75 | 3.00 | ↑290 |
| Japan | (0.10) | | | | | | | | | | | | | | (0.10) | |
| China, People's Rep. of | 2.95 | | | ↓0.10 | | | | | | | ↓0.10 | | | | 2.75 | ↓20 |
| Indonesia | 3.50 | | | | | | | | | | ↑0.25 | ↑0.50 | ↑0.50 | | 4.75 | ↑125 |
| Korea, Rep. of | 0.75 | ↑0.25 | | ↑0.25 | | | ↑0.25 | ↑0.25 | | ↑0.50 | ↑0.25 | | ↑0.50 | | 3.00 | ↑225 |
| Malaysia | 1.75 | | | | | | | ↑0.25 | | ↑0.25 | | ↑0.25 | ↑0.25 | | 2.75 | ↑100 |
| Philippines | 2.00 | | | | | | | ↑0.25 | ↑0.25 | ↑0.75 | ↑0.50 | ↑0.50 | | | 4.25 | ↑225 |
| Singapore | – | | ↑ | | | | ↑ | | | ↑ | | | ↑ | | – | – |
| Thailand | 0.50 | | | | | | | | | | ↑0.25 | ↑0.25 | | | 1.00 | ↑50 |
| Viet Nam | 4.00 | | | | | | | | | | | ↑1.00 | ↑1.00 | | 6.00 | ↑200 |

( ) = negative.

Notes:
1. Data coverage is from 5 November 2021 to 4 November 2022.
2. For the People's Republic of China, data used in the chart are for the 1-year medium-term lending facility rate. While the 1-year benchmark lending rate is the official policy rate of the People's Bank of China, market players use the 1-year medium-term lending facility rate as a guide for the monetary policy direction of the People's Bank of China.
3. The up (down) arrow for Singapore signifies monetary policy tightening (loosening) by its central bank. The Monetary Authority of Singapore utilizes the Singapore dollar nominal effective exchange rate (S$NEER) to guide its monetary policy.

Sources: Various central bank websites.

In the US, monetary policy continued to tighten. At the September Federal Open Market Committee (FOMC) meeting, the Federal Reserve raised the federal funds target rate by 75 bps for the third consecutive time and signaled it would continue reducing its bond holdings and pursue additional rate hikes. The Federal Reserve raised market expectations for more aggressive rate hikes during the Jackson Hole meeting on 25 August, implying that it was willing to allow some weakness in the economy to tame inflation. At the September FOMC meeting, the Federal Reserve updated its forecast for the federal funds rate for 2022 and 2023 to 4.4% and 4.6%, respectively, from June's forecasts of 3.4% and 3.8%. The market interpreted this as continued aggressive rate hikes in coming FOMC meetings. During its 2–3 November meeting, the Federal Reserve maintained its aggressive stance and raised the federal funds target rate range by 75 bps as expected. Furthermore, the Federal Reserve implied that interest rates may rise higher than previously expected, albeit at a moderating pace. As a result, the market expected a 61.5% chance of a 50 bps rate hike and a 38.5% probability of a 75 bps hike at the December FOMC meeting, as indicated by Fed Watch as of 4 November.

US inflation remained elevated in July–September but showed signs of possibly having peaked. Inflation recorded moderating readings of 8.5% year-on-year (y-o-y) (July) and 8.3% y-o-y (August), following June's record-high reading of 9.1% y-o-y. Inflation fell further in September and October to 8.2% y-o-y and 7.7% y-o-y, respectively. At the September FOMC meeting, the Federal Reserve slightly raised its full-year personal consumption expenditures inflation forecasts for 2022 and 2023 to 5.4% and 2.8%, respectively, from its June forecasts of 5.2% and 2.6%.

The US labor market remained robust but also showed some weakening signs. October nonfarm payrolls added 261,000 new jobs, lower than September's 315,000 and August's 292,000. The unemployment rate remained low but inched up slightly to 3.7% in October, from 3.5% in September, and was at par with the August reading. Amid more global headwinds, in September the Federal Reserve significantly revised downward its GDP growth forecasts for 2022 and 2023 to 0.2% and 1.2%, respectively, from June's forecasts of 1.7% for both years. Likewise, the forecasts for the unemployment rate for 2022 and 2023 were revised up to 3.8% and 4.4% from 3.7% and 3.9%, respectively.

In the euro area, the European Central Bank (ECB) continued to use monetary tightening in its efforts to tame inflation. Despite the ECB's aggressive monetary policy tightening, as evidenced by two consecutive rate hikes of 75 bps each announced on 8 September and 27 October, inflation in the euro area rose to a record high of 10.6% y-o-y in October from 9.9% y-o-y in September and 9.1% y-o-y in August, largely driven by high energy costs. The ECB expects to continue raising interest rates as inflationary pressure is projected to persist for an extended period on mounting energy and food prices, demand pressure from the reopening of the economy, and continued supply chain bottlenecks. In September, the ECB revised upward its inflation projections for 2022 and 2023 to 8.1% and 5.5%, respectively, from its June projections of 6.8% and 3.5%. To support market liquidity, the ECB also announced it would continue reinvesting in full the principal payments for maturing securities under its asset purchase and pandemic emergency purchase programs until at least the end of 2024. Similar to the US, the ECB expects a substantial slowdown in the euro area economy in the second half of 2022, owing to mounting headwinds including soaring energy prices, persistent supply bottlenecks, and geopolitical risks, particularly the Russian invasion of Ukraine. Although the euro area's GDP growth forecast for 2022 was revised up slightly to 3.1% in September (from June's 2.8%), forecasted growth for 2023 was significantly revised downward to 0.9% from 2.1%. In Q3 2022, the euro area reported a GDP growth of 2.1% y-o-y, down from 4.3% y-o-y in the previous quarter.

Contrary to monetary tightening in major advanced economies, Japan maintained an accommodative monetary policy stance amid moderate inflation and weak economic growth. Japan's economy contracted an annualized 1.2% in the third quarter (Q3) of 2022, a reversal from an annualized growth of 4.6% in the second quarter (Q2). Compared with other advanced economies, Japan's inflation rose modestly to 2.6% y-o-y in July, 3.0% y-o-y in both August and September, and 3.7% y-o-y in October, but this was still above the Bank of Japan's 2.0% target. Nevertheless, the Bank of Japan maintained its short-term policy rate target at –0.1%, its 10-year Japan Government Bond yield target at zero, and left unchanged the target amounts of its asset purchases at its 21–22 September and 27-28 October monetary policy meetings. Its accommodative monetary policy relative to the rest of the world's major economies has weighed on the Japanese yen, which depreciated more than 20% against the US dollar from the beginning of 2022 to 4 November.

Bond yields climbed in emerging East Asia between 31 August and 4 November, driven by higher bond yields in major advanced markets as well as higher interest rates due to domestic monetary tightening. In September and October, central banks in major member economies of the Association of Southeast Asian Nations, as well as the Bank of Korea, raised policy rates to quell elevated inflation and safeguard financial stability amid aggressive monetary tightening by the Federal Reserve (Table B). Despite monetary tightening in the region, inflationary pressure persisted in most emerging East Asian markets on rising food and energy prices, and, to a lesser extent, pending supply chain disruptions (**Figure A**). The dimming economic outlook in the region and tightening financial conditions weighed on investment sentiment across the region (**Box 1**).

Among regional bond markets, Viet Nam and the Philippines recorded the sharpest rise overall in government bond yields. Viet Nam's 2-year and 10-year bond yields rose 172 bps and 139 bps, respectively, during the review period. This was largely driven by the State Bank of Vietnam's two consecutive 100 bps hike of the refinancing rate on 23 September and 25 October to keep inflation below the full-year target of 4.0% (Table B). Year-to-date consumer price inflation in Viet Nam recorded 3.6% in August and further climbed

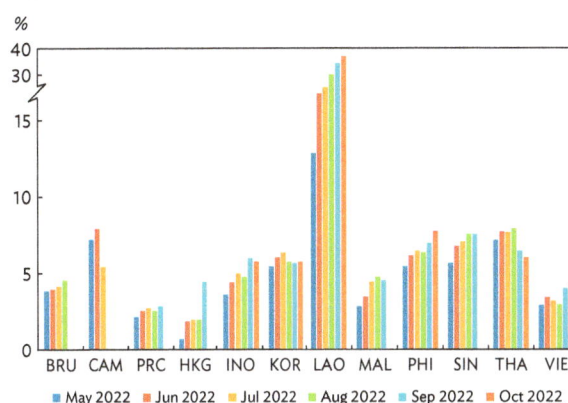

**Figure A: Inflation in Select Emerging East Asian Markets**

Legend: ■ May 2022  ■ Jun 2022  ■ Jul 2022  ■ Aug 2022  ■ Sep 2022  ■ Oct 2022

BRU = Brunei Darussalam; CAM = Cambodia; PRC = China, People's Rep. of; HKG = Hong Kong, China; INO = Indonesia; KOR = Korea, Rep. of; LAO = Lao People's Democratic Republic; MAL = Malaysia; PHI = Philippines; SIN = Singapore; THA = Thailand; VIE = Viet Nam.
Note: Data for the PRC; Hong Kong, China; Malaysia; and Singapore up to September 2022; Brunei Darussalam up to August 2022; and Cambodia up to July 2022.
Sources: Various local sources.

## Box 1: Economic Outlook in Developing Asia

Relaxed coronavirus disease (COVID-19) restrictions are lifting economic activity in many economies, but headwinds have also strengthened.[a] Elevated commodity prices due to the Russian invasion of Ukraine, aggressive monetary tightening in advanced economies, and recurrent COVID-19 lockdowns in the People's Republic of China are dimming economic prospects. Signs of a global slowdown are already evident in weaker export orders and worsening financial conditions. With these developments, developing Asia's forecasted growth in 2022 was revised down to 4.3% in the most recent *Asian Development Outlook 2022 Update* from 5.2% in April. The growth forecast for 2023 has also been revised down to 4.9% from 5.3% in April (**Table B1**).

In East Asia, the People's Republic of China's economy grew 2.5% in the first half (H1) of 2022, following 8.1% growth in 2021, as the services sector struggled due to COVID-19 lockdowns. Growth in 2022 also slowed in the Republic of Korea and Taipei,China in H1 2022 to 3.0% and 3.4%, respectively, from 4.2% and 8.5% in H1 2021, with net exports making a relatively smaller contribution to growth in both economies due to softer global demand (**Figure B1**). A decline in export orders suggests that this trend will continue and points to tepid growth for these and other export-driven economies in 2022 and 2023. Overall, East Asia

is expected to grow 3.2% in 2022, compared with the 4.7% *Asian Development Outlook 2022* forecast made in April. The subregion's growth forecast for 2023 was also lowered from 4.5% to 4.2%.

In contrast, the reopening of markets and borders in Southeast Asia is strengthening consumption and boosting growth. In Malaysia, private consumption grew 11.5% in H1 2022 on the back of spending for services and government assistance that bolstered incomes. In the Philippines, household consumption was also the main driver, rising 9.3% as COVID-19 restrictions were eased. With this rebound in spending, Malaysia and the Philippines posted some of the strongest economic growth in the region in H1 2022 at 6.9% and 7.8%, respectively. This drove the 2022 forecast for the subregion up to 5.1% from a 4.9% forecast made in April. Nevertheless, the glum global outlook is weighing on Southeast Asian's 2023 growth prospects, prompting a downward revision in the forecast from 5.2% to 5.0%.

High global food and energy prices are driving inflation higher, though there is considerable variation across the region. In the Caucasus and Central Asia, inflation appears to be accelerating, reaching 14.3% year-on-year (y-o-y) in August, while South Asia saw inflation of 10.9% y-o-y in August,

**Table B1: Gross Domestic Product Growth and Inflation Forecasts** (% per year)

| | GDP Growth | | | | Inflation | | | |
|---|---|---|---|---|---|---|---|---|
| | 2022 | | 2023 | | 2022 | | 2023 | |
| | ADO 2022 | Update | ADO 2022 | Update | ADO 2022 | Update | ADO 2022 | Update |
| **Developing Asia** | 5.2 | 4.3 | 5.3 | 4.9 | 3.7 | 4.5 | 3.1 | 4.0 |
| **Developing Asia excluding the PRC** | 5.5 | 5.3 | 5.8 | 5.3 | 5.1 | 6.6 | 4.2 | 5.5 |
| **East Asia** | 4.7 | 3.2 | 4.5 | 4.2 | 2.4 | 2.5 | 2.0 | 2.5 |
| Hong Kong, China | 2.0 | 0.2 | 3.7 | 3.7 | 2.3 | 2.0 | 2.0 | 2.0 |
| People's Republic of China | 5.0 | 3.3 | 4.8 | 4.5 | 2.3 | 2.3 | 2.0 | 2.5 |
| Republic of Korea | 3.0 | 2.6 | 2.6 | 2.3 | 3.2 | 4.5 | 2.0 | 3.0 |
| Taipei,China | 3.8 | 3.4 | 3.0 | 3.0 | 1.9 | 2.8 | 1.6 | 2.0 |
| **Southeast Asia** | 4.9 | 5.1 | 5.2 | 5.0 | 3.7 | 5.2 | 3.1 | 4.1 |
| Indonesia | 5.0 | 5.4 | 5.2 | 5.0 | 3.6 | 4.6 | 3.0 | 5.1 |
| Malaysia | 6.0 | 6.0 | 5.4 | 4.7 | 3.0 | 2.7 | 2.5 | 2.5 |
| Philippines | 6.0 | 6.5 | 6.3 | 6.3 | 4.2 | 5.3 | 3.5 | 4.3 |
| Singapore | 4.3 | 3.7 | 3.2 | 3.0 | 3.0 | 5.5 | 2.3 | 2.3 |
| Thailand | 3.0 | 2.9 | 4.5 | 4.2 | 3.3 | 6.3 | 2.2 | 2.7 |
| Viet Nam | 6.5 | 6.5 | 6.7 | 6.7 | 3.8 | 3.8 | 4.0 | 4.0 |

( ) = negative, ADO = Asian Development Outlook, GDP = gross domestic product.
Source: ADO 2022 Update.

[a] This box was written by Irfan Qureshi (economist) and David Keith de Padua (economics officer) in the Economic Research and Regional Cooperation Department of the Asian Development Bank.

*continued on next page*

Box 1   *continued*

**Figure B1: Demand-Side Contributions to Growth**

Percentage points

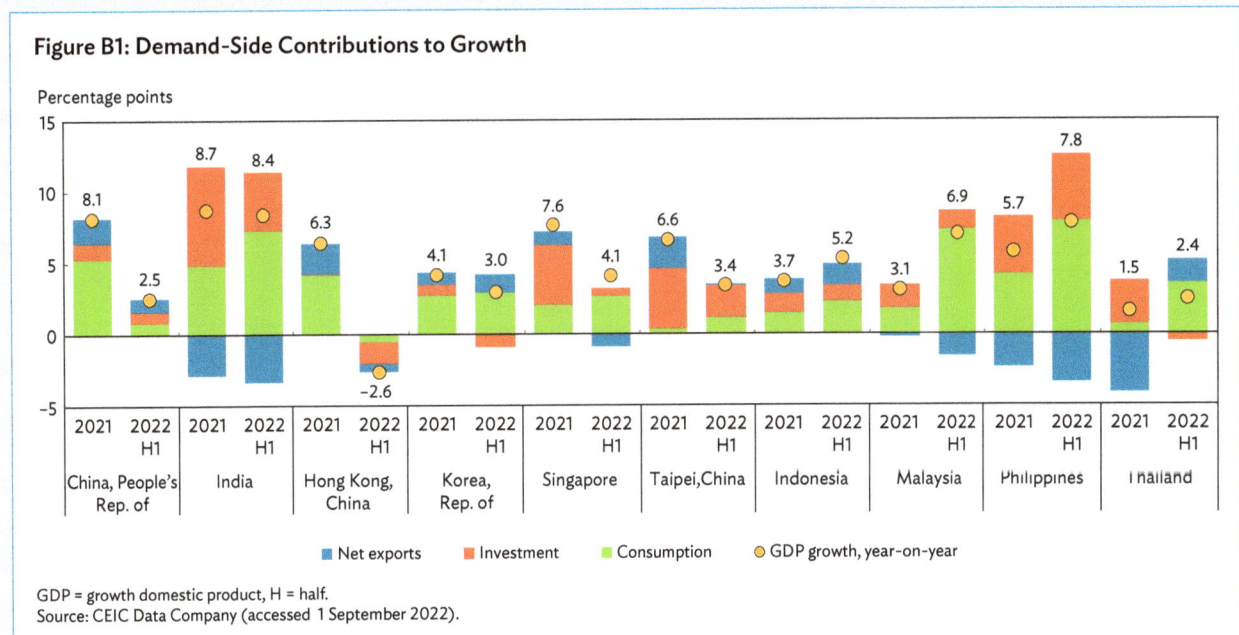

GDP = growth domestic product, H = half.
Source: CEIC Data Company (accessed 1 September 2022).

driven by high double-digit inflation in Pakistan and Sri Lanka. Inflation in East Asia remained relatively manageable at 2.8%. With inflation expected to moderate in the Republic of Korea and Taipei,China, and slower growth in Hong Kong, China mitigating inflationary pressure, inflation in the subregion is expected to slow to 2.5% in 2022 and remain at this level in 2023 (Table B1). In Southeast Asia, inflation accelerated from 3.0% y-o-y in January to 5.5% y-o-y in August, largely reflecting higher energy and food prices. Supply disruptions, higher cost of credit, and reduced production due to bad

weather have led to higher prices across food groups. The prices of maize in the Philippines, eggs in Singapore, and meat in Thailand have all increased. Rice prices, a staple in the region, also saw an uptick, reaching USD439 per metric ton in September. India, the world's largest rice-exporting country, started restricting exports in September, threatening to push rice prices higher. With price pressures mounting, headline inflation in developing Asia is expected to reach 4.5% in 2022, up from the 3.7% forecast made in April. Similarly, the inflation forecast for 2023 was raised to 4.0% from 3.1%.

to 4.0% in September and 4.2% in October. Economic growth in Viet Nam accelerated to 13.7% y-o-y in the third quarter (Q3) of 2022 from 7.7% y-o-y in the prior quarter. Meanwhile, 2-year and 10-year bond yields in the Philippines rose by 132 bps and 136 bps, respectively, following the Bangko Sentral ng Pilipinas' aggressive monetary tightening, with consecutive rate hikes every month from May through September for a cumulative 225 bps increase. The Bangko Sentral ng Pilipinas further raised rates by another 75 bps in November. Consumer price inflation has steadily risen in the Philippines since March, with October inflation reaching 7.7% y-o-y, the fastest pace since December 2008 and the second-highest in the region among markets that have released October inflation data.

Regional currencies collectively depreciated against the US dollar, which strengthened on the Federal Reserve's accelerated monetary tightening. During the review period, regional currencies posted average depreciations against the US dollar of 3.8% (simple average) and 4.2% (GDP-weighted average) (**Figure B**). Currency depreciation accelerated across the region after 13 September when August inflation data for the US came in at a higher-than-expected level, thus implying that aggressive monetary tightening would continue. Given the accelerated monetary tightening, the region witnessed rapid currency depreciation in September and October, with a monthly average of 2.7% (GDP-weighted average), compared to monthly average GDP-weighted exchange rate declines of 1.2% during the first 9 months of 2022,

**Figure B: Changes in Select Emerging East Asian Currencies**

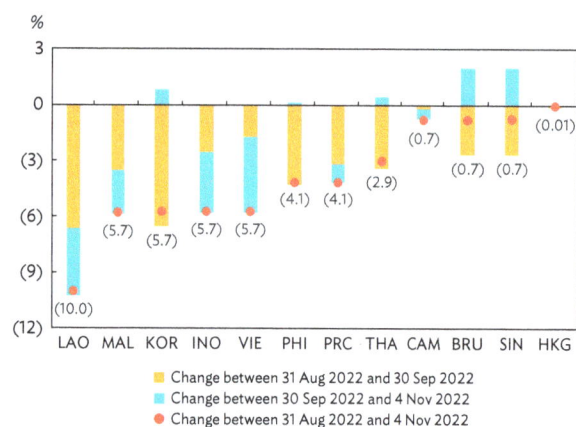

( ) = negative; BRU = Brunei Darussalam; CAM = Cambodia;
PRC = China, People's Rep. of; HKG = Hong Kong, China; INO = Indonesia;
KOR = Korea, Rep. of; LAO = Lao People's Democratic Republic;
MAL = Malaysia; PHI = Philippines; SIN = Singapore; THA = Thailand;
VIE = Viet Nam.
Note: A positive (negative) value for the FX rate indicates the appreciation
(depreciation) of the local currency against the United States dollar.
Source: *AsianBondsOnline* computations based on Bloomberg LP data.

**Figure C: Changes in Credit Default Swap Spreads in Select Emerging East Asian Markets** (senior 5-year)

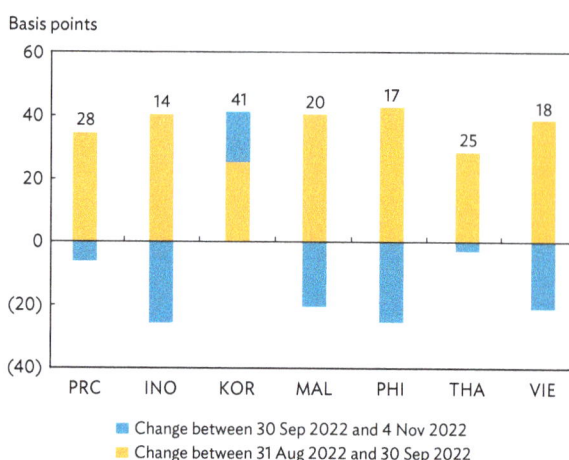

( ) = negative; GDP = gross domestic product; PRC = China, People's Rep. of;
INO = Indonesia; KOR = Korea, Rep. of; MAL = Malaysia; PHI = Philippines;
THA = Thailand; VIE = Viet Nam.
Note: Figures refer to change between 31 August 2022 and 4 November 2022.
Source: *AsianBondsOnline* computations based on Bloomberg LP data.

1.7% during Q2 2022, and 1.9% during Q3 2022. During the entire review period from 31 August to 4 November, the Lao People's Democratic Republic posted the region's largest currency depreciation (10.0%) on high inflationary pressure, financial stress, and declining foreign reserves.

A dimming global economic outlook and tightening financial conditions soured investment sentiment in emerging markets. During the review period, negative sentiment pushed up risk premiums across the region. As a typical risk premium measure, credit default swap (CDS) spreads widened by 28 bps (GDP-weighted) and 23 bps (simple average) during the review period from 31 August to 4 November (**Figure C**). During September and October, the region witnessed a monthly average GDP-weighted change of 24 bps in the CDS spread, compared with the monthly average GDP-weighted monthly changes in CDS spreads of 7 bps during the first 9 months of 2022, 9 bps during Q2 2022, and 7 bps during Q3 2022.

Equity markets in emerging East Asia also weakened between 31 August and 4 November by 7.4% (simple average) and 7.5% (market-weighted average) (**Figure D**). The largest decline was noted in Viet Nam (22.1%) as equities were weighed down by the consecutive rate hikes of 100 bps each in September and October by the

State Bank of Vietnam. The downward price pressure was further exacerbated by the triggering of margin calls, while negative news about stock manipulations and the rumor of a bank default also dampened investor sentiment. Next was Hong Kong, China (19.0%), which was dragged down by heightened investor concerns over continued negative domestic GDP growth during the first 3 quarters of 2022 and the PRC's weakened growth outlook and pandemic containment measures. Equity markets in the Philippines and the Republic of Korea retreated by 6.0% and 5.0%, respectively, during the review period. Equities in the Philippines declined over aggressive rate hikes by its central bank in response to rising inflation and a weakening currency. The Republic of Korea posted losses on continued equity outflows. The US ban on semiconductor exports to the PRC also negatively affected Korean semiconductor firms with exposure to the PRC market.

The retreat in regional equity markets can be partly attributed to net foreign capital outflows of USD5.6 billion during the review period (**Figure E**). All markets except Indonesia and the Republic of Korea posted foreign equity outflows, with the PRC posting the largest net outflows of USD7.8 billion. A negative outlook—generated by uncertainty over the impact of coronavirus disease (COVID-19) containment measures and the

**Figure D: Movements in Equity Indexes in Select Emerging East Asian Markets**

1 January 2022 = 100

ASEAN = Association of Southeast Asian Nations, COVID = coronavirus disease, EEA = emerging East Asia, FOMC = Federal Open Market Committee, PRC = People's Republic of China, US = United States.
Notes:
1. Equity market indexes included in ASEAN are the Jakarta Stock Exchange Composite Index, Kuala Lumpur Composite Index, Philippine Stock Exchange Index, Straits Times Index, Stock Exchange of Thailand Index, and Vietnam Ho Chi Minh Stock Index.
2. Data as of 4 November 2022.
Source: *AsianBondsOnline* computations based on Bloomberg LP data.

**Figure E: Foreign Capital Flows in Equity Markets in Select Emerging East Asian Markets**

USD billion

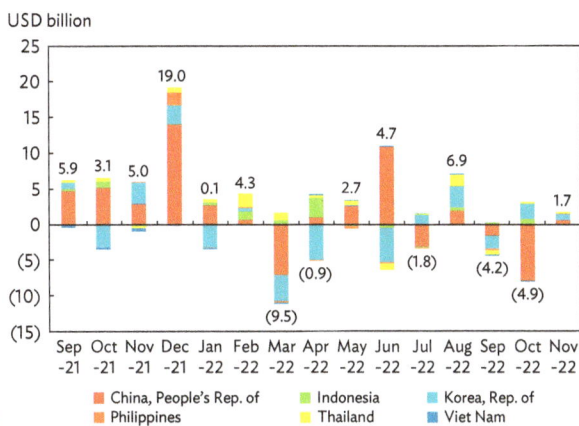

( ) = outflows, USD = United States dollar.
Notes:
1. Data coverage is from 1 September 2021 to 4 November 2022.
2. Figures refer to net inflows (net outflows) for each month.
Source: Institute of International Finance.

recent US announcement of export restrictions that could impact its semiconductor industry—continued to hamper the PRC's economy. Excluding Indonesia, all other member markets of the Association of Southeast Asian Nations recorded aggregate capital outflows of USD0.5 billion. Indonesia's equity market recorded net capital inflows of USD0.9 billion as some companies benefited from rising oil prices.

Net outflows were recorded in most regional bond markets in September as accelerated US monetary tightening not only subdued investment sentiment over risky assets but also made yields on emerging East Asian bonds relatively less attractive (**Figure F**). The loss of yield attractiveness was very evident in the PRC and Indonesia, which recorded the region's largest outflows of USD5.0 billion and USD1.9 billion, respectively, in September. This was largely because the PRC maintained an easing monetary stance, while Bank Indonesia's interest rate hikes lagged those of other regional markets up until September. Bank Indonesia subsequently raised rates by 50 bps each in October and November.

The outlook for regional financial conditions remained tilted to the downside. In the short term, subdued growth outlooks in major advanced economies and the PRC, uncertainties regarding the containment of COVID-19 and inflationary pressure, ongoing monetary tightening globally and in the region, and the possibility of larger-than-expected fallout from the Russian invasion of Ukraine will continue to erode investment sentiment. Nevertheless, the financial sector in emerging East Asia remained resilient to persistent headwinds not only because of sound economic fundamentals such as sufficient reserves and healthy fiscal and trade balances, but also because of improved institutional quality and more developed domestic capital markets, especially local

**Figure F: Foreign Capital Flows in Local Currency Bond Markets in Select Emerging East Asian Markets**

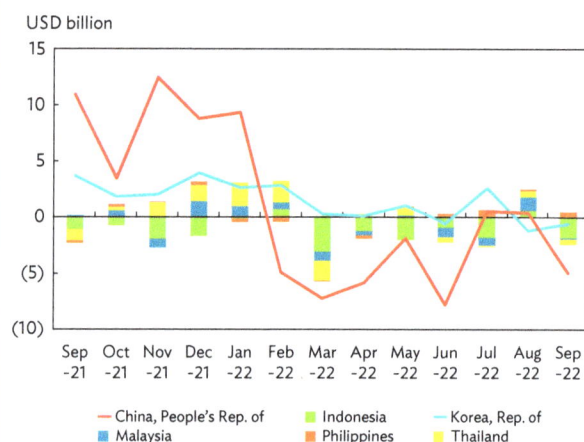

( ) = negative, USD = United States dollar.
Notes:
1.  The Republic of Korea and Thailand provided data on bond flows. For the People's Republic of China, Indonesia, Malaysia, and the Philippines, month-on-month changes in foreign holdings of local currency government bonds were used as a proxy for bond flows.
2.  Data are as of 30 September 2022.
3.  Figures were computed based on 30 September 2022 exchange rates and do not include currency effects.
Sources: People's Republic of China (Bloomberg LP); Indonesia (Directorate General of Budget Financing and Risk Management, Ministry of Finance); Republic of Korea (Financial Supervisory Service); Malaysia (Bank Negara Malaysia); Philippines (Bureau of the Treasury); and Thailand (Thai Bond Market Association).

currency bond markets (**Box 2**). Over the medium term, as many major regional economies commit to transition to net zero emissions, the region's financial sector faces asset vulnerability issues, especially in high-emitting sectors, as well as large financing gaps for investments in low-emission projects and the transitioning of high-emitting sectors. Providing enough financing while ensuring a resilient and timely transition calls for further development of the sustainable finance market and innovative financing solutions (**Box 3**).

## Box 2: Institutional Quality as a Shock Absorber for Asian Capital Flows in Crisis Times

Institutional quality comprises an important pull factor for international capital flows (Alfaro, Kalemli-Ozcan, and Volosovych 2009; Pagliari, Hannan, and Kaufman 2017).[a] Economies with higher levels of institutional quality tend to have more liquid financial markets and less vulnerability to sharp reversals of capital flows during times of crisis, and they are able to attract global capital flows that are less short-term and volatile in nature, such as foreign direct investment (FDI) and portfolio equity investment. In addition, high levels of institutional quality are associated with less external debt exposure, more export-oriented FDI policies, and more liberalized trade and capital accounts. While numerous studies exist on the benefits of enhanced institutional quality for economic growth, productivity, and economic development (e.g., Knack and Keefer 1995; Mauro 1995; Hall and Jones 1999; Rodrik, Subramanian, and Trebbi 2004), there is less work on the role of institutions as a buffer against economic and financial shocks.

New Asian Development Bank Institute research by Beirne and Panthi (2022) contributes to this literature in the Asian context. Focusing on 12 Asian economies from 1996 to 2020—split between economies that have high and low levels of institutional quality—they empirically test the role of institutions as a resilience mechanism for international capital flows during episodes of elevated financial stress. They also examine the impact of the resilience of gross domestic product (GDP) per capita due to institutions. The main findings from the paper are summarized in **Figure B2**.

In the case of FDI, while elevated financial stress reduces the marginal effect of institutions in economies with high institutional quality by a factor of around two, the overall effect remains positive and significant. For these economies, therefore, institutions have an important role to play in supporting the resilience of FDI. By contrast, the institutions of economies with lower levels of institutional development

[a]   This box was written by John Beirne (vice-chair of research and senior research fellow) and Pradeep Panthi (research associate) of the Asian Development Bank Institute.

**Box 2**  *continued*

### Figure B2: Impact of Institutions on Capital Flows and Gross Domestic Product per Capita in Asia

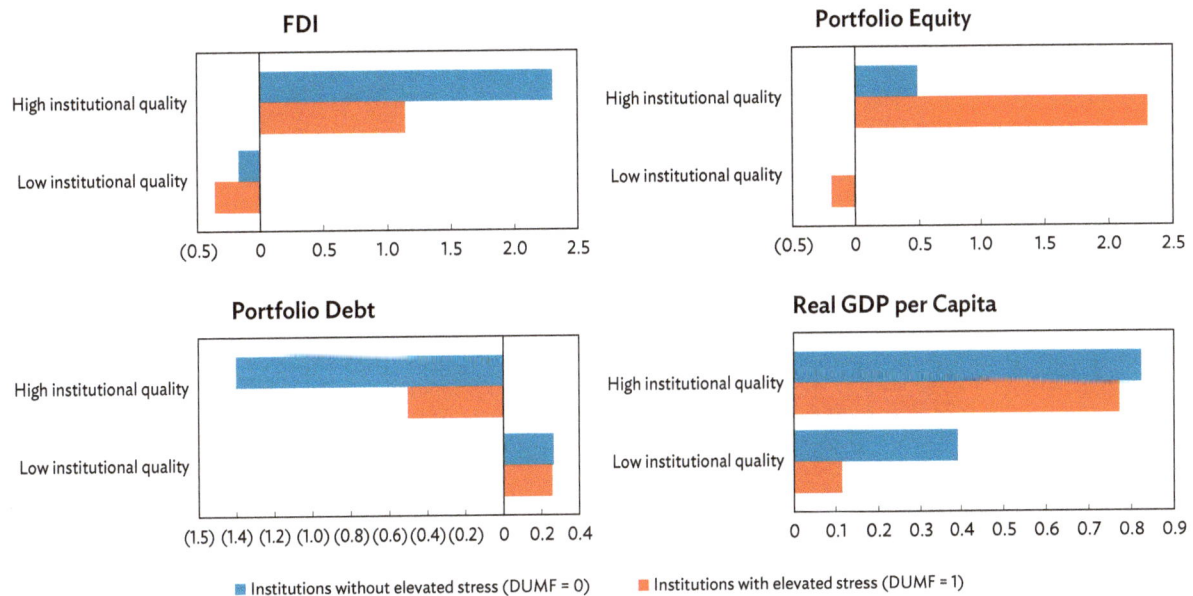

( ) = negative, FDI = net foreign direct investment, DUMF = dummy for elevated financial stress, GDP = gross domestic product.

Notes: The figure reports the total (significant) marginal effects from a panel regression analysis. Capital flow measures are net inflows as a share of GDP. The measure used for institutions is based on a principal component analysis of six components of institutions: (i) control of corruption, (ii) government effectiveness, (iii) voice and accountability, (iv) political stability and absence of violence, (v) the rule of law, and (vi) regulatory quality. High institutional quality reflects economies in the sample with institutional quality above the long-term historical average, while low institutional quality refers to economies below the average. The former group comprises Hong Kong, China; Japan; the Republic of Korea; Malaysia; and Singapore. The latter group comprises the People's Republic of China, India, Indonesia, Pakistan, the Philippines, Sri Lanka, and Thailand.

Source: Beirne and Panthi (2022).

do not exhibit positive effects on FDI, even in normal times. Elevated financial stress reduces net FDI inflows for these economies. On portfolio equity, there is some evidence to suggest portfolio-rebalancing effects and safe-haven flows to economies with high institutional quality during crisis times. For these economies, while institutions positively affect equity even in normal times, the effect is magnified more than fourfold in crisis times. While enhancing resilience, it also may suggest that investors rebalance their portfolios toward these economies in times of elevated financial stress. For economies with low-quality institutions, there is no effect of institutions on equity in normal times, whereas a reduction in net equity inflows is evident in crisis times.

Turning to the capital flows that are more volatile in nature, net portfolio debt for economies with lower levels of institutional quality can be somewhat resilient during crisis times, with debt stabilized, although the magnitudes of the effects are small. For economies with high institutional development, even in normal times, institutions are associated with a reduction in net inflows of portfolio debt.

The effect is less pronounced in crisis times (i.e., the marginal effect of institutions is less negative), which is also likely related to portfolio rebalancing effects. These economies also typically attract more stable and longer-term capital flows overall. For real GDP per capita, a threshold effect is evident, whereby the institutions of economies with high levels of institutional quality have twice the effect on economic development in normal times than those of economies with low levels of institutional development. In times of elevated financial stress, the marginal effect of economies with high institutional quality remains largely constant, whereas the effect declines substantially for economies with low institutional quality. This implies that institutions in the former group bolster the resilience of real GDP per capita to heightened financial tensions.

Beirne and Panthi (2022) also examine the subcomponents of institutions to identify which are important for the resilience of real GDP per capita and capital flows. For capital flows, political stability is a key institutional factor for crisis resilience with respect to portfolio equity. However, we also

*continued on next page*

**Box 2**  *continued*

observe an important role for regulatory quality, both for FDI and equity. Higher regulatory quality helps to support the resilience of these types of capital flows, which are longer-term and more stable in nature. This can also be an important factor affecting the effectiveness of macroprudential policy in managing capital flows (e.g., Beirne and Friedrich 2017). For real GDP per capita, the main source of resilience due to institutions comes from a strong rule of law and political stability.

While developing solid institutions is a gradual, long-term endeavor, policy makers, in particular in emerging economies, should intertwine their macroeconomic policy frameworks with measures to enhance institutional quality. This can have important implications for stabilizing capital flows and reducing exposure to financial shocks. Strong institutions can also have a strong role to play in terms of both enhancing the absorptive capacity of economies in the face of shocks and accelerating their recovery speed. As policy makers seek to improve the resilience of their economies to macrofinancial disturbances, it follows that structural reforms aimed at improving the quality of institutions should be central to the policy agenda over the medium to long term. A more granular understanding of the subcomponents of institutional quality at the global level, particularly with regard to harmonized cross-country data available over a long period, would provide the basis for more targeted structural policies for enhancing long-term macrofinancial resilience.

**References**

Alfaro, Laura, Sebnem Kalemli-Ozcan, and Vadym Volosovych. 2009. "Capital Flows in a Globalized World: The Role of Policies and Institutions." In *Capital Controls and Capital Flows in Emerging Economies: Policies, Practices, and Consequences*, edited by S. Edwards. Chicago: University of Chicago Press.

Beirne, John, and Christian Friedrich. 2017. "Macroprudential Policies, Capital Flows, and the Structure of the Banking Sector." *Journal of International Money and Finance* 75 (2017): 47–68.

Beirne, John, and Pradeep Panthi. 2022. "Institutional Quality and Macrofinancial Resilience in Asia." Asian Development Bank Institute Working Paper 1336.

Hall, Robert E., and Charles I. Jones. 1999. "Why Do Some Countries Produce So Much More Output per Worker Than Others?" *Quarterly Journal of Economics* 114 (1): 83–116.

Knack, Steven, and Philip Keefer. 1995. "Institutions and Economic Performance: Cross-Country Tests Using Alternative Institutional Measures." *Economics and Politics* 7 (3): 207–27.

Mauro, Paolo. 1995. "Corruption and Growth." *Quarterly Journal of Economics* 110 (3): 681–712.

Pagliari, Maria S., and Swarnali A. Hannan. 2017. "The Volatility of Capital Flows in Emerging Markets: Measures and Determinants." IMF Working Papers 2017 (041). Washington, DC: International Monetary Fund.

Rodrik, Dani, Arvind Subramanian, and Francesco Trebbi. 2004. "Institutions Rule: The Primacy of Institutions over Geography and Integration in Economic Development." *Journal of Economic Growth* 9 (2): 131–65.

# Box 3: Financing the Energy Transition in Emerging Asia

As the region prepares for the next wave of development, energy transition will be critical in the fight against climate change.

**Emerging Asia is reliant on coal, and existing coal-fired power plants are relatively young.**[a] Coal accounts for about half of the region's energy mix and is still subsidized by the government in some markets. Phasing out young coal fleets is a key step to achieving the emission reductions needed to limit global warming to 1.5°C. There are two options: (i) retiring plants early or (ii) repurposing plants to an alternative clean energy solution. However, the retirement of coal plants in emerging Asia is a challenge. The region's average remaining life span of coal-fired power plants operating from 2000 to 2022 is still higher than the world average (**Figure B3.1**).

**Emerging Asia's coal-fired power plant capacity has declined despite renewable energy capacity increasing in the past decade.** The capacity of new coal-fired power plants declined by 41.9% in 2020 from 2011, while total renewable energy capacity increased by almost 200% (**Figure B3.2**). While coal phase-out is a major step in energy transition,

this should be coordinated with a sustained expansion of renewable energy. The falling costs and increasing availability of clean energy solutions offers tremendous opportunities in renewable energy expansion, with solar and wind energy leading the growth in emerging Asia.

**Despite the increase in renewable energy capacity, the energy transition score in emerging Asia is still lower than the world average.** The average Energy Transition Index (ETI) of emerging Asian economies for 2021 was 56.1, compared with the world average of 59.3 and the advanced economies average of 68.2. The ETI is a benchmark measure of a country's energy transition progress based on the current energy system and transition readiness. Some Asian economies like Singapore, Georgia, Malaysia, Azerbaijan, the Republic of Korea, and Thailand have surpassed the world average ETI (**Figure B3.3**).

**Renewable investments have been increasing, but energy transition requires more than USD1 trillion under a net zero emissions scenario by 2050.**[b] In 2020, emerging Asia received USD3.0 billion of public flows in renewable investments, up by more than 200% from USD928.5 million in 2000, while peaking in 2017 at USD8.7 billion (**Figure B3.4**). Although climate financing has accelerated with the types of instruments available, it is still short of the USD100 billion per year commitment made at the virtual

### Figure B3.1: Average Remaining Life Span of Coal-Fired Power Plants Operating in Emerging Asia

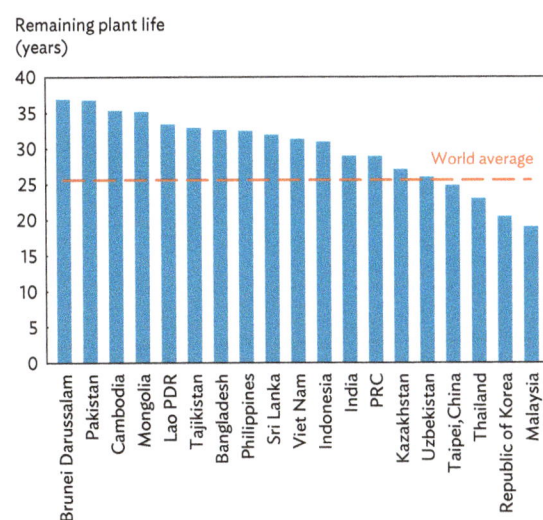

Remaining plant life (years)

Lao PDR = Lao People's Democratic Republic, PRC = People's Republic of China.
Source: Global Energy Monitor. Global Coal Plant Tracker (accessed 31 July 2022).

### Figure B3.2: New Coal-Fired Power Plants and Renewable Energy Capacity in Emerging Asia

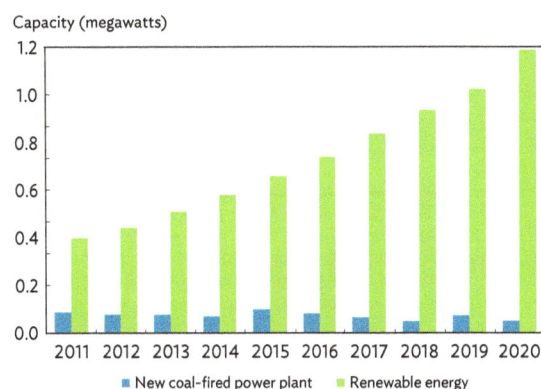

Capacity (megawatts)

■ New coal-fired power plant    ■ Renewable energy

Sources: Global Energy Monitor. Global Coal Plant Tracker (accessed 31 July 2022) and International Renewable Energy Agency. 2021. *Renewable Capacity Statistics 2021*. Abu Dhabi.

---

[a] This box was written by Sylvia Chen (senior sustainable officer) of Amundi and Mai Lin Villaruel (economics officer) in the Economic Research and Regional Cooperation Department of the Asian Development Bank.
[b] International Energy Agency. 2021. *Financing Clean Energy Investment*. Paris.

*continued on next page*

**Box 3**  *continued*

component of the United Nations Biodiversity Conference in 2021. For emerging Asia, the focus will be twofold: (i) coal phase-out and (ii) renewable energy expansion. Much effort has been devoted to finding innovative solutions for accelerating coal phase-out while minimizing the risk of stranded coal assets in emerging Asia. The Energy Transition Mechanism announced by the Asian Development Bank at COP26 aims to resolve this issue.[c] Another focus is the growing popularity of corporate renewable Power Purchase Agreements, which have contributed to renewable energy development in emerging Asia.

**Sustainable bond markets channel private funding to support energy transition.** Green bonds are a popular solution to fund projects with positive climate and environmental benefits (**Figure B3.5**). Green bond issuance for energy sector projects in emerging Asia reached USD14.5 billion in 2021, increasing almost 300% from 2010. While green bonds channel funds to environmentally friendly projects, instruments such as sustainability-linked and transition bonds are also useful tools to finance energy transition, offering opportunities for conventional facilities to achieve sustainability goals such as improving overall environmental performance. The first sustainability-linked bonds in the energy sector in emerging Asia were issued

in 2020, totaling USD270.1 million in their first year of issuance before jumping to USD5.3 billion in 2021. Transition bond issuance in emerging Asia has also recently picked up following the region's inaugural issuance of a transition bond aligned with the International Capital Market Association's *Climate Transition Finance Handbook in 2021*. As a critical measure to help emerging Asian economies accelerate toward net zero emissions, the transition finance market has significant growth potential.

**Figure B3.4: Public Investment Flows in Renewables in Emerging Asia**

Amount (2020 USD billion)

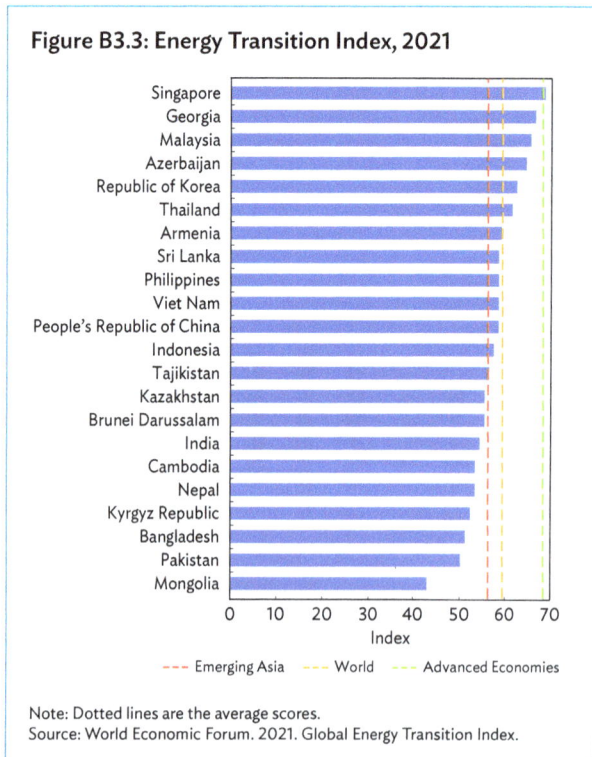

USD = United States dollar.
Notes: Public flows are financial flows in the form of commitments originating from public institutions like governments, multilateral development banks, and other public finance institutions. A commitment represents a legal contract to mobilize financial funds directed to one or more countries. These flows are corrected for currency exchange rates and inflation to a base year.
Source: International Renewable Energy Agency. Statistics—Renewable Energy Finance Flows (accessed 5 October 2022).

**Figure B3.3: Energy Transition Index, 2021**

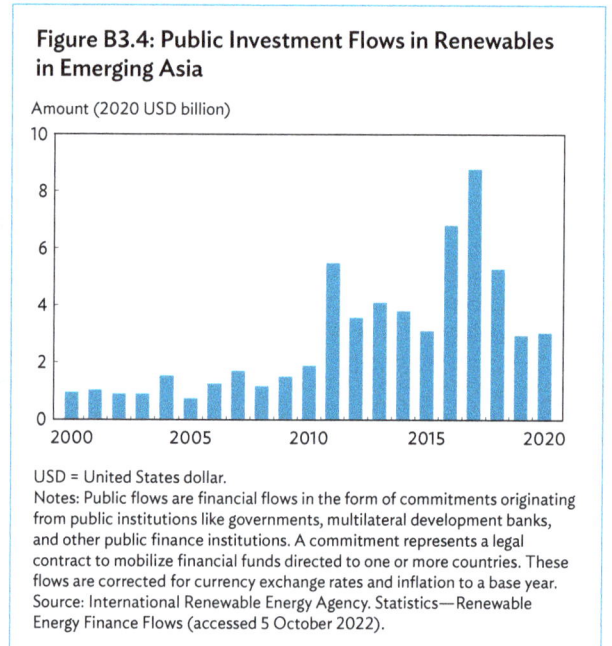

Note: Dotted lines are the average scores.
Source: World Economic Forum. 2021. Global Energy Transition Index.

**Figure B3.5: Sustainable Bond Issuance in Emerging Asia's Energy Sector**

USD billion

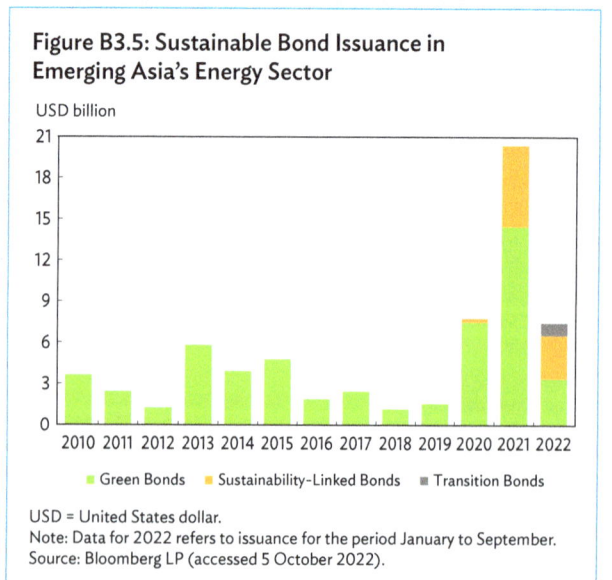

USD = United States dollar.
Note: Data for 2022 refers to issuance for the period January to September.
Source: Bloomberg LP (accessed 5 October 2022).

---

[c]  Asian Development Bank. 2021. *Energy Transition Mechanism Explainer: How ETM Will Support Climate Action in Southeast Asia*. 3 November.

# Bond Market Developments in the Third Quarter of 2022

## Size and Composition

Emerging East Asia's local currency bond market reached a size of USD22.0 trillion at the end of September.

Emerging East Asia's local currency (LCY) bond market expanded 2.3% quarter-on-quarter (q-o-q) in the third quarter (Q3) of 2022 to reach a size of USD22.0 trillion at the end of September.[2] Overall growth eased from 3.1% q-o-q in the second quarter (Q2) of 2022 as expansions in both the government and corporate bond segments slowed. Growth in the region's LCY bond market during the review period was largely capped by a slowdown in the market of the People's Republic of China (PRC). Rising borrowing costs and heightened economic uncertainties also affected the region's bond market. Interest rates rose as most regional central banks raised their policy rates to combat inflation and in response to the United States (US) Federal Reserve's aggressive monetary policy tightening. Uncertainties from slowing global growth, persistent global inflation, geopolitical risks, and the impacts of the US Federal Reserve's prolonged monetary policy tightening cycle became more pronounced during the review period.

Eight out of nine LCY bond markets in emerging East Asia recorded positive q-o-q growth in Q3 2022, while the market of Viet Nam showed negative q-o-q growth (**Figure 1a**). Among those that experienced positive q-o-q expansions, seven markets (Hong Kong, China; Indonesia; the Republic of Korea; Malaysia; the Philippines; Singapore; and Thailand) posted faster q-o-q growth in Q3 2022 than in the prior quarter. The markets of Hong Kong, China and Indonesia showed the fastest q-o-q expansions, while the markets of the PRC and the Republic of Korea experienced the weakest q-o-q growth in Q3 2022.

On a year-on-year (y-o-y) basis, growth in emerging East Asia's LCY bond market also slowed to 12.5% in Q3 2022 from 14.0% in the previous quarter. The markets

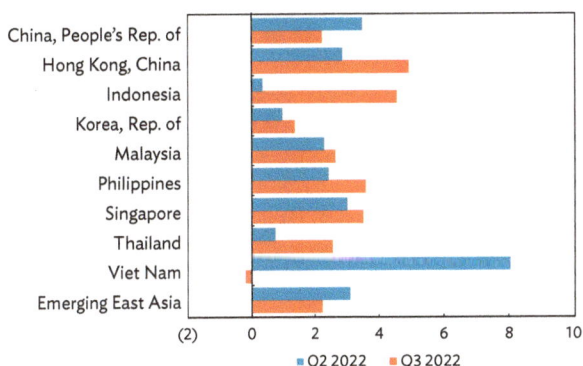

**Figure 1a: Growth of Select Emerging East Asian Local Currency Bond Markets in the Second and Third Quarters of 2022** (q-o-q, %)

q-o-q = quarter-on-quarter, Q2 = second quarter, Q3 = third quarter.
Notes:
1. For Singapore, corporate bonds outstanding are based on *AsianBondsOnline* estimates.
2. Growth rates are calculated from local currency base and do not include currency effects.
3. Emerging East Asia growth figures are based on 30 September 2022 currency exchange rates and do not include currency effects.
Sources: People's Republic of China (CEIC Data Company); Hong Kong, China (Hong Kong Monetary Authority); Indonesia (Bank Indonesia; Directorate General of Budget Financing and Risk Management, Ministry of Finance; and Indonesia Stock Exchange); Republic of Korea (KG Zeroin Corporation and The Bank of Korea); Malaysia (Bank Negara Malaysia); Philippines (Bureau of the Treasury and Bloomberg LP); Singapore (Monetary Authority of Singapore, Singapore Government Securities, and Bloomberg LP); Thailand (Bank of Thailand); and Viet Nam (Bloomberg LP and Vietnam Bond Market Association).

of Viet Nam and Singapore recorded the fastest y-o-y growth, while the markets of Thailand and the Republic of Korea showed the slowest y-o-y expansions in Q3 2022. All nine markets posted positive y-o-y growth, although five (the PRC, the Republic of Korea, the Philippines, Singapore, and Viet Nam) of the nine markets experienced slower y-o-y expansions in Q3 2022 than in Q2 2022 (**Figure 1b**). The markets of Hong Kong, China; Indonesia; and Malaysia experienced faster y-o-y growth in Q3 2022 than in the previous quarter while Thailand grew at the same pace from Q2 2022.

The PRC remained home to the region's largest LCY bond market. At the end of September, the PRC's LCY bond market reached a size of USD17.7 trillion, accounting for

---

[2] Emerging East Asia is defined to include member states of the Association of Southeast Asian Nations (ASEAN) plus the People's Republic of China; Hong Kong, China; and the Republic of Korea.

**Figure 1b: Growth of Select Emerging East Asian Local Currency Bond Markets in the Second and Third Quarters of 2022** (y-o-y, %)

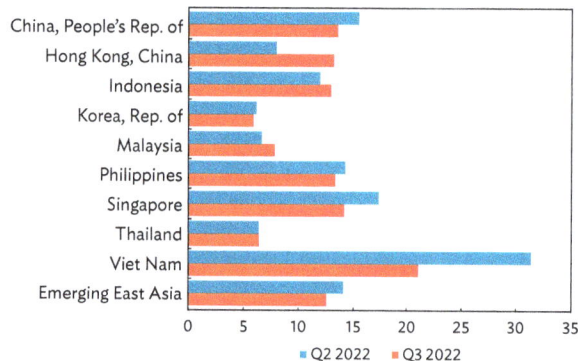

Q2 = second quarter, Q3 = third quarter, y-o-y = year-on-year.
Notes:
1. For Singapore, corporate bonds outstanding are based on *AsianBondsOnline* estimates.
2. Growth rates are calculated from local currency base and do not include currency effects.
3. Emerging East Asia growth figures are based on 30 September 2022 currency exchange rates and do not include currency effects.
Sources: People's Republic of China (CEIC Data Company); Hong Kong, China (Hong Kong Monetary Authority); Indonesia (Bank Indonesia; Directorate General of Budget Financing and Risk Management, Ministry of Finance; and Indonesia Stock Exchange); Republic of Korea (KG Zeroin Corporation and The Bank of Korea); Malaysia (Bank Negara Malaysia); Philippines (Bureau of the Treasury and Bloomberg LP); Singapore (Monetary Authority of Singapore, Singapore Government Securities, and Bloomberg LP); Thailand (Bank of Thailand); and Viet Nam (Bloomberg LP and Vietnam Bond Market Association).

80.2% of the region's total bond stock. Overall growth in the PRC's LCY bond market dropped to 2.2% q-o-q in Q3 2022 from 3.5% q-o-q in Q2 2022, as expansions in both the government and corporate segments slowed. Growth in LCY government bonds outstanding dipped to 2.8% q-o-q in Q3 2022 from 4.3% q-o-q in the previous quarter, due primarily to a contraction in issuance, as local government bond annual quotas had been nearly fulfilled in earlier quarters. Growth in government bonds was supported by expansions in Treasury and other government bonds (4.9% q-o-q), policy bank bonds (3.8% q-o-q), and local government bonds (0.8% q-o-q). Meanwhile, growth in the PRC's corporate bond market eased to 1.2% q-o-q in Q3 2022 from 2.0% q-o-q in the previous quarter, amid a worsening property market slump and "zero-COVID" restrictions. On a y-o-y basis, the PRC's LCY bond market expanded 13.5% in Q3 2022, down from 15.4% in Q2 2022.

With an outstanding bond stock of USD2.1 trillion at the end of September, the Republic of Korea's LCY bond market continued to be the second-largest in the region. Its share of the region's total bond market slipped to

9.4% at the end of September. The Republic of Korea's LCY bond market posted 1.3% q-o-q growth in Q3 2022, up from 1.0% q-o-q in the prior quarter. Growth in the government bond segment rose to 1.8% q-o-q in Q3 2022 from 1.6% q-o-q in Q2 2022, due primarily to faster growth in other government bonds. Growth in other government bonds picked up, rising 3.0% q-o-q in Q3 2022 from 1.9% q-o-q in the previous quarter. The stock of central government bonds rose 2.1% q-o-q in Q3 2022, down from 3.4% q-o-q in the previous quarter. The Bank of Korea's bonds outstanding continued to contract, dropping 2.3% q-o-q in Q3 2022 following a 10.2% q-o-q decline in the prior quarter. On the other hand, growth in the corporate bond market inched up to 1.0% q-o-q in Q3 2022 from 0.5% q-o-q in the previous quarter. On a y-o-y basis, growth in the Republic of Korea's LCY bond market eased to 5.9% in Q3 2022 from 6.1% in Q2 2022.

Hong Kong, China's LCY bonds outstanding totaled USD350.1 billion at the end of September. Overall growth rose to 4.9% q-o-q in Q3 2022 from 2.9% q-o-q in the previous quarter, driven by faster growth in both the government and corporate bond segments. Government bonds outstanding expanded 3.7% in Q3 2022, up from 1.5% in Q2 2022. The faster growth in government bonds in Q3 2022 stemmed from stronger growth in outstanding Exchange Fund Bills and Hong Kong Special Administrative Region (HKSAR) bonds, as well as a narrower contraction in outstanding Exchange Fund Notes. The review period saw record issuance of 3-year floating rate Silver Bonds, which are bonds intended for senior citizens. Meanwhile, growth in the corporate bond segment accelerated to 6.2% q-o-q in Q3 2022 from 4.4% q-o-q in the previous quarter. On an annual basis, Hong Kong, China's LCY bond market expanded 13.2% y-o-y in Q3 2022, up from 7.9% y-o-y in the prior quarter.

The aggregate LCY bond stock of the members of the Association of Southeast Asian Nations (ASEAN) amounted to USD1,938.0 billion at the end of September, with growth rising to 3.1% q-o-q in Q3 2022 from 2.0% in Q2 2022. Annual growth eased to 11.1% y-o-y in Q3 2022 from 11.8% y-o-y in the previous quarter. ASEAN members' share of emerging East Asia's total LCY bond market rose slightly to 8.8% in Q3 2022 from 8.7% in Q2 2022. The ASEAN LCY bond market remained dominated by government bonds. Total government bonds among all ASEAN markets amounted to USD1,426.1 billion at the end of September, comprising 73.6% of the total ASEAN LCY bond market. Outstanding corporate bonds amounted to USD0.5 billion, or 26.4% of the total market. The LCY bond markets of Singapore, Thailand, and Malaysia remained the region's largest, while Viet Nam accounted for the smallest LCY bond market in ASEAN.

Singapore's LCY bond market expanded 3.5% q-o-q in Q3 2022 to reach a size of USD464.3 billion at the end of September. The rate of q-o-q growth in Q3 2022 outpaced that of the previous quarter (3.0% q-o-q). The faster expansion in Q3 2022 stemmed solely from the government bond segment as the corporate bond segment recorded a marginal contraction. Growth in outstanding government bonds accelerated to 5.1% q-o-q in Q3 2022 from 3.8% q-o-q in the preceding quarter. The strong growth in government bonds was supported by expansions in Singapore Government Securities (1.4% q-o-q) and Monetary Authority of Singapore (MAS) bills (8.8% q-o-q). The review period saw the inaugural issuance of Singapore's sovereign green bonds worth SGD2.4 billion. Meanwhile, Singapore's stock of outstanding LCY corporate bonds recorded a marginal contraction in Q3 2022 amid rising borrowing costs. The MAS tightened its monetary policy in July and October to arrest rising inflation. On a y-o-y basis, Singapore's LCY bond market expanded 14.1% in Q3 2022, down from 17.3% in Q2 2022.

Thailand's outstanding LCY bond stock totaled USD410.7 billion at the end of September. Quarterly growth rose to 2.6% q-o-q in Q3 2022 from 0.7% q-o-q in the preceding quarter, driven by a recovery in the government bond segment. Government bonds outstanding expanded 2.3% q-o-q in Q3 2022, reversing the 0.7% q-o-q decline in Q2 2022. The rebound in the government bond segment stemmed from growth in government bonds and Treasury bills (3.8% q-o-q) and state-owned enterprise and other bonds (1.9% q-o-q), as well as a narrower contraction in Bank of Thailand (BOT) bonds outstanding. Meanwhile, growth in the corporate bond market dropped to 3.4% q-o-q in Q3 2022 from 4.6% q-o-q in Q2 2022, mainly due to higher borrowing costs. The BOT raised its benchmark raised by 25 basis points (bps) each in August and September after holding it at a record low rate of 0.50% for over 2 years. On a y-o-y basis, growth in Thailand's LCY bond market was unchanged at 6.4% in Q2 2022 and Q3 2022.

Outstanding LCY bonds in Malaysia amounted to USD399.6 billion at the end of September, with quarterly growth inching up to 2.6% in Q3 2022 from 2.3% in the prior quarter. The higher overall growth was driven primarily by a faster expansion in the corporate bond segment. The outstanding LCY government bond stock rose 3.2% q-o-q in Q3 2022 versus 4.1% q-o-q in Q2 2022. Central government bonds continued to drive most of the growth in total government bonds. Renewed issuance of Bank Negara Malaysia bills also contributed to overall growth in government bonds during the review period. Meanwhile, expansion in corporate bonds outstanding picked up, rising to 1.9% q-o-q in Q3 2022 from a tepid pace of 0.1% q-o-q in the previous quarter. On an annual basis, Malaysia' LCY bond market expanded 7.8% y-o-y in Q3 2022, up from 6.6% y-o-y in Q2 2022.

Malaysia's *sukuk* (Islamic bond) market remained the largest in emerging East Asia with total *sukuk* outstanding amounting to USD255.1 billion at the end of September on growth of 3.9% q-o-q in Q3 2022. Government *sukuk* outstanding amounted to USD111.6 billion, representing nearly half (49.3%) of Malaysia's total LCY government bond stock. Meanwhile, corporate *sukuk* dominated Malaysia's LCY corporate bond market—outstanding corporate *sukuk* totaled USD143.6 billion, or 82.8% of the total corporate bond market.

Indonesia's LCY bond market reached a size of USD377.4 billion at the end of September on growth of 4.5% q-o-q and 12.9% y-o-y in Q3 2022. Growth accelerated from 0.3% q-o-q and 11.9% y-o-y in Q2 2022. Faster quarterly growth in Q3 2022 stemmed from a stronger expansion in the government bond segment combined with a rebound in the corporate bond segment. Growth in LCY government bonds outstanding jumped to 4.6% q-o-q in Q3 2022 from 0.6% q-o-q in the previous quarter, driven by robust growth in central government bonds. Central banks bonds and nontradable bonds, on the other hand, recorded contractions during the review period. Meanwhile, Indonesia's corporate bond market rebounded in Q3 2022 on positive business sentiment as Indonesia's economic recovery gained ground. LCY corporate bonds outstanding rose 4.1% q-o-q after declining 2.3% q-o-q in the prior quarter as issuance rebounded.

Indonesia's *sukuk* market reached a size of USD70.5 billion at the end of September after rising 7.1% q-o-q. *Sukuk* outstanding comprised 18.7% of Indonesia's LCY bond market. Government *sukuk* outstanding amounted to USD67.9 billion, comprising 19.6% of Indonesia's LCY government bond market. Outstanding corporate *sukuk* totaled USD2.6 billion, representing 8.7% of Indonesia's LCY corporate bond market.

The outstanding stock of LCY bonds in the Philippines stood at USD188.6 billion at the end of September. Overall growth accelerated to 3.6% q-o-q in Q3 2022 from 2.4% q-o-q in Q2 2022 as the government issued Retail Treasury Bonds in September and corporate bonds recovered. Government bonds outstanding posted 3.9% q-o-q growth in Q3 2022, down from 4.1% q-o-q in the previous quarter. Treasury bonds increased during the period but contractions were noted in Bangko Sentral ng Pilipinas securities and other government bonds. Corporate bonds outstanding rose 1.4% q-o-q in Q3 2022, reversing the 7.1% q-o-q decline in the previous quarter. On an annual basis, growth in the Philippines' LCY bond market moderated to 13.3% y-o-y in Q3 2022 from 14.2% y-o-y in the prior quarter.

At the end of September, Viet Nam's LCY bond market remained the smallest in emerging East Asia with an outstanding bond stock of USD97.4 billion. Viet Nam's LCY bond market contracted 0.2% q-o-q in Q3 2022, driven by a decline in the government bond segment combined with a slowdown in the corporate bond segment. Outstanding LCY government bonds fell 2.0% q-o-q in Q3 2022, reversing the 7.4% q-o-q gain posted in the prior quarter. Contractions in the State Bank of Vietnam's (SBV) outstanding bills and government-guaranteed and municipal bonds drove the decline in government bonds during the review period. Meanwhile, growth in corporate bonds outstanding plunged to 4.1% q-o-q in Q3 2022 from 9.5% q-o-q in Q2 2022 amid rising borrowing costs. The SBV raised its policy rate by 100 bps each in September and October after holding it steady since October 2020. On a y-o-y basis, Viet Nam's LCY bond market expanded 21.1% in Q3 2022, down from 31.4% in the previous quarter.

Government bonds continued to dominate emerging East Asia's LCY bond market. The region's aggregate LCY government bond stock totaled USD14.0 trillion at the end of September, accounting for 63.6% of the region's total LCY bond market (**Table 1**). Growth in the region's government bonds declined to 2.8% q-o-q

in Q3 2022 from 3.9% q-o-q in Q2 2022. Except for Viet Nam, all of the region's LCY government bond markets saw positive q-o-q growth in Q3 2022, supported by gains in issuance in nearly all markets except the PRC and the Republic of Korea. Both the PRC and the Republic of Korea frontloaded borrowing in the first half of the year to boost economic recovery. Annual growth in emerging East Asia's LCY government bond stock moderated to 14.3% in Q3 2022 from 15.6% in Q2 2022.

The market of the PRC remained the largest in the region, comprising 82.2% of the region's LCY government bond market at the end of September. A distant second was the Republic of Korea's, which represented 6.3% of the region's total LCY government bond market at the end of the review period. Meanwhile, ASEAN member economies accounted for 10.2% of the region's government bond market. Within ASEAN, the largest government bond markets were those of Indonesia and Singapore, while the smallest were those of the Philippines and Viet Nam.

At the end of the review period, emerging East Asia's LCY government bonds remained concentrated in medium- to long-term tenors (**Figure 2**). About 54% of the region's total government bonds had maturities of over 5 years. Apart from the PRC; Hong Kong, China; and the Philippines; all markets in the region had over half of their government bonds concentrated in tenors of greater than 5 years. Hong Kong, China's government bonds remained dominated by shorter-dated bonds due to robust market demand for short-term securities. About 80.0% of Hong Kong, China's government bonds had maturities of 1–3 years, while only 10.8% had maturities of more than 5 years.

Emerging East Asia's corporate bond market amounted to USD8.0 trillion at the end of September, comprising 36.4% of the region's total LCY bond stock. Growth dipped to 1.3% q-o-q and 9.6% y-o-y in Q3 2022 from 1.8% q-o-q and 11.5% y-o-y in the prior quarter. Except for the market of Singapore, all of the region's LCY corporate bond markets showed positive q-o-q growth in Q3 2022. Hong Kong, China; Indonesia; the Republic of Korea; Malaysia; and the Philippines posted faster q-o-q growth in Q3 2022 versus Q2 2022. However, the slower expansion in the corporate bond market in the PRC and, to a lesser extent, in Thailand and Viet Nam capped the region's LCY corporate bond growth during the review period.

## Table 1: Size and Composition of Select Emerging East Asian Local Currency Bond Markets

| | Q3 2021 | | Q2 2022 | | Q3 2022 | | Growth Rate (LCY-base %) | | | | Growth Rate (USD-base %) | | | |
|---|---|---|---|---|---|---|---|---|---|---|---|---|---|---|
| | Amount (USD billion) | % share | Amount (USD billion) | % share | Amount (USD billion) | % share | Q3 2021 | | Q3 2022 | | Q3 2021 | | Q3 2022 | |
| | | | | | | | q-o-q | y-o-y | q-o-q | y-o-y | q-o-q | y-o-y | q-o-q | y-o-y |
| **China, People's Rep. of** | | | | | | | | | | | | | | |
| Total | 17,190 | 100.0 | 18,368 | 100.0 | 17,676 | 100.0 | 3.9 | 12.8 | 2.2 | 13.5 | 4.1 | 18.9 | (3.8) | 2.8 |
| Government | 11,043 | 64.2 | 11,898 | 64.8 | 11,512 | 65.1 | 4.1 | 13.4 | 2.8 | 15.1 | 4.3 | 19.5 | (3.2) | 4.2 |
| Corporate | 6,146 | 35.8 | 6,469 | 35.2 | 6,164 | 34.9 | 3.7 | 11.8 | 1.2 | 10.7 | 3.9 | 17.8 | (4.7) | 0.3 |
| **Hong Kong, China** | | | | | | | | | | | | | | |
| Total | 312 | 100.0 | 334 | 100.0 | 350 | 100.0 | 0.1 | 6.1 | 4.9 | 13.2 | (0.2) | 5.6 | 4.9 | 12.2 |
| Government | 161 | 51.6 | 176 | 52.7 | 183 | 52.1 | 3.0 | 8.2 | 3.7 | 14.4 | 2.7 | 7.7 | 3.7 | 13.5 |
| Corporate | 151 | 48.4 | 158 | 47.3 | 168 | 47.9 | (2.9) | 4.1 | 6.2 | 11.8 | (3.1) | 3.6 | 6.2 | 10.9 |
| **Indonesia** | | | | | | | | | | | | | | |
| Total | 356 | 100.0 | 369 | 100.0 | 377 | 100.0 | 3.6 | 23.9 | 4.5 | 12.9 | 5.0 | 28.8 | 2.3 | 6.1 |
| Government | 326 | 91.7 | 339 | 92.0 | 347 | 92.0 | 4.0 | 27.3 | 4.6 | 13.3 | 5.3 | 32.3 | 2.3 | 6.5 |
| Corporate | 29 | 8.3 | 29 | 8.0 | 30 | 8.0 | (0.2) | (4.2) | 4.1 | 8.4 | 1.1 | (0.5) | 1.8 | 1.9 |
| **Korea, Rep. of** | | | | | | | | | | | | | | |
| Total | 2,365 | 100.0 | 2,253 | 100.0 | 2,071 | 100.0 | 1.6 | 7.6 | 1.3 | 5.9 | (3.4) | 6.3 | (8.0) | (12.4) |
| Government | 996 | 42.1 | 956 | 42.4 | 883 | 42.6 | 1.9 | 10.4 | 1.8 | 7.1 | (3.1) | 9.0 | (7.6) | (11.4) |
| Corporate | 1,369 | 57.9 | 1,296 | 57.6 | 1,188 | 57.4 | 1.4 | 5.7 | 1.0 | 5.0 | (3.6) | 4.41 | (8.4) | (13.2) |
| **Malaysia** | | | | | | | | | | | | | | |
| Total | 411 | 100.0 | 410 | 100.0 | 400 | 100.0 | 1.5 | 8.5 | 2.6 | 7.8 | 0.6 | 7.8 | (2.4) | (2.7) |
| Government | 224 | 54.6 | 230 | 56.3 | 226 | 56.6 | 1.5 | 10.6 | 3.2 | 11.8 | 0.6 | 9.8 | (1.9) | 0.9 |
| Corporate | 186 | 45.4 | 179 | 43.7 | 173 | 43.4 | 1.4 | 6.1 | 1.9 | 3.1 | 0.5 | 5.4 | (3.2) | (7.0) |
| **Philippines** | | | | | | | | | | | | | | |
| Total | 191 | 100.0 | 194 | 100.0 | 189 | 100.0 | 4.4 | 20.0 | 3.6 | 13.3 | (0.1) | 14.1 | (2.9) | (1.5) |
| Government | 163 | 85.3 | 169 | 86.8 | 164 | 87.1 | 6.2 | 28.0 | 3.9 | 15.8 | 1.7 | 21.7 | (2.6) | 0.7 |
| Corporate | 28 | 14.7 | 26 | 13.2 | 24 | 12.9 | (5.1) | (11.9) | 1.4 | (0.9) | (9.2) | (16.2) | (4.9) | (13.8) |
| **Singapore** | | | | | | | | | | | | | | |
| Total | 430 | 100.0 | 463 | 100.0 | 464 | 100.0 | 6.4 | 21.6 | 3.5 | 14.1 | 5.4 | 22.3 | 0.3 | 8.0 |
| Government | 291 | 67.7 | 321 | 69.3 | 327 | 70.4 | 8.0 | 26.3 | 5.1 | 18.6 | 7.1 | 27.0 | 1.8 | 12.2 |
| Corporate | 139 | 32.3 | 142 | 30.7 | 138 | 29.6 | 3.0 | 12.8 | (0.03) | 4.7 | 2.1 | 13.4 | (3.2) | (1.0) |
| **Thailand** | | | | | | | | | | | | | | |
| Total | 430 | 100.0 | 427 | 100.0 | 411 | 100.0 | 2.5 | 3.9 | 2.6 | 6.4 | 40.6 | 54.9 | (3.9) | (4.6) |
| Government | 312 | 72.5 | 307 | 71.9 | 294 | 71.7 | 2.2 | 2.8 | 2.3 | 5.2 | 38.0 | 50.0 | (4.2) | (5.6) |
| Corporate | 119 | 27.5 | 120 | 28.1 | 116 | 28.3 | 3.4 | 6.7 | 3.4 | 9.5 | 47.8 | 69.7 | (3.2) | (1.9) |
| **Viet Nam** | | | | | | | | | | | | | | |
| Total | 84 | 100.0 | 100 | 100.0 | 97 | 100.0 | 8.3 | 23.7 | (0.2) | 21.1 | 9.5 | 26.0 | (2.6) | 15.5 |
| Government | 63 | 74.4 | 70 | 70.3 | 67 | 69.1 | 4.3 | 9.8 | (2.0) | 12.4 | 5.4 | 11.8 | (4.4) | 7.2 |
| Corporate | 22 | 25.6 | 30 | 29.7 | 30 | 30.9 | 22.0 | 96.1 | 4.1 | 46.1 | 23.3 | 99.7 | 1.6 | 39.4 |
| **Emerging East Asia** | | | | | | | | | | | | | | |
| Total | 21,769 | 100.0 | 22,917 | 100.0 | 22,035 | 100.0 | 3.6 | 12.3 | 2.3 | 12.5 | 3.7 | 17.7 | (3.9) | 1.2 |
| Government | 13,580 | 62.4 | 14,468 | 63.1 | 14,004 | 63.6 | 3.9 | 13.5 | 2.8 | 14.3 | 4.3 | 19.3 | (3.2) | 3.1 |
| Corporate | 8,189 | 37.6 | 8,450 | 36.9 | 8,031 | 36.4 | 3.1 | 10.4 | 1.3 | 9.6 | 2.7 | 15.1 | (5.0) | (1.9) |
| **Japan** | | | | | | | | | | | | | | |
| Total | 11,428 | 100.0 | 9,659 | 100.0 | 9,084 | 100.0 | (0.6) | 4.9 | 0.3 | 3.4 | (0.8) | (0.6) | (6.0) | (20.5) |
| Government | 10,601 | 92.8 | 8,957 | 92.7 | 8,417 | 92.7 | (0.7) | 4.9 | 0.2 | 3.3 | (0.8) | (0.6) | (6.0) | (20.6) |
| Corporate | 828 | 7.2 | 702 | 7.3 | 667 | 7.3 | (0.02) | 5.5 | 1.3 | 4.8 | (0.2) | (0.02) | (5.0) | (19.4) |

( ) = negative, LCY = local currency, q-o-q = quarter-on-quarter, Q2 = second quarter, Q3 = third quarter, USD = United States dollar, y-o-y = year-on-year.

Notes:
1. For Singapore, corporate bonds outstanding are based on *AsianBondsOnline* estimates.
2. Corporate bonds include issues by financial institutions.
3. Bloomberg LP end-of-period LCY–USD rates are used.
4. For LCY base, emerging East Asia growth figures are based on 30 September 2022 currency exchange rates and do not include currency effects.

Sources: People's Republic of China (CEIC Data Company); Hong Kong, China (Hong Kong Monetary Authority); Indonesia (Bank Indonesia; Directorate General of Budget Financing and Risk Management, Ministry of Finance; and Indonesia Stock Exchange); Republic of Korea (KG Zeroin Corporation and The Bank of Korea); Malaysia (Bank Negara Malaysia); Philippines (Bureau of the Treasury and Bloomberg LP); Singapore (Monetary Authority of Singapore, Singapore Government Securities, and Bloomberg LP); Thailand (Bank of Thailand); Viet Nam (Bloomberg LP and Vietnam Bond Market Association); and Japan (Japan Securities Dealers Association).

**Figure 2: Maturity Structure of Local Currency Government Bonds Outstanding in Select Emerging East Asian Markets**

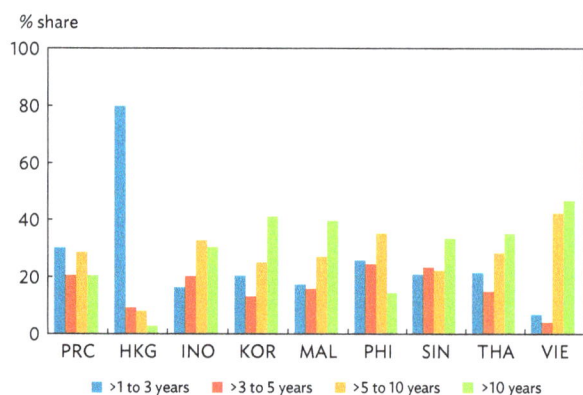

PRC = China, People's Rep. of; HKG = Hong Kong, China; INO = Indonesia; KOR = Korea, Rep. of; MAL = Malaysia; PHI = Philippines; SIN = Singapore; THA = Thailand; VIE = Viet Nam.
Notes:
1. Government bonds include Treasury bills and bonds.
2. Data as of 30 September 2022.
Source: *AsianBondsOnline*.

**Table 2: Size and Composition of Select Emerging East Asian Local Currency Bond Markets** (% of GDP)

| | Q3 2021 | Q2 2022 | Q3 2022 |
|---|---|---|---|
| **China, People's Rep. of** | | | |
| Total | 99.4 | 104.6 | 105.3 |
| Government | 63.8 | 67.7 | 68.6 |
| Corporate | 35.5 | 36.8 | 36.7 |
| **Hong Kong, China** | | | |
| Total | 86.1 | 92.1 | 96.7 |
| Government | 44.4 | 46.6 | 50.4 |
| Corporate | 41.7 | 43.6 | 46.3 |
| **Indonesia** | | | |
| Total | 31.0 | 30.1 | 30.2 |
| Government | 28.5 | 27.7 | 27.8 |
| Corporate | 2.6 | 2.4 | 2.4 |
| **Korea, Rep. of** | | | |
| Total | 147.7 | 150.6 | 151.4 |
| Government | 62.2 | 63.9 | 64.6 |
| Corporate | 85.5 | 86.6 | 86.8 |
| **Malaysia** | | | |
| Total | 125.1 | 125.9 | 125.1 |
| Government | 68.3 | 70.8 | 70.8 |
| Corporate | 56.8 | 55.1 | 54.3 |
| **Philippines** | | | |
| Total | 51.6 | 51.9 | 52.1 |
| Government | 44.0 | 45.0 | 45.4 |
| Corporate | 7.6 | 6.8 | 6.7 |
| **Singapore** | | | |
| Total | 112.2 | 114.8 | 115.1 |
| Government | 76.0 | 79.6 | 81.0 |
| Corporate | 36.2 | 35.2 | 34.1 |
| **Thailand** | | | |
| Total | 91.0 | 90.2 | 90.2 |
| Government | 66.0 | 64.8 | 64.7 |
| Corporate | 25.1 | 25.4 | 25.6 |
| **Viet Nam** | | | |
| Total | 23.6 | 26.3 | 25.2 |
| Government | 17.6 | 18.5 | 17.4 |
| Corporate | 6.1 | 7.8 | 7.8 |
| **Emerging East Asia** | | | |
| Total | 97.5 | 101.4 | 101.6 |
| Government | 60.8 | 64.0 | 64.6 |
| Corporate | 36.7 | 37.4 | 37.0 |
| **Japan** | | | |
| Total | 234.5 | 241.3 | 241.3 |
| Government | 217.5 | 223.8 | 223.6 |
| Corporate | 17.0 | 17.5 | 17.7 |

GDP = gross domestic product, Q2 = second quarter, Q3 = third quarter.
Notes:
1. Data for GDP is from CEIC. Q3 2022 GDP figure carried over from Q2 2022 for Singapore.
2. For Singapore, corporate bonds outstanding are based on *AsianBondsOnline* estimates.
Sources: People's Republic of China (CEIC Data Company); Hong Kong, China (Hong Kong Monetary Authority); Indonesia (Bank Indonesia; Directorate General of Budget Financing and Risk Management, Ministry of Finance; and Indonesia Stock Exchange); Republic of Korea (KG Zeroin Corporation and The Bank of Korea); Malaysia (Bank Negara Malaysia); Philippines (Bureau of the Treasury and Bloomberg LP); Singapore (Monetary Authority of Singapore, Singapore Government Securities, and Bloomberg LP); Thailand (Bank of Thailand); Viet Nam (Bloomberg LP and Vietnam Bond Market Association); and Japan (Japan Securities Dealers Association).

The corporate bond markets of the PRC and the Republic of Korea remained the largest in emerging East Asia. Together, the two markets accounted for 91.5% of the region's total corporate bonds outstanding at the end of September. Meanwhile, the combined shares of ASEAN member economies comprised 6.4% of the region's total corporate bond stock. Within ASEAN, Malaysia and Singapore remained home to the two largest LCY corporate bond markets, while Indonesia and the Philippines had the two smallest LCY corporate bond markets in the region at the end of September.

The value of LCY bonds outstanding in emerging East Asia at the end of Q3 2022 was equivalent to 101.6% of the region's total gross domestic product (GDP), marginally higher than 101.4% in Q2 2022 (**Table 2**). The increase in the share of outstanding government bonds to GDP was offset by a decline in the share of outstanding corporate bonds to GDP. The share of government bonds to GDP rose to 64.6% at the end of September from 64.0% at the end of June, while the share of corporate bonds outstanding to GDP fell to 37.0% from 37.4% in the same period.

At the end of the review period, four economies in the region logged LCY bonds-to-GDP shares surpassing 100% in Q3 2022. The leader of the pack was the Republic of Korea with 151.4%, followed by Malaysia (125.1%), Singapore (115.1%), and the PRC (105.3%). As in previous quarters, Viet Nam lagged all economies in the region with a bonds-to-GDP share of only 25.2%.

Six economies recorded an increase in the size of the LCY bond market as a percentage of GDP from Q2 2022 to Q3 2022: the PRC; Hong Kong, China; Indonesia; the Republic of Korea; the Philippines; and Singapore. Except for the PRC, all five economies also showed an increase in their respective government-bonds-to-GDP shares. For the corporate bonds-to-GDP share, only the Republic of Korea, Thailand, and Hong Kong, China logged an expansion from Q2 2022 to Q3 2022.

In Q3 2022, the largest government-bonds-to-GDP share in emerging East Asia was in Singapore (81.0%), while Viet Nam had the smallest (17.4%). The Republic of Korea had the largest share of LCY corporate bonds to GDP at 86.8%, while Indonesia had the smallest at 2.4%.

## Foreign Investor Holdings and Foreign Bond Flows

Emerging East Asia posted net foreign bond outflow of USD5.5 billion in the third quarter of 2022, largely due to the People's Republic of China; shares of foreign holdings also declined.

Foreign holdings of emerging East Asian LCY government bond markets declined further in Q3 2022 as the Federal Reserve and other major central banks reiterated their commitment to aggressive monetary tightening to abate high inflation (**Figure 3**). The rise in US Treasury yields and the strengthening of the US dollar continued to mute foreign demand in regional bond markets, particularly in the month of September.

The region experienced a reprieve from outflows in July and August, with some LCY government bond markets posting net inflows (**Figure 4**). This was due to the temporary shift in global risk sentiment

### Figure 3: Foreign Holdings of Local Currency Government Bonds in Select Asian Markets (% of total)

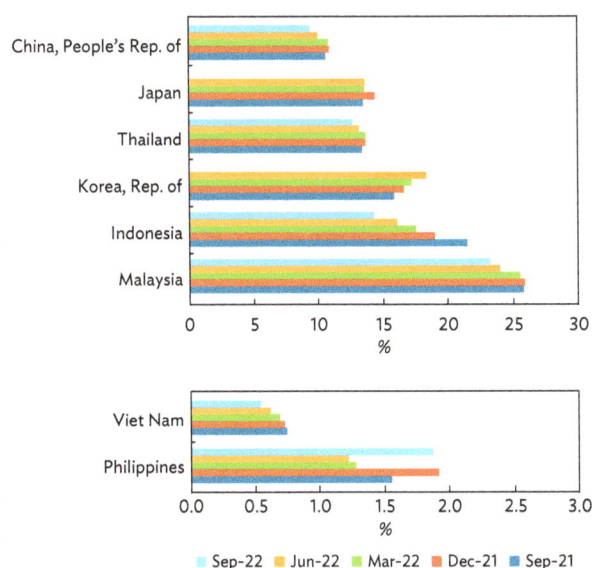

Note: Data are as of 30 September 2022 except for Japan and the Republic of Korea (30 June 2022).
Source: *AsianBondsOnline* calculations based on data from local market sources.

### Figure 4: Foreign Capital Flows in Select Emerging East Asian Local Currency Bond Markets

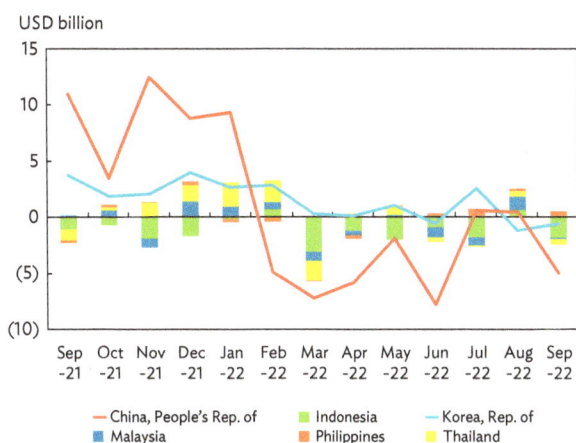

( ) = negative, USD = United States dollar.
Notes:
1. The Republic of Korea and Thailand provided data on bond flows. For the People's Republic of China, Indonesia, Malaysia, and the Philippines, month-on-month changes in foreign holdings of local currency government bonds were used as a proxy for bond flows.
2. Data are as of 30 September 2022.
3. Figures were computed based on 30 September 2022 exchange rates and do not include currency effects.
Sources: People's Republic of China (Bloomberg LP); Indonesia (Directorate General of Budget Financing and Risk Management, Ministry of Finance); Republic of Korea (Financial Supervisory Service); Malaysia (Bank Negara Malaysia); Philippines (Bureau of the Treasury); and Thailand (Thai Bond Market Association).

as market participants expected a slowdown in the aggressive monetary tightening of the Federal Reserve. In addition, inflation in the US started to peak in June with July data starting to show a slowdown in inflation. In July, the region posted aggregate net inflows of USD0.8 billion, led by inflows in the LCY bond market of the Republic of Korea. In August, net inflows rose to USD1.5 billion with nearly all markets posting net inflows. However, in September, nearly all markets posted net foreign outflows except the Philippines. This was largely driven by the Jackson Hole speech in late August when the Federal Reserve reiterated its commitment to fight inflation via aggressive monetary tightening, sending a signal that it would not be paring back rate increases in the near-term contrary to market expectations. Outflows were exacerbated in the PRC due to ongoing economic weakness. The Federal Reserve subsequently delivered another 75 bps rate hike at its 20–21 September monetary policy meeting.

Foreign investors returned to the PRC's LCY government bond market in July, posting marginal net inflows of USD0.5 billion following net outflows from February to June. The inflows were largely due to an improvement in domestic bonds' negative interest rate differential with US Treasury yields, which declined during the month. The relative stability of the Chinese yuan in July also contributed to the increase in demand for domestic bonds. In August, net foreign inflows slightly declined to USD0.3 billion, while September posted outflows of USD5.0 billion, driven by the divergence in monetary policy with the US that led to the depreciation of the Chinese yuan. Foreign holdings of the PRC's LCY government bond market fell to 9.4% in Q3 2022 from 10.0% in Q2 2022.

In the Republic of Korea, the domestic government bond market posted quarterly net inflows of USD0.5 billion in Q3 2022, slightly higher than the USD0.3 billion posted in Q2 2022. However, this was low compared to quarterly inflows in recent years. Although the Republic of Korea remained a safe haven for foreign investors relative to its peers, as evidenced by the USD2.5 billion of net inflows in July, it has not been spared by the capital outflows from the region as US Treasury yields rose at a faster pace than domestic bond yields. This resulted in USD1.3 billion and USD0.7 billion of net outflows in August and September, respectively, which were largely driven by expectations of a continuation of aggressive monetary tightening by the Federal Reserve. Despite recent rate hikes by the Bank of Korea, the pace of the central bank's increases

was slower compared to its US counterpart. In addition, a sharp depreciation of the Korean won, the weakest currency in the region year-to-date, also reduced the attractiveness of the returns of domestic bonds. Foreign holdings rose to 18.4% in Q2 2022 from 17.2% in Q1 2022, based on current available data.

Malaysia's foreign holdings share fell to 23.3% in Q3 2022 from 24.1% in Q2 2022, but it continued to have the highest share in the region. The quarterly decline of 0.7 percentage points was less than the 1.5 percentage points decline from Q1 2022 to Q2 2022. The falling foreign holdings share occurred in spite of the USD0.3 billion of net inflows registered in Q3 2022, reversing the USD1.1 billion of net outflows in Q2 2022, as the USD1.2 billion of net inflows in August more than offset outflows of USD0.7 billion and USD0.1 billion in July and September, respectively. Despite the rate hike by the Bank Negara Malaysia in September, foreign investors still sold Malaysian bonds as rates remained low compared to US Treasuries amid the aggressive rate hikes of the Federal Reserve.

The foreign holdings share in Indonesia's LCY government bond market fell to 14.3% in Q3 2022 from 16.1% in Q2 2022 as net foreign outflows continued during the most recent quarter. Foreign investors sold a net USD3.3 billion of LCY bonds in Q3 2022, slightly lower than the USD4.5 billion of outflows in Q2 2022. This was largely driven by USD1.9 billion of net outflows in both July and September, which more than offset the USD0.5 billion of net inflows recorded in August. Despite the end of the accommodative stance of Bank Indonesia in August, when it started to raise policy rates, the narrowing yield premiums of domestic bonds over US Treasury yields continued to make Indonesian LCY bonds less attractive to foreign investors.

In Thailand, foreign investors sold a net USD0.02 billion of LCY government bonds in Q3 2022, a reversal from the USD0.6 billion of net inflows posted in the previous quarter. The net quarterly outflows were driven by USD0.1 billion and USD0.5 billion of net outflows in July and September, respectively, which offset the marginal USD0.6 billion net inflows in August. Similar to Indonesia, the slower pace of rate hikes by the Bank of Thailand relative to the Federal Reserve and the weakening of the Thai baht contributed to the foreign outflows from its LCY bond market. As a result, foreign holdings of Thailand's LCY government bond market declined further to 12.7% in Q3 2022 from 13.2% in Q2 2022.

In the Philippines, the LCY government bond market registered net foreign inflows of USD0.6 billion, USD0.1 billion, and USD0.4 billion in July, August, and September, respectively. However, the LCY bond market's foreign holdings share remained negligible at 1.9% in Q3 2022. In Viet Nam, the foreign holdings share also remained negligible at 0.5% in Q3 2022, slightly lower than 0.6% in Q2 2022.

Given the continued outflows from the region's LCY bond markets that resulted in declining shares of foreign holdings, domestic investor groups saw an increase in their corresponding shares in recent quarters. This highlights the continued contribution of domestic investors to market stability amid a foreign sell-off in the region. For example, banks and insurance companies and pension funds registered increases in their shares in most markets in the region (**Figure 5**). Central banks also increased in their participation, particularly in Indonesia and Thailand.

## Local Currency Bond Issuance

Emerging East Asia issued a total of USD2.2 trillion of local currency bonds in the third quarter of 2022.

Q3 2022 marked the sixth consecutive quarter where regional bond market issuance tallied over USD2.0 trillion. As the Federal Reserve maintained its aggressive monetary tightening stance, issuers turned to the LCY

bond market to support their financing needs, but they were also cautious amid uncertainty and rising borrowing costs. While regional central banks tightened their monetary policies, the pace of rate hikes remained relatively subdued with some markets only raising rates starting in August (Indonesia, Thailand) or September (Viet Nam).

Total issuance of LCY bonds in emerging East Asia tallied USD2.2 trillion in Q3 2022, a decline of 1.1% q-o-q from a 13.6% q-o-q hike in Q2 2022 (**Figure 6**). Overall growth was dragged down by the 12.0% q-o-q contraction in the issuance of Treasury and other government bonds during the quarter. On a y-o-y basis, growth in Treasury and other government bond issuance also eased.

While issuance of Treasury instruments slowed during the quarter, they continued to account for a substantial share of emerging East Asia's issuance volume in Q3 2022 (**Figure 7**). Newly issued Treasury and other government bonds comprised 42.3% of the region's issuance total during the quarter. It also accounted for a 66.2% share of the regional government bond issuance total. Treasury and other government bond issuance declined to USD948.6 billion in Q3 2022. The larger markets of the PRC and the Republic of Korea tapered issuance of Treasury and other government bonds, dragging down the regional total. Similarly, Thailand reduced its issuance during the quarter as it had already met its borrowing plan total before the end of its fiscal year in September. On the

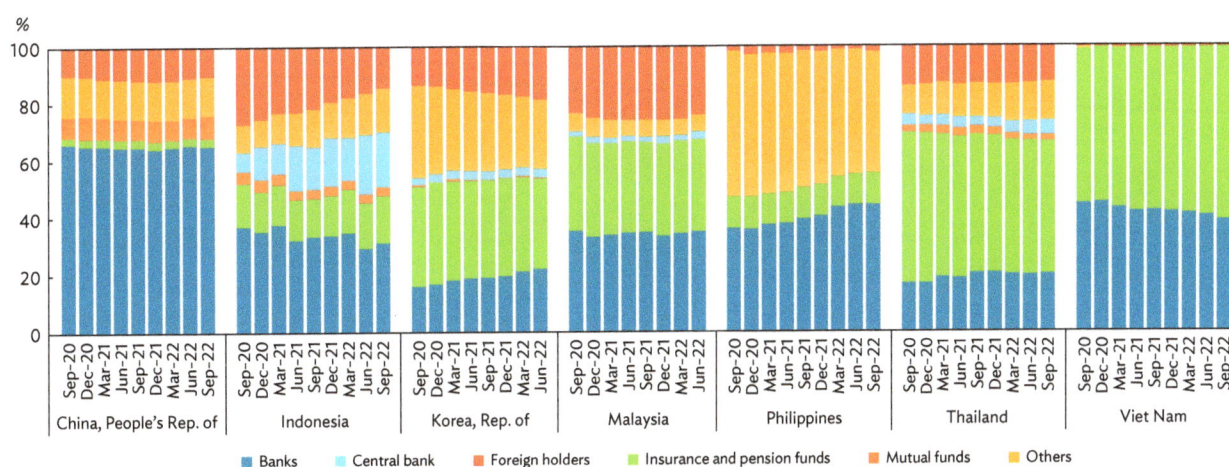

**Figure 5: Investor Profiles of Local Currency Government Bonds in Select Emerging East Asian Markets**

Notes:
1. Data for the Republic of Korea and Malaysia are up to 30 June 2022.
2. "Others" include government institutions, individuals, securities companies, custodians, private corporations, and all other investors not elsewhere classified.
Source: *AsianBondsOnline*.

**Figure 6: Local Currency Bond Issuance in Select Emerging East Asian Markets**

USD trillion

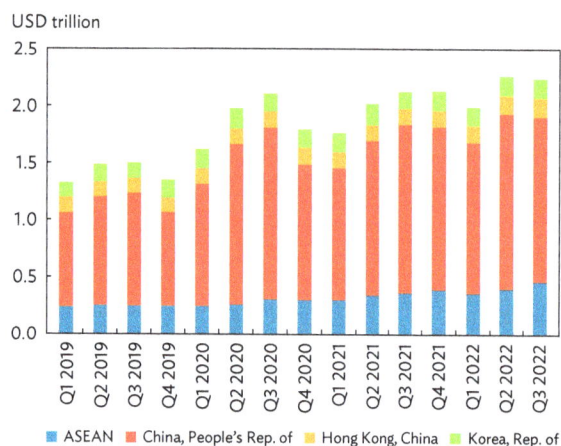

ASEAN = Association of Southeast Asian Nations, Q1 = first quarter, Q2 = second quarter, Q3 = third quarter, Q4 = fourth quarter, USD = United States dollar.
Note: Figures were computed based on 30 September 2022 currency exchange rates and do not include currency effects.
Source: *AsianBondsOnline*.

**Figure 7: Share in Bond Issuance by Type of Bonds in Select Emerging East Asian Markets**

Share of total (%)

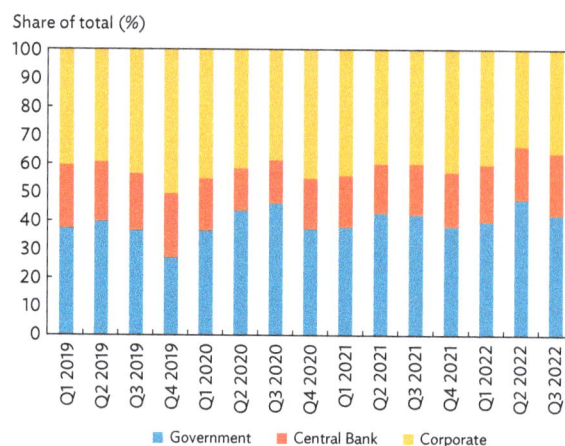

Q1 = first quarter, Q2 = second quarter, Q3 = third quarter, Q4 = fourth quarter, USD = United States dollar.
Note: Figures were computed based on 30 September 2022 currency exchange rates and do not include currency effects.
Source: *AsianBondsOnline*.

other hand, some governments continued to secure funding to support fiscal measures and spur economic recovery, while also taking advantage of interest rates that remained low in the region.

The maturity structure of the region's LCY Treasury bond issuance shifted toward longer-term tenors in Q3 2022. Treasury bonds with maturities of over 5 years accounted for 60.5% of the region's total issuance, inching up from 48.6% in Q2 2022 (**Figure 8**). This reflected improved capacity of investors to absorb longer-term durations. Bonds with maturities of 5 years or less comprised 39.5% of the regional issuance volume in Q3 2022, down from 51.4% in the preceding quarter.

Corporate bond issuance rebounded in Q3 2022, largely driven by higher issuance from the PRC as it eased monetary policy, leading to lower borrowing costs. Regional corporate bond issuance totaled USD808.1 billion on growth of 5.7% q-o-q, reversing the 4.7% q-o-q contraction in Q2 2022. Four out of nine markets in the region saw increased q-o-q issuance of corporate bonds during the quarter, including the PRC, Indonesia, the Republic of Korea, and the Philippines. On an annual basis, corporate bond issuance declined 4.9% y-o-y, a slowdown from the 5.2% y-o-y contraction in Q2 2022. Corporate bonds accounted for 36.1% of emerging East Asia's bond issuance total during the quarter.

**Figure 8: Maturity Structure of Local Currency Government Bond Issuance in Select Emerging East Asian Markets**

%

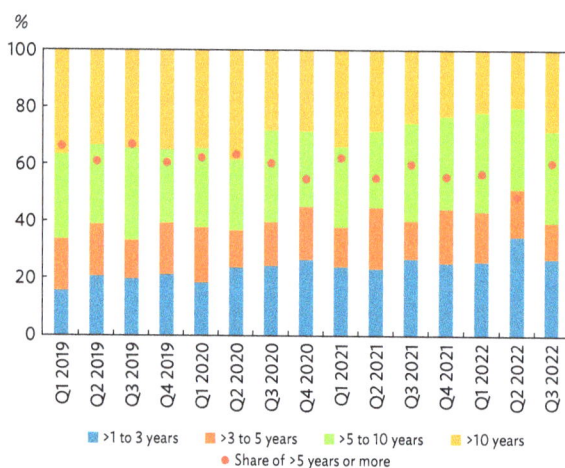

Q1 = first quarter, Q2 = second quarter, Q3 = third quarter, Q4 = fourth quarter.
Note: Figures were computed based on 30 September 2022 currency exchange rates and do not include currency effects.
Source: *AsianBondsOnline* computations based on various local sources.

Among all bond segments, central bank bonds posted the fastest expansion in issuance at 14.7% q-o-q and 28.3% y-o-y. This was up from 6.6% q-o-q and 21.6% y-o-y in Q2 2022. Most central banks engaged in market operations to mop-up liquidity amid persistent high inflation levels across the region. All regional central banks except one saw q-o-q increases in the issuance of central bank instruments. The sole exception was the Bangko Sentral ng Pilipinas, which tapered its issuance amid aggressive policy rate hikes in recent months. Central bank issuance totaled USD484.1 billion in emerging East Asia, accounting for 21.6% of the regional issuance volume in Q3 2022.

Overall, seven out of nine regional markets saw higher LCY bond issuance in Q3 2022 compared with Q2 2022 (**Table 3**). The markets of Hong Kong, China; Indonesia; Malaysia; the Philippines; Singapore; Thailand; and Viet Nam posted increased issuance during the quarter. In contrast, the PRC and the Republic of Korea had lower issuance volumes compared with Q2 2022. On a y-o-y basis, the majority of emerging East Asian markets recorded higher bond sales, with only the PRC, Indonesia, and Thailand posting declines.

LCY bond issuance in the PRC totaled USD1,443.2 billion in Q3 2022, posting a contraction of 5.9% q-o-q after gaining 16.3% q-o-q in Q2 2022. Lower bond sales stemmed from a 14.2% q-o-q drop in the issuance of Treasury and other government bonds during the quarter. Local authorities had mostly used up the special bond quota for issuing local government bonds following directives from the government for its utilization by the end of June to boost infrastructure activities. To further prop up the economy, the State Council announced an increase of CNY500 billion in its special bond quota in August that was to be utilized by October.

Corporate bond issuance in the PRC rebounded in Q3 2022 on growth of 7.2% q-o-q, reversing the 8.8% q-o-q decline in the preceding quarter. Monetary easing by the People's Bank of China encouraged firms to tap the bond market for funding and take advantage of lower borrowing costs. On a y-o-y basis, LCY bond issuance in the PRC dropped 2.2% in Q3 2022. The PRC accounted for 64.4% of the region's aggregate issuance volume in Q3 2022, down from 67.7% in Q2 2022.

LCY bond sales in the Republic of Korea tallied USD164.6 billion, posting a decline of 5.0% q-o-q in Q3 2022. Overall growth was dragged down by the 23.7% q-o-q contraction in the issuance of Treasury and other government bonds as the Republic of Korea engaged in a frontloading policy in the first half of the year. Central bank issuance climbed the most among all

bond segments, up 11.7% q-o-q following a 21.2% q-o-q contraction in Q2 2022. Corporate bond issuance grew a modest 2.4% q-o-q as corporates borrowed from the bond market in anticipation of further policy rate hikes by the Bank of Korea. Overall issuance on an annual basis rose to 10.6% y-o-y in Q3 2022, a reversal from the 6.3% y-o-y decline in Q2 2022.

In Hong Kong, China, LCY bond issuance reached USD159.6 billion in Q3 2022, inching up 2.1% q-o-q. Issuance of government bonds expanded 3.5% q-o-q, driven largely by an increase in the issuance of HKSAR bonds. The majority of HKSAR bond issuance during the quarter was from the issuance of Silver Bonds amounting to HKD45.0 billion. Exchange Fund Bills and Exchange Fund Notes also contributed to the q-o-q gain in issuance during the quarter. Corporate bond issuance contracted 3.3% q-o-q in Q3 2022 amid rising borrowing costs. Hong Kong, China largely tracks movements in US interest rates as its currency is pegged to the US dollar. On an annual basis, LCY bond issuance in Hong Kong, China grew at a faster pace of 16.1% y-o-y in Q3 2022 versus 12.7% y-o-y in Q2 2022.

ASEAN member economies collectively raised USD473.3 billion from the sale of LCY bonds in Q3 2022, accounting for 21.1% of emerging East Asia's issuance total. Growth quickened by 17.8% q-o-q and 29.6% y-o-y in Q3 2022, up from 10.4% q-o-q and 17.0% y-o-y in the preceding quarter. All six ASEAN markets had increased issuance activities in Q3 2022. Singapore, Thailand, the Philippines, and Indonesia were the largest issuers of LCY bonds in the ASEAN space, accounting for 56.8%, 12.4%, 9.9%, and 9.3% shares of total issuance, respectively.

Singapore continued to account for the largest issuance volume among ASEAN member economies in Q3 2022. Total issuance reached USD268.9 billion, with growth easing to 14.4% q-o-q from 16.1% q-o-q in Q2 2022. Much of the growth was contributed by the government bond segment, largely from increased issuance of central bank bills to help contain inflationary pressure. Singapore is among the markets in emerging East Asia with relatively high inflation. Issuance of Treasury and other government bonds also contributed to the overall growth but to a lesser extent. On the other hand, corporate bond issuance contracted a significant 25.2% q-o-q amid elevated borrowing cost as the Monetary Authority of Singapore

**Table 3: Local Currency Bond Issuance in Select Emerging East Asian Market** (gross)

| | Q3 2021 | | Q2 2022 | | Q3 2022 | | Growth Rate (LCY-base %) | | Growth Rate (USD-base %) | |
|---|---|---|---|---|---|---|---|---|---|---|
| | Amount (USD billion) | % share | Amount (USD billion) | % share | Amount (USD billion) | % share | Q3 2022 | | Q3 2022 | |
| | | | | | | | q-o-q | y-o-y | q-o-q | y-o-y |
| **China, People's Rep. of** | | | | | | | | | | |
| Total | 1,629 | 100.0 | 1,629 | 100.0 | 1,443 | 100.0 | (5.9) | (2.2) | (11.4) | (11.4) |
| Government | 848 | 52.1 | 996 | 61.1 | 804 | 55.7 | (14.2) | 4.7 | (19.2) | (5.1) |
| Central Bank | 0 | 0.0 | 0 | 0.0 | 0 | 0.0 | – | – | – | – |
| Treasury and Other Govt. | 848 | 52.1 | 996 | 61.1 | 804 | 55.7 | (14.2) | 4.7 | (19.2) | (5.1) |
| Corporate | 781 | 47.9 | 633 | 38.9 | 639 | 44.3 | 7.2 | (9.7) | 0.9 | (18.2) |
| **Hong Kong, China** | | | | | | | | | | |
| Total | 139 | 100.0 | 156 | 100.0 | 160 | 100.0 | 2.1 | 16.1 | 2.1 | 15.1 |
| Government | 113 | 81.8 | 125 | 79.6 | 129 | 80.7 | 3.5 | 14.6 | 3.5 | 13.7 |
| Central Bank | 109 | 78.9 | 121 | 77.3 | 123 | 76.8 | 1.5 | 13.0 | 1.4 | 12.1 |
| Treasury and Other Govt. | 4 | 2.9 | 3.6 | 2.3 | 6 | 3.9 | 71.9 | 58.1 | 71.9 | 56.8 |
| Corporate | 25 | 18.2 | 32 | 20.4 | 31 | 19.3 | (3.3) | 22.8 | (3.4) | 21.8 |
| **Indonesia** | | | | | | | | | | |
| Total | 48 | 100.0 | 34 | 100.0 | 44 | 100.0 | 31.9 | (1.8) | 29.0 | (7.7) |
| Government | 46 | 95.2 | 32 | 94.0 | 41 | 91.7 | 28.6 | (5.4) | 25.8 | (11.1) |
| Central Bank | 27 | 57.0 | 22 | 65.0 | 23 | 52.0 | 5.4 | (10.4) | 3.1 | (15.8) |
| Treasury and Other Govt. | 18 | 38.2 | 10 | 29.1 | 18 | 39.8 | 80.4 | 2.1 | 76.5 | (4.0) |
| Corporate | 2 | 4.8 | 2 | 6.0 | 4 | 8.3 | 83.3 | 71.0 | 79.3 | 60.7 |
| **Korea, Rep. of** | | | | | | | | | | |
| Total | 180 | 100.0 | 191 | 100.0 | 165 | 100.0 | (5.0) | 10.6 | (13.8) | (8.5) |
| Government | 78 | 43.4 | 79 | 41.5 | 61 | 36.9 | (15.5) | 6.0 | (23.3) | (22.3) |
| Central Bank | 27 | 15.0 | 18 | 9.6 | 19 | 11.2 | 11.7 | (17.1) | 1.4 | (31.4) |
| Treasury and Other Govt. | 51 | 28.4 | 61 | 31.9 | 42 | 25.7 | (23.7) | (0.2) | (30.7) | (17.4) |
| Corporate | 102 | 56.6 | 112 | 58.5 | 104 | 63.1 | 2.4 | 23.3 | (7.0) | 2.0 |
| **Malaysia** | | | | | | | | | | |
| Total | 21 | 100.0 | 25 | 100.0 | 26 | 100.0 | 7.2 | 36.3 | 1.9 | 23.0 |
| Government | 12 | 55.9 | 15 | 60.6 | 16 | 63.5 | 12.4 | 54.9 | 6.9 | 39.9 |
| Central Bank | 0 | 0.0 | 0.2 | 0.8 | 0.9 | 3.5 | 388.2 | – | 364.1 | – |
| Treasury and Other Govt. | 12 | 55.9 | 15 | 59.8 | 15 | 60.0 | 7.6 | 46.4 | 2.3 | 32.1 |
| Corporate | 9 | 44.1 | 10 | 39.4 | 9 | 36.5 | (0.7) | 12.7 | (5.6) | 1.7 |
| **Philippines** | | | | | | | | | | |
| Total | 42 | 100.0 | 43 | 100.0 | 47 | 100.0 | 15.5 | 28.0 | 0.03 | 2.8 |
| Government | 41 | 97.7 | 42 | 96.2 | 45 | 95.4 | 14.7 | 25.0 | (1.1) | 0.0 |
| Central Bank | 26 | 62.3 | 32 | 73.1 | 28 | 60.7 | (4.1) | 24.6 | (10.1) | 8.4 |
| Treasury and Other Govt. | 15 | 35.4 | 10 | 23.1 | 16 | 34.7 | 74.0 | 25.7 | 27.2 | (14.7) |
| Corporate | 1 | 2.3 | 2 | 3.8 | 2 | 4.6 | 37.7 | 154.0 | 29.0 | 120.9 |
| **Singapore** | | | | | | | | | | |
| Total | 205 | 100.0 | 243 | 100.0 | 269 | 100.0 | 14.4 | 38.3 | 10.8 | 30.9 |
| Government | 200 | 97.4 | 239 | 98.5 | 266 | 99.0 | 15.0 | 40.6 | 11.4 | 33.0 |
| Central Bank | 174 | 84.8 | 209 | 86.2 | 237 | 88.3 | 17.1 | 44.0 | 13.4 | 36.2 |
| Treasury and Other Govt. | 26 | 12.6 | 30 | 12.2 | 29 | 10.7 | 0.5 | 17.9 | (2.7) | 11.6 |
| Corporate | 5 | 2.6 | 4 | 1.5 | 3 | 1.0 | (25.2) | (46.2) | (27.6) | (49.1) |
| **Thailand** | | | | | | | | | | |
| Total | 69 | 100.0 | 61 | 100.0 | 59 | 100.0 | 1.9 | (5.3) | (4.5) | (15.1) |
| Government | 55 | 79.9 | 44 | 72.5 | 44 | 74.8 | 5.2 | (11.3) | (1.4) | (20.5) |
| Central Bank | 37 | 53.4 | 25 | 40.5 | 28 | 48.0 | 20.8 | (14.9) | 13.2 | (23.7) |
| Treasury and Other Govt. | 18 | 26.5 | 20 | 32.0 | 16 | 26.9 | (14.4) | (4.0) | (19.8) | (13.9) |
| Corporate | 14 | 20.1 | 17 | 27.5 | 15 | 25.2 | (6.9) | 18.3 | (12.8) | 6.1 |

*continued on next page*

**Table 3** *continued*

| | Q3 2021 | | Q2 2022 | | Q3 2022 | | Growth Rate (LCY-base %) | | Growth Rate (USD-base %) | |
|---|---|---|---|---|---|---|---|---|---|---|
| | | | | | | | Q3 2022 | | Q3 2022 | |
| | Amount (USD billion) | % share | Amount (USD billion) | % share | Amount (USD billion) | % share | q-o-q | y-o-y | q-o-q | y-o-y |
| **Viet Nam** | | | | | | | | | | |
| Total | 9 | 100.0 | 12 | 100.0 | 29 | 100.0 | 158.8 | 244.3 | 152.5 | 228.4 |
| Government | 5 | 52.9 | 9 | 74.4 | 27 | 93.0 | 223.8 | 505.3 | 215.9 | 477.4 |
| Central Bank | 0 | 0.0 | 7 | 62.2 | 25 | 86.4 | 259.6 | – | 250.8 | – |
| Treasury and Other Govt. | 5 | 52.9 | 1 | 12.2 | 2 | 6.6 | 40.8 | (56.9) | 37.4 | (58.9) |
| Corporate | 4 | 47.1 | 3 | 25.6 | 2 | 7.0 | (29.8) | (49.2) | (31.5) | (51.5) |
| **Emerging East Asia** | | | | | | | | | | |
| Total | 2,342 | 100.0 | 2,395 | 100.0 | 2,241 | 100.0 | (1.1) | 5.4 | (6.4) | (4.3) |
| Government | 1,398 | 59.7 | 1,581 | 66.0 | 1,433 | 63.9 | (4.5) | 12.1 | (9.4) | 2.5 |
| Central Bank | 401 | 17.1 | 435 | 18.1 | 484 | 21.6 | 14.7 | 28.3 | 11.4 | 20.7 |
| Treasury and Other Govt. | 997 | 42.6 | 1,146 | 47.9 | 949 | 42.3 | (12.0) | 5.4 | (17.2) | (4.8) |
| Corporate | 944 | 40.3 | 814 | 34.0 | 808 | 36.1 | 5.7 | (4.9) | (0.7) | (14.4) |
| **Japan** | | | | | | | | | | |
| Total | 502 | 100.0 | 412 | 100.0 | 373 | 100.0 | (3.4) | (3.3) | (9.4) | (25.7) |
| Government | 464 | 92.5 | 384 | 93.3 | 347 | 92.9 | (3.7) | (2.9) | (9.7) | (25.3) |
| Central Bank | 10 | 2.0 | 16 | 3.9 | 0 | 0.0 | (100.0) | (100.0) | – | (100.0) |
| Treasury and Other Govt. | 454 | 90.5 | 368 | 89.3 | 347 | 92.9 | 0.5 | (0.7) | (5.7) | (23.6) |
| Corporate | 38 | 7.5 | 28 | 6.7 | 26 | 7.1 | 1.3 | (9.0) | (5.1) | (30.1) |

( ) = negative, – = not applicable, LCY = local currency, q-o-q = quarter-on-quarter, Q2 = second quarter, Q3 = third quarter, USD = United States dollar, y-o-y = year-on-year.
Notes:
1.  Corporate bonds include issues by financial institutions.
2.  Bloomberg LP end-of-period LCY–USD rates are used.
3.  For LCY base, emerging East Asia growth figures are based on 30 September 2022 currency exchange rates and do not include currency effects.
Sources: People's Republic of China (CEIC Data Company); Hong Kong, China (Hong Kong Monetary Authority); Indonesia (Bank Indonesia; Directorate General of Budget Financing and Risk Management, Ministry of Finance; and Indonesia Stock Exchange); Republic of Korea (KG Zeroin Corporation and The Bank of Korea); Malaysia (Bank Negara Malaysia); Philippines (Bureau of the Treasury and Bloomberg LP); Singapore (Singapore Government Securities and Bloomberg LP); Thailand (Bank of Thailand); Viet Nam (Bloomberg LP, Hanoi Stock Exchange, and Vietnam Bond Market Association); and Japan (Japan Securities Dealers Association).

engaged in monetary tightening measures. On a y-o-y basis, LCY bond issuance in Singapore grew at a faster pace of 38.3% in Q3 2022 versus 29.0% in Q2 2022.

In Thailand, total bond sales in Q3 2022 reached USD58.6 billion on growth of 1.9% q-o-q. The rise in issuance during the quarter stemmed solely from a recovery in the government bond segment. Government bond issuance rebounded, with the 5.2% q-o-q growth in Q3 2022 reversing the 5.9% q-o-q decline in the previous quarter. Meanwhile, corporate bond issuance contracted 6.9% q-o-q in Q3 2022 amid rising borrowing costs as the BOT started monetary policy tightening during the quarter. On an annual basis, bond issuance in Thailand contracted at a faster pace of 5.3% y-o-y in Q3 2022 than 1.7% y-o-y in Q2 2022.

LCY bond issuance growth in the Philippines accelerated to 15.5% q-o-q in Q3 2022 after rising a marginal 0.3% q-o-q in the prior quarter. Total issuance reached USD46.9 billion, buoyed by higher sales of Treasury and other government bonds, as well as corporate bonds. In September, the government raised PHP420.4 billion from the sale of its 28th series of Retail Treasury Bonds, which carried a maturity of 5.5 years and a coupon rate of 5.75%. About PHP108.5 billion of the amount came from a debt switch of bonds that will mature later this year and early next year. Corporate bond issuance also rebounded in Q3 2022, climbing 37.7% q-o-q after contracting 40.2% q-o-q in Q2 2022. In contrast, issuance of central bank bills declined 4.1% q-o-q, as the Bangko Sentral ng Pilipinas aggressively raised policy rates starting in May to quell inflationary pressure and stabilize the domestic currency. Compared with the same period a year earlier, bond issuance growth rose to 28.0% y-o-y in Q3 2022 from 15.8% y-o-y in Q2 2022.

In Indonesia, bond issuance rebounded strongly, with growth surging to 31.9% q-o-q after contracting 22.4% q-o-q in Q2 2022. Issuance volume tallied

USD44.2 billion in Q3 2022, with growth recorded across all bond types, reversing the contraction from the prior quarter. Issuance of Treasury and other government bonds nearly doubled from Q2 2022. Aside from regular Treasury auctions and private placement issuance, the government also raised IDR27.0 trillion from the sale of *sukuk ritel* (retail Islamic bonds) in September. The *sukuk ritel* carried a maturity of 3 years and a coupon rate of 5.90%. Corporate bond issuance also recovered in Q3 2022, rising 83.3% q-o-q. Firms rushed to issue bonds ahead of expectations of higher borrowing costs. Bank Indonesia was among the few central banks in the region that tightened its policy rate starting in August. On a y-o-y basis, however, LCY bond issuance contracted at a slower pace of 1.8% in Q3 2022 versus a decline of 8.8% in Q2 2022.

LCY bond sales in Viet Nam more than doubled in Q3 2022, with issuance rising to USD29.2 billion. Strong issuance growth was maintained at 158.8% q-o-q, which was broadly the same pace of expansion during the preceding quarter. Growth was largely buoyed by the high volume of issuance from the central bank, which accounted for 86.4% of Viet Nam's issuance total during the quarter The SBV opted to engage in open market operations to stabilize the exchange rate, holding off on raising rates and doing so only in September with a 100 bps hike to contain inflationary pressure. Due to the short-term maturity of SBV bills, the large volume of issuance had no significant impact on Viet Nam's outstanding bond stock at the end of September. Treasury and other government bonds also contributed to the growth, rising 40.8% q-o-q. In contrast, issuance of corporate bonds contracted 29.8% q-o-q, following a strong expansion of 120.5% q-o-q in Q2 2022. On an annual basis, Viet Nam's issuance growth surged a substantial 244.3% y-o-y in Q3 2022, up from 25.7% y-o-y in Q2 2022.

In Malaysia, bond issuance growth moderated to 7.2% q-o-q in Q3 2022, after climbing 35.5% q-o-q in Q2 2022, to reach USD25.5 billion, the smallest issuance amount among ASEAN peers. Growth was solely driven by government bond issuance, which rose 12.4% q-o-q, moderating from 33.7% q-o-q growth in Q2 2022. Both the central government and the central bank increased issuance during the quarter. In contrast, corporate bond issuance contracted a marginal 0.7% q-o-q over rising borrowing costs. The Bank Negara Malaysia raised policy rates by 25 bps in both July and September. On a y-o-y

basis, Malaysia's bond issuance growth accelerated to 36.3% in Q3 2022 from 9.0% in the preceding quarter.

## Cross-Border Bond Issuance

### Emerging East Asia's cross-border bond issuance reached USD8.0 billion in Q3 2022

Cross border bond issuance in emerging East Asia totaled USD8.0 billion in Q3 2022, a 20.6% q-o-q increase from the USD6.6 billion raised in the previous quarter. Hong Kong, China continued to comprise the largest share of the region's quarterly aggregate issuance volume at 80.7% (**Figure 9**). Other economies that registered cross-border bond issuances in Q3 2022 include the Republic of Korea, the Lao People's Democratic Republic (Lao PDR), Malaysia, and Singapore. Monthly issuance volumes amounted to USD2.1 billion, USD3.7 billion, and USD2.2 billion, respectively, in July, August, and September.

Hong Kong, China continued to dominate the region with an aggregate issuance volume of USD6.4 billion, a 32.3% q-o-q increase from USD4.9 billion in Q2 2022. Eleven institutions from Hong Kong, China raised funds via cross-border issuances during the quarter, and all bonds were denominated in Chinese yuan. Firms from the transportation sector continued to have the largest collective issuance volume in Q3 2022 at USD2.4 billion. China Merchants Group, a PRC state-owned company based in Hong Kong, China that is primarily involved in

**Figure 9: Origin Economies of Select Intra-Emerging East Asian Bond Issuance in the Third Quarter of 2022**

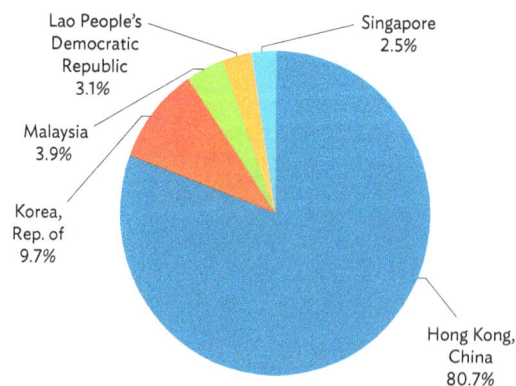

Lao People's Democratic Republic 3.1%
Singapore 2.5%
Malaysia 3.9%
Korea, Rep. of 9.7%
Hong Kong, China 80.7%

Source: *AsianBondsOnline* calculations based on Bloomberg LP data.

shipping and integrated transportation, led the group with total issuance of USD2.1 billion via multiple short-term bonds and one perpetual bond. MTR Corporation, which operates the Mass Transit Railway in Hong Kong, China, raised a total of USD199.6 million via two 2-year green bonds and a 3-year bond. Firms involved in consumer products comprised the second-largest group and accounted for nearly a third of the total issuance volume in Hong Kong, China. The two companies from this sector were China Mengniu Dairy, which issued USD1.9 billion worth of short-term bonds, and China Tourism with USD210.8 million. The other notable issuers from Hong Kong, China were China Power International Development and Pioneer Reward with USD702.6 million each.

The Republic of Korea registered the second-largest aggregate issuance volume in emerging East Asia at USD777.0 million for a 9.7% share of the regional total. The Export–Import Bank of Korea issued USD393.7 million worth of 1-year and 2-year bonds denominated in Chinese yuan, Hong Kong dollars, and Singapore dollars. State-owned Korea Development Bank issued USD198.4 million worth of multi-tenor bonds denominated in Chinese yuan and Hong Kong dollars. Other issuers of cross-border bonds from the Republic of Korea were Hyundai Capital (USD114.4 million) and the Industrial Bank of Korea (USD70.5 million).

Cagamas Global, Malaysia's state-owned mortgage corporation, was the sole issuer of cross-border bonds in Malaysia in Q3 2022, raising a total of USD313.5 million worth of SGD-denominated 1-year bonds.

In the Lao PDR, Xayaburi Power Company issued USD222.5 million worth of multitranche THB-denominated green bonds in July to repay and refinance loans used for the funding of its hydropower plant. The other issuer, EDL-Generation Public Company, which is involved in the generation and wholesale of electricity in the Lao PDR, raised USD25.8 million worth of THB-denominated bonds.

In Singapore, Korea Development Bank-Singapore issued USD148.3 million of 3-year bonds denominated in Chinese yuan and Hong Kong dollars. Meanwhile, Nomura International Fund raised USD54.9 million via issuance of multi-tenor Chinese yuan bonds.

The top 10 issuers in the region had an aggregate issuance volume of USD7.1 billion and accounted for 88.7% of the regional total in Q3 2022. Seven out of the top 10 issuers were from Hong Kong, China, while the rest were from the Republic of Korea, Malaysia, and the Lao PDR. The top four issuers were from Hong Kong, China, including China Merchants Group, Mengniu Dairy, China Power International, and Pioneer Reward.

The Chinese yuan remained the predominant issuance currency for cross-border bonds in the region in Q3 2022 with a share of 85.0% and a total volume of USD6.8 billion (**Figure 10**). Firms from Hong Kong, China, the Republic of Korea, and Singapore issued cross-border bonds denominated in Chinese yuan. Bonds denominated in Hong Kong dollars followed with a 6.5% share of cross-border bond issuance and a total volume of USD515.7 million. Other currencies used in cross-border issuance were the Singapore dollar (5.4%, USD429.9 million) and the Thai baht (3.1%, USD248.3 million).

Issuance of cross-border bonds in emerging East Asia in Q3 2022 were largely concentrated in three sectors. The transportation sector comprised 32.6% of the regional issuance for the quarter, slightly higher than its 31.0% share in Q2 2022, with aggregate issuance volume of USD2.6 billion (**Figure 11**). China Merchants Group accounted for a large share of this total with issuance of USD2.1 billion. The financial sector with an aggregate issuance volume of USD2.5 billion also comprised almost

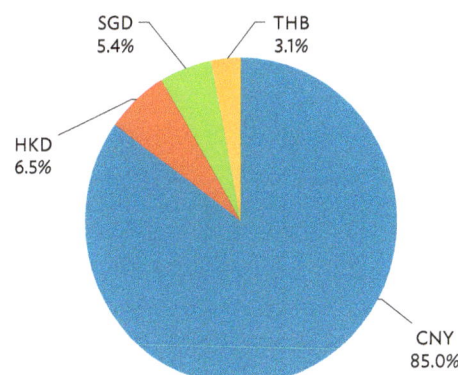

**Figure 10: Currency Shares of Select Intra-Emerging East Asian Bond Issuance in the Third Quarter of 2022**

SGD 5.4%
THB 3.1%
HKD 6.5%
CNY 85.0%

CNY = Chinese yuan, HKD = Hong Kong dollar, SGD = Singapore dollar, THB = Thai baht.
Source: *AsianBondsOnline* calculations based on Bloomberg LP data.

**Figure 11: Select Intra-Emerging East Asian Bond Issuance by Sector**

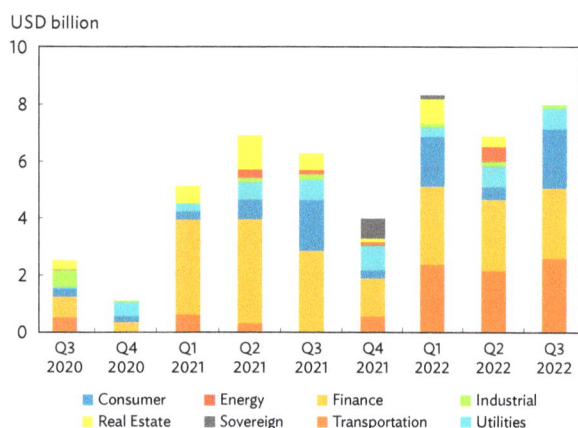

USD billion

Q1 = first quarter, Q2 = second quarter, Q3 = third quarter, Q4 = fourth quarter, USD = United States dollar.
Note: Figures were computed based on 30 September 2022 exchange rates to avoid currency effects.
Source: *AsianBondsOnline* calculations based on Bloomberg LP data.

a third of the regional total with a share of 30.8%, which was lower than its 35.6% share in Q2 2022. The two largest issuers from this industry include Pioneer Reward (USD702.6 million) and the Export–Import Bank of Korea (USD393.7 million). Companies involved in consumer products raised a total of USD2.1 billion in Q3 2022, comprising 26.1% of the regional total, which was well up from 6.4% in the previous quarter. The largest issuer from this industry was China Mengniu Dairy (USD1.9 billion). The issuance shares of companies from the utilities (USD728.4 million) and industrial (USD114.4 million) sectors declined in Q3 2022 to 9.1% and 1.4%, respectively, from 10.7% and 2.3% in Q2 2022.

## G3 Currency Bond Issuance

A total of USD189.8 billion worth of G3 currency bonds was issued from January to September in emerging East Asia.

During the January–September review period, emerging East Asian economies raised USD189.8 billion through the G3 currency bonds issuance, a contraction of 37.3% y-o-y from USD302.6 billion in the same period in 2021 (**Table 4**).[3] Only the Republic of Korea among all economies in the region logged an increased volume of

issuance of G3 currency bonds during the review period, expanding its bond issuance size denominated in all three G3 currencies. Large contractions in G3 issuances were registered in all other emerging East Asian economies due to the strong performance of the US dollar resulting from Federal Reserve rate hikes meant to temper inflationary pressure. There were also significantly fewer issuing companies from all economies in the region, except for the PRC and the Republic of Korea, during the first 9 months of 2022 compared to the same period in 2021.

Of the total amount of G3 currency bonds issued in emerging East Asia in the first 3 quarters of 2022, 93.4% was denominated in US dollars, 5.7% in euros, and 0.9% in Japanese yen. The region's aggregate USD-denominated bond issuance during the January–September period was USD177.2 billion, a drop of 37.3% y-o-y from January–September 2021 on tepid issuance activity from all economies in the region except the Republic of Korea. EUR-denominated bond issuance amounted to USD10.8 billion during the review period, a decline of 39.5% y-o-y brought about by the decline in issuances from the PRC and the absence of fundraising activities in most other regional markets. During the first 9 months of 2022, bonds denominated in Japanese yen totaled USD1.8 billion, falling 5.2% y-o-y due to sluggish issuance from Hong Kong, China; Indonesia; and Malaysia compared with a year earlier.

Entities from the PRC continued to lead emerging East Asia in the issuance of G3 currency bonds, issuing the equivalent of USD110.7 billion in January–September 2022. The Republic of Korea was a distant second with USD36.2 billion, followed by Hong Kong, China with USD12.1 billion. During the review period, all emerging East Asian economies used the US dollar as their currency of choice in their G3 fundraising activities.

From January to September, a y-o-y decline in the issuance of G3 currency bonds was registered in nearly all economies in the region: the Philippines (−67.2%); Hong Kong, China (−64.7%); Malaysia (−61.4%); Indonesia (−49.7%); Singapore (−35.8%); the PRC (−34.8%); and Thailand (−34.2%). Only the Republic of Korea posted growth with a 3.6% y-o-y increase. No G3 currency bonds were issued in Viet Nam

---

[3]  G3 currency bonds are denominated in either euros, Japanese yen, or US dollars.

**Table 4: G3 Currency Bond Issuance in Select Asian Markets**

| 2021 | | | January–September 2022 | | |
|---|---|---|---|---|---|
| Issuer | Amount (USD billion) | Issue Date | Issuer | Amount (USD billion) | Issue Date |
| **China, People's Rep. of** | **217.4** | | **China, People's Rep. of** | **110.7** | |
| Industrial and Commercial Bank of China 3.200% Perpetual | 6.2 | 24-Sep-21 | Easy Tactic 7.50% 2027 | 2.2 | 11-Jul-22 |
| China Development Bank 0.380% 2022 | 2.0 | 10-Jun-21 | China Construction Bank 2.85% 2032 | 2.0 | 21-Jan-22 |
| Prosus 3.061% 2031 | 1.9 | 13-Jul-21 | Easy Tactic 7.50% 2028 | 1.6 | 11-Jul-22 |
| Others | 207.4 | | Others | 104.9 | |
| **Hong Kong, China** | **39.7** | | **Hong Kong, China** | **12.1** | |
| Hong Kong, China (Sovereign) 0.000% 2026 | 1.4 | 24-Nov-21 | Airport Authority Hong Kong 2.50% 2032 | 1.2 | 12-Jan-22 |
| NWD Finance 4.125% Perpetual | 1.2 | 10-Jun-21 | Airport Authority Hong Kong 3.25% 2052 | 1.2 | 12-Jan-22 |
| Hong Kong, China (Sovereign) 0.625% 2026 | 1.0 | 2-Feb-21 | Airport Authority Hong Kong 1.75% 2027 | 1.0 | 12-Jan-22 |
| Others | 36.1 | | Others | 8.7 | |
| **Indonesia** | **26.4** | | **Indonesia** | **11.7** | |
| Indonesia (Sovereign) 3.05% 2051 | 2.0 | 12-Jan-21 | Perusahaan Penerbit SBSN Indonesia III 4.400% 2027 | 1.8 | 6-Jun-22 |
| Perusahaan Penerbit SBSN Indonesia III 1.50% 2026 | 1.3 | 9-Jun-21 | Perusahaan Penerbit SBSN Indonesia III 4.700% 2032 | 1.5 | 6-Jun-22 |
| Indonesia (Sovereign) 1.85% 2031 | 1.3 | 12-Jan-21 | Freeport Indonesia 5.315% 2032 | 1.5 | 14-Apr-22 |
| Others | 21.9 | | Others | 7.0 | |
| **Korea, Rep. of** | **43.9** | | **Korea, Rep. of** | **36.2** | |
| Posco 0.00% 2026 | 1.2 | 1-Sep-21 | Export–Import Bank of Korea 4.00% 2024 | 1.0 | 15-Sep-22 |
| Korea Housing Finance Corporation 0.01% 2026 | 1.1 | 29-Jun-21 | Korea Development Bank 2.00% 2025 | 1.0 | 24-Feb-22 |
| SK Hynix 1.50% 2026 | 1.0 | 19-Jan-21 | Export–Import Bank of Korea 4.25% 2027 | 1.0 | 15-Sep-22 |
| Others | 40.6 | | Others | 33.2 | |
| **Malaysia** | **16.0** | | **Malaysia** | **5.0** | |
| Petronas Capital 3.404% 2061 | 1.8 | 28-Apr-21 | Misc Capital Two (Labuan) 3.75% 2027 | 0.6 | 6-Apr-22 |
| Petronas Capital 2.480% 2032 | 1.3 | 28-Apr-21 | Bank Negara Malaysia 0.00% 2022 | 0.6 | 25-Jan-22 |
| Others | 13.0 | | Others | 3.8 | |
| **Philippines** | **10.8** | | **Philippines** | **2.7** | |
| Philippines (Sovereign) 3.200% 2046 | 2.3 | 6-Jul-21 | Philippines (Sovereign) 4.200% 2047 | 1.0 | 29-Mar-22 |
| Philippines (Sovereign) 1.375% 2026 | 1.1 | 8-Oct-21 | Philippines (Sovereign) 3.556% 2032 | 0.8 | 29-Mar-22 |
| Others | 7.5 | | Others | 1.0 | |
| **Singapore** | **16.5** | | **Singapore** | **9.0** | |
| BOC Aviation 1.625% 2024 | 1.0 | 29-Apr-21 | DBS Bank 2.375% 2027 | 1.5 | 17-Mar-22 |
| Temasek Financial I 2.750% 2061 | 1.0 | 2-Aug-21 | United Overseas Bank 0.387% 2025 | 1.5 | 17-Mar-22 |
| Others | 14.5 | | Others | 6.1 | |
| **Thailand** | **4.1** | | **Thailand** | **2.4** | |
| Bangkok Bank in Hong Kong, China 3.466% 2036 | 1.0 | 23-Sep-21 | GC Treasury Center 4.4% 2032 | 1.0 | 30-Mar-22 |
| GC Treasury Center 2.980% 2031 | 0.7 | 18-Mar-21 | Bangkok Bank in Hong Kong, China 4.3% 2027 | 0.8 | 15-Jun-22 |
| Others | 2.4 | | Others | 0.7 | |
| **Viet Nam** | **1.6** | | **Viet Nam** | **–** | |
| **Emerging East Asia Total** | **376.4** | | **Emerging East Asia Total** | **189.8** | |
| **Memo Items:** | | | **Memo Items:** | | |
| **India** | **23.7** | | **India** | **6.7** | |
| Vedanta Resources 8.95% 2025 | 1.2 | 11-Mar-21 | Reliance Industries 3.625% 2052 | 1.8 | 12-Jan-22 |
| Others | 22.5 | | Others | 5.0 | |
| **Sri Lanka** | **0.8** | | **Sri Lanka** | **0.02** | |
| Sri Lanka (Sovereign) 7.95% 2024 | 0.2 | 3-May-21 | Sri Lanka (Sovereign) 8% 2023 | 0.01 | 24-Jan-22 |
| Others | **0.6** | | Others | **0.01** | |

USD = United States dollar.
Notes:
1. Data exclude certificates of deposit.
2. G3 currency bonds are bonds denominated in either euros, Japanese yen, or US dollars.
3. Bloomberg LP end-of-period rates are used.
4. Figures after the issuer name reflect the coupon rate and year of maturity of the bond.
Source: *AsianBondsOnline* calculations based on Bloomberg LP data.

from January to September 2022 in contrast to the same period in the prior year.

Of all G3 currency bond sales in emerging East Asia from January to September 2022, 58.3% were from issuers in the PRC: USD104.4 billion in US dollars, the equivalent of USD6.1 billion in euros, and the equivalent of USD0.1 billion in Japanese yen. In August, consumer electronics company Lenovo Group raised USD675.0 million from its 7-year USD-denominated convertible bond. Proceeds from the issuance will be used to partially repurchase some of the company's existing convertible bonds and for general corporate funding purposes. From August to September, the Macau, China branch of the Bank of China issued five bonds denominated in US dollars totaling USD16.4 million. The fixed-income securities have periodic distribution rates from 2.20% to 4.25% and tenors from 2 years to 4 years.

During the review period, the Republic of Korea had a 19.1% share of the total issuance of G3 currency bonds from the region: USD32.8 billion was issued in US dollars, the equivalent of USD3.1 billion was in euros, and the equivalent of USD0.3 billion was raised in Japanese yen. In August and September, Hana Bank raised a total of USD220.0 million from six bonds denominated in US dollars. The issuances had tenors of 2 years. and 3 years. In August, Hyundai Capital, a consumer financial services company, issued a JPY-denominated bond worth USD27.6 million, with a tenor of 2 years. The issuance had a coupon rate of 0.77%. About a month later, Hyundai Capital raised USD60.0 million from a 1-year bond with a coupon rate of 4.78%.

From January to September 2022, Hong Kong, China accounted for 6.4% of regional G3 currency bond issuance, comprising USD-denominated bonds totaling USD12.0 billion and JPY-denominated bonds amounting to USD0.1 billion. In September, CNCB (Hong Kong) Investment issued a USD300.0 million 1-year USD-denominated bond. It had a period distribution rate of 4.2132%. In August, Guotai Junan International, an investment holding company, raised USD66.5 million from its issuance of a 1-year bond denominated in US dollars and with a coupon rate of 3.95%.

Amid tepid fundraising activities from most economies in the region, issuance of G3 currency bonds in the ASEAN

region decreased 51.5% y-o-y during the first 9 months of the year.[4] On an aggregate basis, USD30.9 billion worth of G3 currency bonds were issued by entities based in ASEAN, which was lower than the USD63.6 billion recorded in the first 9 months of 2021, with reduced issuance from most economies in the region. ASEAN member economies' regional G3 currency issuance share was 16.3% during the review period, fell from 21.0% in the prior year. Indonesia accounted for the most G3 currency bond issuance among ASEAN members in January–September 2022. This was followed by Singapore, Malaysia, the Philippines, and Thailand.

Indonesian G3 currency bond issuance in the January–September review period was 6.2% of the emerging East Asian total. Most of the economy's issuances were denominated in US dollars, totaling USD11.2 billion, while USD0.6 billion worth of bonds were denominated in Japanese yen. In September, the Government of Indonesia issued three tranches of a callable USD-denominated bond totaling USD2.7 billion. The issuance had tenors of 5 years, 10 years, and 30 years. Proceeds from the global bond will be utilized to repurchase some of the government's outstanding USD-denominated bonds and to fund the state budget. In the same month, Perusahaan Penerbit SBSN Indonesia III, a government special purpose vehicle in charge of issuing Shariah-compliant, foreign-currency-denominated securities, raised USD175.0 million from its dual-tranche issuance of USD-denominated bonds. The bonds had tenors of 3 years and 5 years.

During the review period, a 4.8% share of the issuance of G3 currency bonds in emerging East Asia was from Singaporean issuers, who raised USD7.5 billion in US dollars and the equivalent of USD1.5 billion in euros. In August and September, two banks issued zero-coupon, 30-year callable bonds denominated in US dollars. United Overseas Bank's issuance in September was worth USD70.0 million, while that of DBS Bank's issuance in August was USD40.0 million.

Entities in Malaysia with G3 currency bond issuance comprised 2.6% of the total in emerging East Asia. USD-denominated bond issuance reached USD4.8 billion, while JPY-denominated bonds totaled the equivalent of USD0.2 billion. In August and September, the Bank Negara Malaysia issued four

---

[4]  For the discussion on G3 currency issuance, data for ASEAN include Indonesia, Malaysia, the Philippines, Singapore, Thailand, and Viet Nam.

Bank Negara Interbank Bills totaling USD700.0 million. These are USD-denominated short-term securities used by the central bank to manage the economy's liquidity in the interbank market. Malayan Banking issued 5-year bonds denominated in US dollars in August and September. Totaling USD50.0 million, the bonds have periodic distribution rates of 3.620077% and 3.844122%.

Philippine issuers accounted for a 1.4% share of total emerging East Asian G3 currency bond issuance during the first 9 months of 2022. In terms of currency, entities from the Philippines issued USD2.3 billion worth of USD-denominated bonds and the equivalent of USD0.5 billion in Japanese yen. These amounts were raised in March and April.

During the January–September period, Thai issuers comprised a 1.3% share of all issuances of G3 currency bonds from emerging East Asia, with USD-denominated bonds raising USD2.4 billion. These fundraising activities occurred in March and June.

**Figure 12** presents monthly G3 currency bond sales of emerging East Asia from September 2021 to September 2022, broken down by currency. Issuances picked up in September 2022 after falling in the previous month. Fundraising activities were slow in August as the region

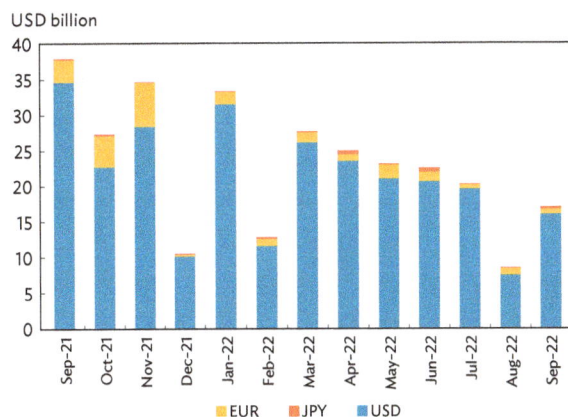

**Figure 12: G3 Currency Bond Issuance in Select Emerging East Asian Markets**

USD billion

EUR = euro, JPY = Japanese yen, USD = United States dollar.
Notes:
1.  G3 currency bonds are denominated in either euros, Japanese yen, or US dollars.
2.  Figures were computed based on 30 September 2022 currency exchange rates and do not include currency effects.
Source: *AsianBondsOnline* calculations based on Bloomberg LP data.

tempered its USD-denominated bond issuances due to the strong performance of the US dollar on account of the Federal Reserve tightening its monetary policy to combat inflationary pressure. Investors in the region resumed their US dollar issuance in September but at a slower pace than in July. The decline in August was driven by reduced issuance from the PRC; Hong Kong, China; the Republic of Korea; and Malaysia. Entities in Indonesia opted not to issue any G3 currency bonds in August. Even as issuance volumes increased in most economies in September, the regional total was dragged down by reduced issuance from the PRC. Meanwhile, there was zero G3 currency issuance from the Philippines and Thailand in Q3 2022.

## Bond Yield Movements

**Yields in most emerging East Asian markets rose as the Federal Reserve continued its aggressive monetary tightening.**

Inflation continues to pressure the global economy, with advanced economies being the most affected. This has led to more aggressive monetary tightening by major central banks in advanced economies and by regional central banks as well.

The most aggressive among advanced economies was the US, where core consumer price inflation rose to a 40-year high in June. In response to persistent inflationary pressure, the Federal Reserve raised the federal funds target range by 75 bps during its 20–21 September meeting. The Federal Reserve also indicated that it intends to continue to raise rates: Its September federal funds rate forecast projects a cumulative 125 bps increase for November and December.

In its 1–2 November meeting, the Federal Reserve, as expected, raised the federal funds rate range by 75 bps. The Federal Reserve also said that the path of interest rates would go higher than expected but with a corresponding decrease in the size of each rate hike and an increase in the number of hikes. Inflation also moderated to 8.2% y-o-y in September and 7.7% y-o-y in October.

The European Central Bank (ECB) has also become more aggressive in its rate hikes as the euro area continued to battle rising inflation. The ECB announced a 75 bps rate hike each on 8 September and 27 October. The central bank also indicated that it would continue to raise rates to ensure that inflation would trend downward toward its target.

The Bank of Japan remained the exception among advanced economy central banks, as it largely left monetary policy unchanged during its 20–21 September and 27-28 October meetings. While inflation has been rising in Japan, it is not near the levels seen in the US and the euro area. Inflation in Japan rose to 3.0% y-o-y in August and September from 2.6% y-o-y in July. The economy also remained weak as GDP contracted an annualized 1.2% in Q3 2022 from a growth of 4.6% in the previous quarter.

Emerging East Asia's LCY government bond yields have mostly followed suit, taking cues from the Federal Reserve as well as movements in domestic prices. The PRC, however, was the region's lone exception as its 2-year yield largely remained stable during the review period (**Figure 13a**), amid continued weakness in the economy that is further exacerbated by "zero-COVID" policies. The PRC was also the sole market in the region that engaged in monetary easing.

Other markets had steep increases in their 2-year yields, particularly in the last week of August, following the Federal Reserve chair's Jackson Hole speech. Another inflection point was on 13 September, after the release of August inflation data for the US that was higher than expected. This was particularly evident in the steep increase in the 2-year yield in Malaysia, which raised its policy rate for the second time in Q3 2022 on 8 September, and in Viet Nam, which hiked its policy rate for the first time in 2 years on 23 September (**Figure 13b**). Malaysia further raised rates by 25 bps in November, while Viet Nam hiked policy rates by another 100 bps in October.

The movements of 10-year yields in emerging East Asia were largely similar to those of 2-year yields, with the PRC as the only market showing relatively stable 10-year yield movement (**Figure 14a**). There was a slight downward trend in the Philippines' 10-year yield in the first half of August following speculation the Federal Reserve might ease its pace of tightening, but the Jackson Hole event completely reversed this sentiment (**Figure 14b**).

Emerging East Asia's yield curves shifted upward between 31 August and 4 November as the Federal Reserve continued its aggressive monetary tightening (**Figure 15**). The steepest rise was noted in Viet Nam, where the yield curve shifted upward by an average of 168 bps, following the SBV's 100 bps rate hikes on 23 September and 25 October. Economic weakness in the PRC has largely counteracted US yield movements, and the PRC's yield shifted slightly upward during the review period by an average of 7 bps.

---

**Figure 13a: 2-Year Local Currency Government Bond Yields**

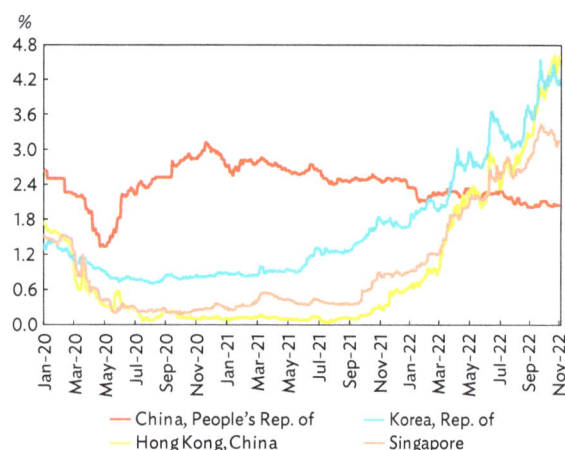

Note: Data coverage is from 1 January 2020 to 4 November 2022.
Source: Based on data from Bloomberg LP.

**Figure 13b: 2-Year Local Currency Government Bond Yields**

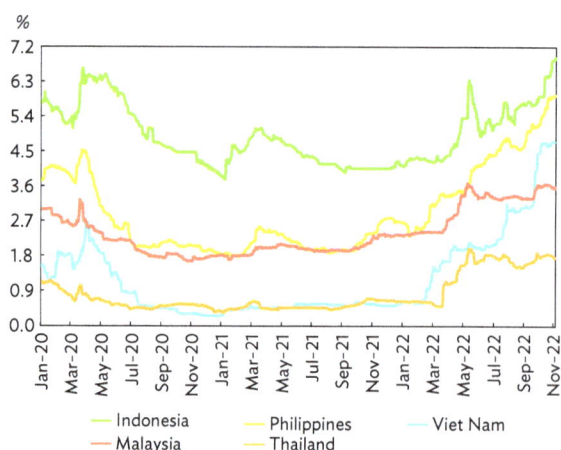

Note: Data coverage is from 1 January 2020 to 4 November 2022.
Source: Based on data from Bloomberg LP.

**Figure 14a: 10-Year Local Currency Government Bond Yields**

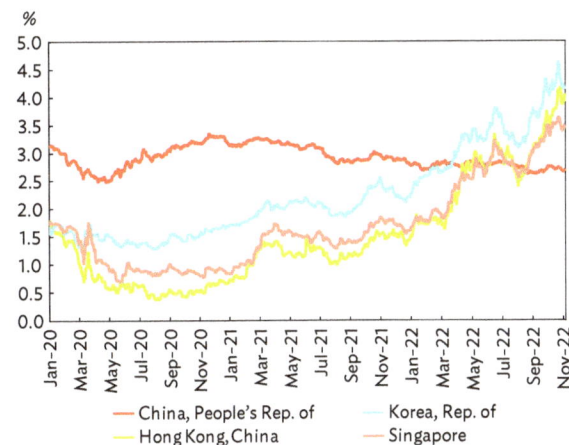

Note: Data coverage is from 1 January 2020 to 4 November 2022.
Source: Based on data from Bloomberg LP.

**Figure 14b: 10-Year Local Currency Government Bond Yields**

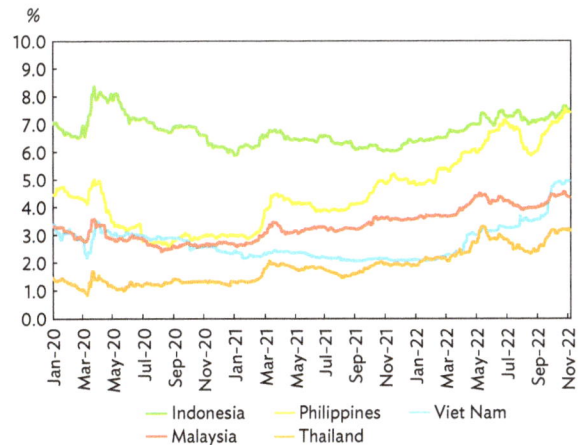

Note: Data coverage is from 1 January 2020 to 4 November 2022.
Source: Based on data from Bloomberg LP.

As a result of the shifts in the yield curve, the 10-year versus 2-year yield spread rose in all markets except Hong Kong, China; Indonesia, the Republic of Korea, and Viet Nam (**Figure 16**).

Both the slowdown in the PRC's economy and concerns over the US economy's trajectory have increased downside risks in emerging East Asian economies; however, so far the impact has been muted. A number of regional economies reported an acceleration in GDP growth from Q2 2022 to Q3 2022, including Indonesia (from 5.5% y-o-y to 5.7% y-o-y), the Republic of Korea (from 2.9% y-o-y to 3.1% y-o-y), Malaysia (from 8.9% y-o-y to 14.2% y-o-y), and Viet Nam (from 7.7% y-o-y to 13.7% y-o-y). The PRC reported 3.9% y-o-y GDP growth in Q3 2022, which was higher than Q2 2022's 0.4% y-o-y but still below the 2022 full-year target of 5.5%. Singapore's GDP growth fell slightly in Q3 2022 to 4.4% y-o-y from 4.5% y-o-y in the previous quarter, while Hong Kong, China's GDP contraction worsened to 4.5% y-o-y in Q3 2022 from 1.3% y-o-y in Q2 2022.

Following advanced economies, inflation in emerging East Asia continued to trend upward, but some economies registered slowing inflation following a decline in global oil prices. Thailand's consumer price inflation fell to 6.0 y-o-y in October from 6.4% y-o-y in September and 7.9% y-o-y in August, but it remained above the central bank's target of 1.0%–3.0% for full-year 2022 (**Figure 17a**). The Republic of Korea's inflation rate

has been broadly stable, rising to 5.7% y-o-y in October from 5.6% y-o-y in September and 5.7% y-o-y in August (**Figure 17b**).

The aggressive monetary hikes in the US placed heavy pressure on central banks in the region. During the review period, nearly all regional central banks raised their policy rates, with the exception of the PRC, which continued to suffer economic weakness (**Table 5**). The biggest movement was in Viet Nam, with the SBV raising its policy rate in September and October after previously being the sole central bank in the region that had left its policy rate unchanged. Indonesia's central bank also became more aggressive, raising the 7-day reverse repurchase rate by 50 bps each in September, October, and November, after previously raising policy rates by only 25 bps on 23 August. Both Malaysia and Thailand raised their policy rates by 25 bps on 8 September and 28 September, respectively. Malaysia's central bank raised its policy rate by another 25 bps on 3 November. The two economies' central banks have been among the least aggressive in the region, with Malaysia's central bank raising rates a total of 100 bps and Thailand's a total of 50 bps for the year.

On the other hand, the Bangko Sentral ng Pilipinas and the Bank of Korea remained the most aggressive central banks in the region this year through 18 November, with the SBV more recently catching up. The Philippines raised policy rates by 50 bps on 23 September and 75 bps on 17 November, while the Republic of Korea raised policy

## Figure 15: Benchmark Yield Curves—Local Currency Government Bonds

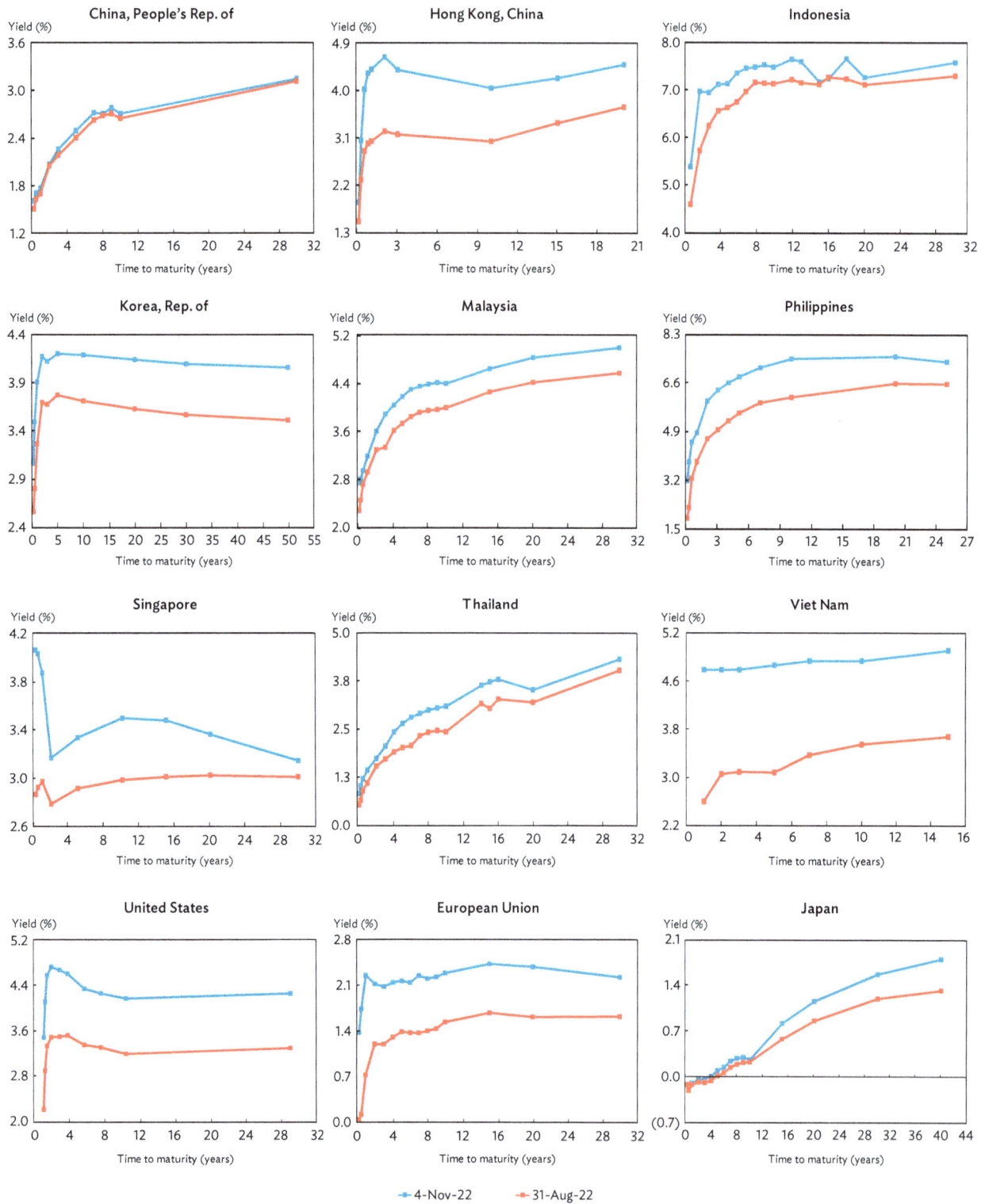

Legend: 4-Nov-22, 31-Aug-22

( ) = negative.
Sources: Based on data from Bloomberg LP and Thai Bond Market Association.

## Figure 16: Yield Spreads between 10-Year and 2-Year Government Bonds

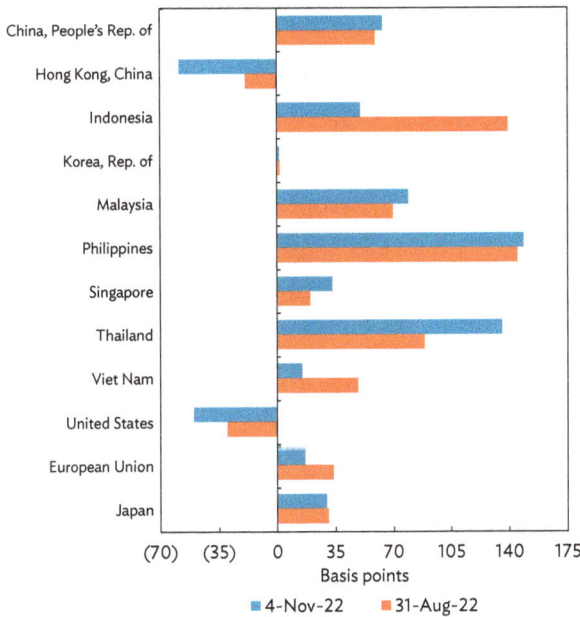

Source: *AsianBondsOnline* computations based on Bloomberg LP data.

rates by 50 bps on 12 October. Cumulative rate hikes in 2022 for the Philippines and the Republic of Korea reached 300 bps and 200 bps, respectively, through 18 November. In the Philippines, inflation continued to remain elevated. The Philippines' inflation rate for October rose to 7.7% y-o-y, the highest since December 2008 and the fastest so far among major regional markets that have released inflation data for the month.

## Corporate spreads for higher-rated bonds fell in most markets.

The spread between AAA-rated yields and government yields fell in the PRC, Malaysia, and Thailand (**Figure 18a**). In contrast, the spread widened in the Republic of Korea, largely influenced by its aggressive monetary tightening stance.

Among lower-rated bonds, the spread rose in the PRC and Malaysia, while it fell in Thailand (**Figure 18b**). In the Republic of Korea, corporate spreads were unchanged.

## Figure 17a: Headline Inflation Rates

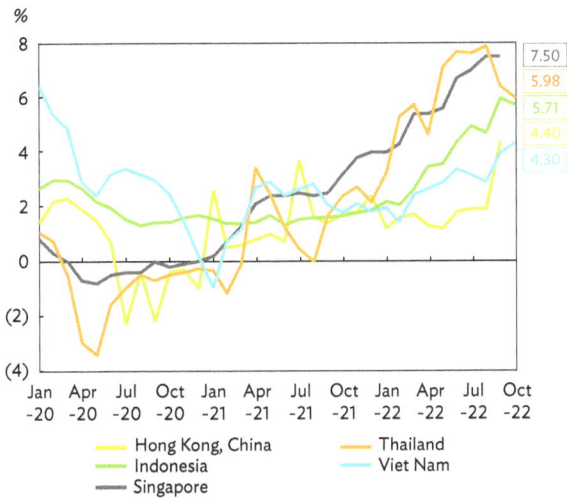

Note: Data coverage is from January 2020 to October 2022 except for Hong Kong, China and Singapore (September 2022).
Source: Based on data from Bloomberg LP.

## Figure 17b: Headline Inflation Rates

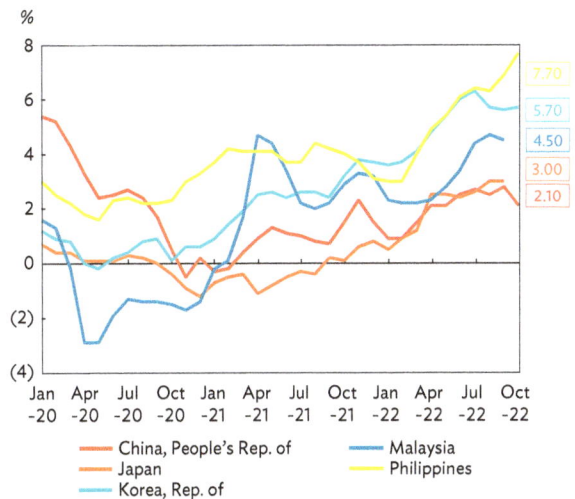

Note: Data coverage is from January 2020 to October 2022 except for Japan and Malaysia (September 2022).
Source: Based on data from Bloomberg LP.

## Table 5: Changes in Monetary Stances in Major Advanced Economies and Select Emerging East Asian Markets

| Economy | Policy Rate 5-Nov-2021 (%) | Rate Change (%) | | | | | | | | | | | | | Policy Rate 4-Nov-2022 (%) | Change in Policy Rates (basis points) |
|---|---|---|---|---|---|---|---|---|---|---|---|---|---|---|---|---|
| | | Nov-2021 | Dec-2021 | Jan-2022 | Feb-2022 | Mar-2022 | Apr-2022 | May-2022 | Jun-2022 | Jul-2022 | Aug-2022 | Sep-2022 | Oct-2022 | Nov-2022 | | |
| United States | 0.25 | | | | | ↑0.25 | | ↑0.50 | ↑0.75 | ↑0.75 | | ↑0.75 | | ↑0.75 | 4.00 | ↑ 375 |
| Euro Area | (0.50) | | | | | | | | | ↑0.50 | | ↑0.75 | | ↑0.75 | 1.50 | ↑200 |
| United Kingdom | 0.10 | | ↑0.15 | ↑0.25 | ↑0.25 | | | ↑0.25 | ↑0.25 | | ↑0.50 | ↑0.50 | | ↑0.75 | 3.00 | ↑290 |
| Japan | (0.10) | | | | | | | | | | | | | | (0.10) | |
| China, People's Rep. of | 2.95 | | ↓0.10 | | | | | | | | ↓0.10 | | | | 2.75 | ↓ 20 |
| Indonesia | 3.50 | | | | | | | | | | ↑0.25 | ↑0.50 | ↑0.50 | | 4.75 | ↑ 125 |
| Korea, Rep. of | 0.75 | ↑0.25 | | ↑0.25 | | | ↑0.25 | ↑0.25 | | ↑0.50 | ↑0.25 | | ↑0.50 | | 3.00 | ↑ 225 |
| Malaysia | 1.75 | | | | | | | ↑0.25 | | ↑0.25 | | ↑0.25 | ↑0.25 | | 2.75 | ↑ 100 |
| Philippines | 2.00 | | | | | | | ↑0.25 | ↑0.25 | ↑0.75 | ↑0.50 | ↑0.50 | | | 4.25 | ↑ 225 |
| Singapore | – | | | ↑ | | | ↑ | | | ↑ | | ↑ | | | – | – |
| Thailand | 0.50 | | | | | | | | | | ↑0.25 | ↑0.25 | | | 1.00 | ↑ 50 |
| Viet Nam | 4.00 | | | | | | | | | | | ↑1.00 | ↑1.00 | | 6.00 | ↑200 |

( ) = negative.
Notes:
1.  Data coverage is from 5 November 2021 to 4 November 2022.
2.  For the People's Republic of China, data used in the chart are for the 1-year medium-term lending facility rate. While the 1-year benchmark lending rate is the official policy rate of the People's Bank of China, market players use the 1-year medium-term lending facility rate as a guide for the monetary policy direction of the People's Bank of China.
3.  The up (down) arrow for Singapore signifies monetary policy tightening (loosening) by its central bank. The Monetary Authority of Singapore utilizes the Singapore dollar nominal effective exchange rate (S\$NEER) to guide its monetary policy.
Sources: Various central bank websites.

### Figure 18a: Credit Spreads—Local Currency Corporates Rated AAA versus Government Bonds

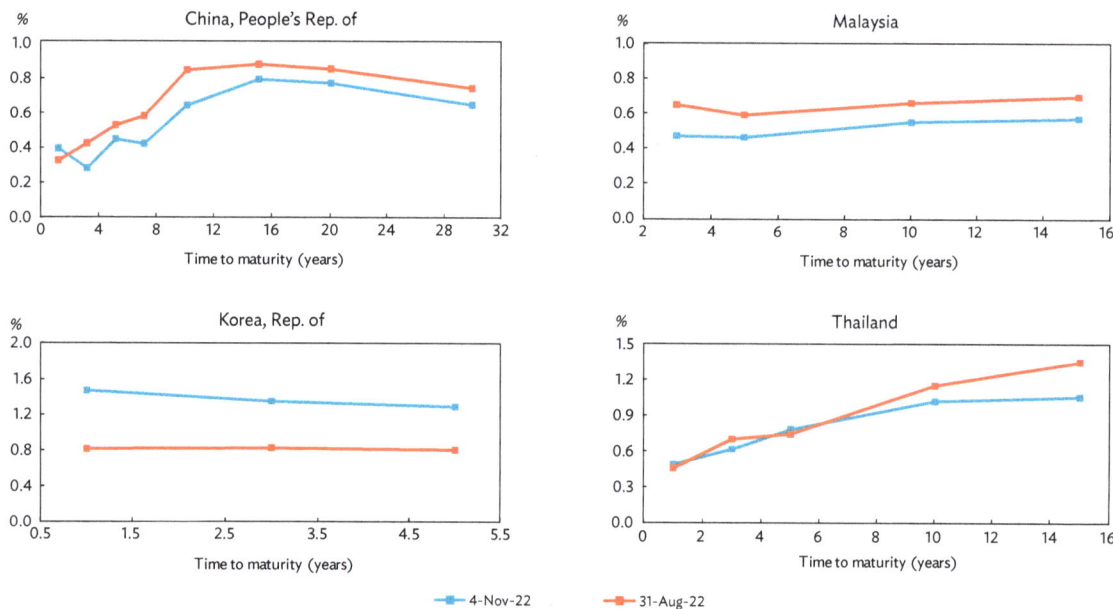

Notes:
1.  Credit spreads are obtained by subtracting government yields from corporate indicative yields.
2.  Corporate yields for Malaysia are as of 30 August 2022 and 31 October 2022.
Sources: People's Republic of China (Bloomberg LP), Republic of Korea (KG Zeroin Corporation), Malaysia (Fully Automated System for Issuing/Tendering Bank Negara Malaysia), and Thailand (Bloomberg LP).

**Figure 18b: Credit Spreads—Lower-Rated Local Currency Corporates versus AAA**

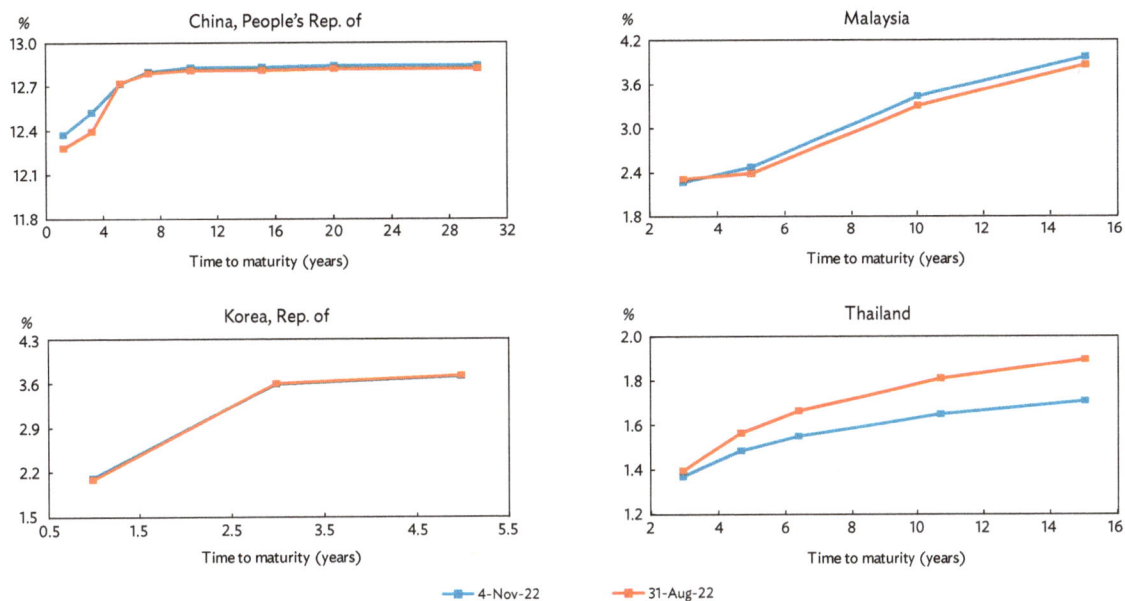

Notes:
1.  Credit spreads are obtained by subtracting government yields from corporate indicative yields.
2.  Corporate yields for Malaysia are as of 30 August 2022 and 31 October 2022.
Sources: People's Republic of China (Bloomberg LP), Republic of Korea (KG Zeroin Corporation), Malaysia (Fully Automated System for Issuing/Tendering Bank Negara Malaysia), and Thailand (Bloomberg LP).

# Recent Developments in ASEAN+3 Sustainable Bond Markets

**ASEAN+3's sustainable bond market growth eased in Q3 2022.**[5,6] The outstanding size of the sustainable bond market in ASEAN+3 totaled USD521.6 billion at the end of September on growth of 1.7% quarter-on-quarter (q-o-q) and 24.9% year-on-year (y-o-y) (**Figure 19**). Growth moderated from the 5.0% q-o-q and 37.1% y-o-y expansions posted in the second quarter (Q2). Overall growth was weighed down by the dimming economic outlook and monetary tightening in regional and global markets. At the end of September, the size of the global sustainable bond market stood at USD3.1 trillion on growth of 4.5% q-o-q and 30.3% y-o-y in Q3 2022, which were faster expansions than those in ASEAN+3. Next to Europe, ASEAN+3 remained the world's second-largest regional sustainable bond market, accounting for 16.9% of the global total. However, the gap between the size of the sustainable bond market in Europe and ASEAN+3 widened to USD983.7 billion at the end of September from USD784.1 billion at the end of June.

**Issuance of sustainable bonds in the region slowed in Q3 2022, amid weakening financial conditions and rising borrowing costs.** Uncertainties in the global economic outlook and tightening financial conditions led to reduced issuance activities in ASEAN+3's sustainable bond market in Q3 2022. Total issuance of sustainable bonds in the region reached USD49.8 billion in Q3 2022 on contractions of 25.3% q-o-q and 24.1% y-o-y (**Figure 20**). Issuance in the People's Republic of China (PRC) declined in United States (US) dollar terms, while issuance in Hong Kong, China and the Republic of Korea also fell during the quarter. Meanwhile, sustainable bond issuance in ASEAN member economies and Japan expanded 34.0% q-o-q and 11.9% q-o-q to reach USD5.7 billion and USD10.9 billion, respectively, during Q3 2022. The growth in issuance lifted the issuance shares of ASEAN members and Japan in ASEAN+3's sustainable bond issuance total from 6.4% and 14.6% in Q2 2022, respectively, to 11.5% and 21.9% in Q3 2022. ASEAN+3's share of the global sustainable issuance total declined to 25.9% in Q3 2022 from 29.5% in Q2 2022.

**ASEAN has a strong presence in the regional sustainable bond market and excels in the issuance of sustainability and sustainability-linked bonds.** Sustainable bonds outstanding in ASEAN markets climbed to USD41.8 billion at the end of September, accounting for 8.0% of the regional sustainable bond total in Q3 2022, which is more than its 5.5% share in the overall LCY bond market in ASEAN+3. ASEAN economies are active players in sustainability bond and sustainability-linked bond markets, accounting for shares of 19.6% and 14.8%, respectively, of the region's

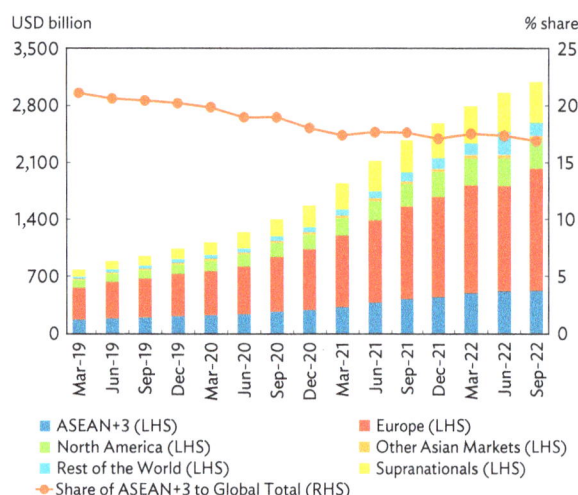

**Figure 19: Sustainable Bonds Outstanding in Global Markets**

ASEAN = Association of Southeast Asian Nations, LHS = left-hand side, RHS = right-hand side, USD = United States dollar.
Notes:
1. ASEAN+3 is defined to include member states of the Association of Southeast Asian Nations (ASEAN) plus the People's Republic of China; Hong Kong, China; Japan; and the Republic of Korea.
2. Data include both local currency and foreign currency issues.
Source: *AsianBondsOnline* computations based on Bloomberg LP data.

---

[5] For the discussion on sustainable bonds, ASEAN+3 is defined to include member states of the Association of Southeast Asian Nations (ASEAN) plus the People's Republic of China; Hong Kong, China; Japan; and the Republic of Korea.
[6] Sustainable bonds include green, social, sustainability, sustainability-linked, and transition bonds.

## Figure 20: Sustainable Bond Issuance in Select ASEAN+3 Markets

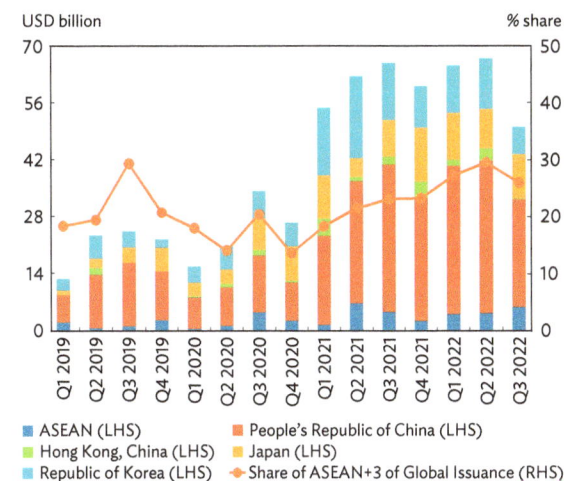

ASEAN = Association of Southeast Asian Nations; LHS = left-hand side; Q = quarter; RHS = right-hand side; USD = United States dollar.
Notes:
1. ASEAN+3 is defined to include member states of the Association of Southeast Asian Nations (ASEAN) plus the People's Republic of China; Hong Kong, China; Japan; and the Republic of Korea.
2. Data include both foreign currency and local currency issues.
Source: *AsianBondsOnline* computations based on Bloomberg LP data.

## Figure 21: Sustainable Bonds Outstanding by Bond Type and Economy Share in Select ASEAN+3 Markets

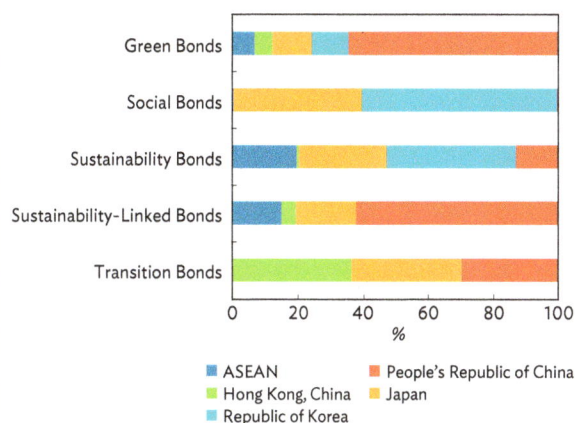

ASEAN = Association of Southeast Asian Nations.
Notes:
1. ASEAN+3 is defined to include member states of the Association of Southeast Asian Nations (ASEAN) plus the People's Republic of China; Hong Kong, China; Japan; and the Republic of Korea.
2. Data as of 30 September 2022 and include both foreign currency and local currency issues.
Source: *AsianBondsOnline* computations based on Bloomberg LP data.

total outstanding bonds of these types at the end of September. As the region's largest sustainable bond market, the PRC accounted for 48.3% of the region's total sustainable bonds outstanding with USD252.2 billion at the end of September, which was more than its corresponding share of 42.8% of ASEAN+3's total bonds outstanding in the same period. The PRC leads the regional green bond and sustainability-linked bond markets, comprising 64.3% and 61.9% of the respective totals at the end of Q3 2022 (**Figure 21**). The Republic of Korea and Japan accounted for 20.9% and 18.4% of the ASEAN+3 sustainable bond market, respectively, at the end of September, with aggregate issuances from both economies dominating the social bond and sustainability bond segments, accounting for 99.2% and 66.6%, respectively, of the regional total for each type of bond.

**ASEAN+3 sustainable bond markets witnessed improved diversification.** The regional sustainable bond market has seen improved diversification in terms of market profile and the issuance of different bond types. This is evidenced by the declining trend in the Herfindahl–Hirschman Index, which is used as common measure of market concentration (**Figure 22**). ASEAN+3's sustainable bond market remains dominated

## Figure 22: Sustainable Bonds Outstanding by Bond Type in Select ASEAN+3 Markets

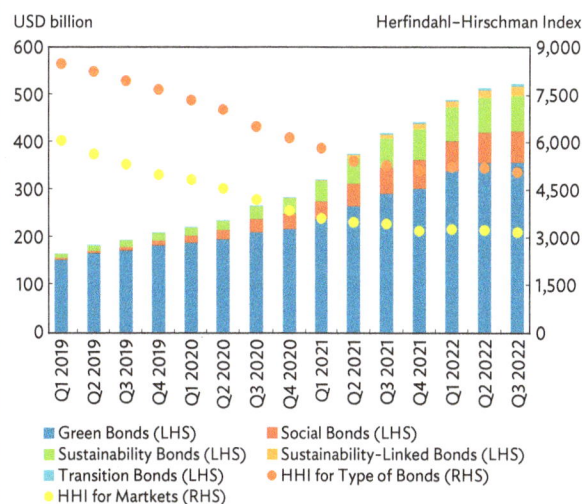

HHI = Herfindahl–Hirschman Index, LHS = left-hand side, Q = quarter, RHS = right-hand side.
ASEAN = Association of Southeast Asian Nations, USD = United States dollar.
Notes:
1. ASEAN+3 is defined to include member states of the Association of Southeast Asian Nations (ASEAN) plus the People's Republic of China; Hong Kong, China; Japan; and the Republic of Korea.
2. Data include both foreign currency and local currency issues.
3. The Herfindahl–Hirschman Index is a commonly accepted measure of market concentration and is calculated by summing the squared market share of each bond type competing in the market.
Source: *AsianBondsOnline* computations based on Bloomberg LP data.

**Figure 23: Sustainable Bond Issuance by Bond Type in Select ASEAN+3 Markets**

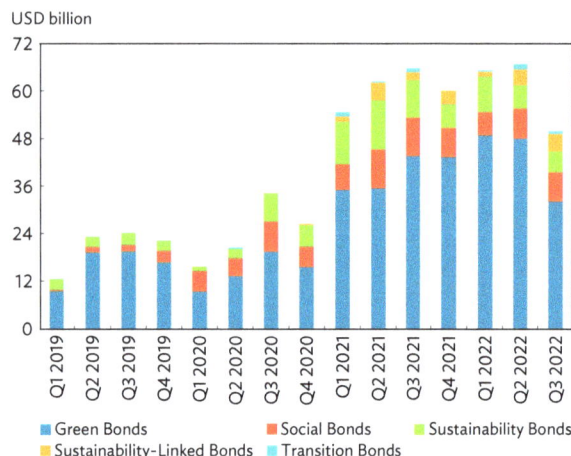

ASEAN = Association of Southeast Asian Nations, Q = quarter, USD = United States dollar.
Notes:
1. ASEAN+3 is defined to include member states of the Association of Southeast Asian Nations (ASEAN) plus the People's Republic of China; Hong Kong, China; Japan; and the Republic of Korea.
2. Data include both foreign currency and local currency issues.
Source: *AsianBondsOnline* computations based on Bloomberg LP data.

**Figure 24: Sustainable Bond Issuance by Sector in Select ASEAN+3 Markets**

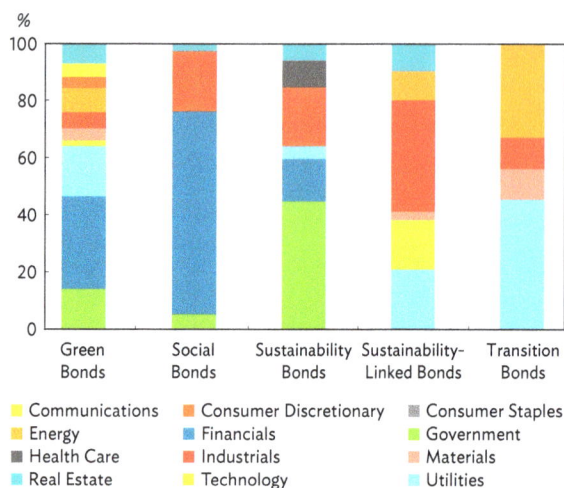

ASEAN = Association of Southeast Asian Nations.
Notes:
1. ASEAN+3 is defined to include member states of the Association of Southeast Asian Nations (ASEAN) plus the People's Republic of China; Hong Kong, China; Japan; and the Republic of Korea.
2. Data reflect issuance for the period 1 July 2022 to 30 September 2022 and include both foreign currency and local currency issues.
Source: *AsianBondsOnline* computations based on Bloomberg LP data.

by green bonds, which comprise 68.2% of the regional sustainable bond total. However, green bonds' share of sustainable bonds outstanding in the market has steadily declined from 91.8% in Q1 2019 as issuance in other sustainable bond segments gradually expands (**Figure 23**).

**The private sector is the leading issuer of sustainable bonds in ASEAN+3.** Sustainable bond issuance in Q3 2022 was dominated by issuances from the private sector, which accounted for 85.5% of the regional total during the quarter (**Figure 24**). In terms of outstanding bonds, 88.7% of ASEAN+3's sustainable bonds at the end of Q3 2022 were from private sector issuers, which contrasts with the ASEAN+3 conventional bond market where government bonds accounted for 75.9% of regional bonds outstanding at the end of September. Among private issuers, financial institutions comprised the largest group, representing 38.7% of total private sector issuance in Q3 2022. While the public sector's share of sustainable bond issuance in ASEAN+3 remains small, its share inched up to 14.5% in Q3 2022 from 10.2% in the prior quarter. Q3 2022 saw three sovereign issuances, all of which were in the domestic currency: Indonesia's IDR4.4 trillion sovereign green bond, Singapore's SGD2.4 billion sovereign green bond, and

Thailand's THB35.0 billion sovereign sustainability bond. The public sector segment of ASEAN+3's sustainable bond market has thus shown good potential for further expansion.

**The ASEAN+3 sustainable bond market largely provides short- to medium-term financing.**
Outstanding sustainable bonds in the region were largely concentrated in short-term to medium-term tenors, with maturities between 1 year and 5 years accounting for 77.0% of the sustainable bond total at the end of September, which is in contrast to the much smaller corresponding share of 35.6% in Europe's sustainable bond market (**Figure 25**). The average size-weighted tenor of outstanding sustainable bonds in ASEAN+3 at the end of September was 4.4 years, substantially lower than the average size-weighted tenor of ASEAN+3's total bond market of 7.5 years. With the issuance of some longer-tenor bonds during the quarter, the average-size weighted tenor of ASEAN+3's sustainable bond issuance climbed to 6.5 years in Q3 2022 from 4.7 years in the prior quarter. For example, longer-tenored sustainable bond issued in Q3 2022 included Singapore's 50-year sovereign green bond, Malaysia's Pengurusan Air Selangor 20-year green bond and 20-year sustainability bond,

**Figure 25: Maturity and Currency Profiles of Sustainable Bonds Outstanding in Select ASEAN+3 Markets**

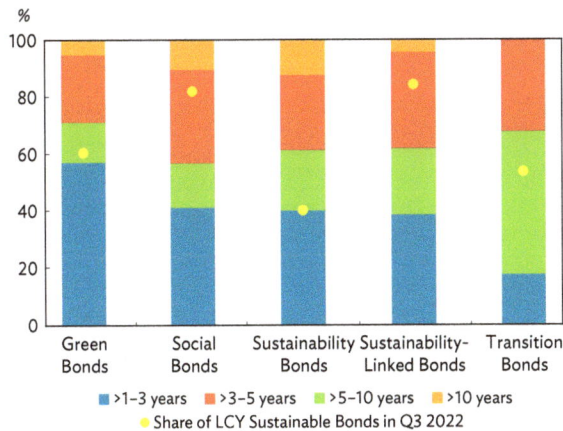

ASEAN = Association of Southeast Asian Nations, LCY = local currency.
Notes:
1. ASEAN+3 is defined to include member states of the Association of Southeast Asian Nations (ASEAN) plus the People's Republic of China; Hong Kong, China; Japan; and the Republic of Korea.
2. Data as of 30 September 2022 and include both foreign currency and local currency issues.
Source: *AsianBondsOnline* computations based on Bloomberg LP data.

and Singapore's Public Utilities Board 30-year green bond. Turning to the currency profile, local-currency-denominated bonds accounted for a majority of outstanding sustainable bonds in the region at the end of September, representing 61.0% of the region's sustainable bond market; however, this share was much lower than LCY bonds' corresponding share of 95.0% of ASEAN+3's total bond market.

# Policy and Regulatory Developments

## People's Republic of China

### People's Bank of China Eases Foreign Borrowing Limits

In October, the People's Bank of China raised the ratio for the cross-border borrowing of firms and banks from 1.00 to 1.25. The move will allow companies to issue more foreign debt.

## Hong Kong, China

### Hong Kong Monetary Authority Announces Tentative Issuance for Hong Kong Special Administrative Region Government Bonds

On 30 September, the Hong Kong Monetary Authority announced the tentative issuance schedule for Hong Kong Special Administrative Region (HKSAR) bonds under the Institutional Bond Issuance Programme for the period between October 2022 and March 2023. The issuance schedule included planned issuances of bonds with tenors ranging from 1 year to 20 years. Of note are two planned switch tenders. The first such switch tender will involve issuance of a 3-year HKSAR bond in exchange for the early redemption of a 15-year HKSAR bond with an original maturity of March 2032. The other switch tender will involve the issuance of a 3-year bond in exchange for the early redemption of a 15-year bond with an original maturity of March 2036. Switch tender operations are intended to promote liquidity in the bond market by allowing market participants to switch bonds with different maturities through a competitive tender.

## Indonesia

### Indonesian Parliament Approves the 2023 State Budget

In September, the Indonesian Parliament approved the government's proposed budget for 2023, setting the deficit at IDR598.2 trillion or the equivalent of 2.8% of gross domestic product (GDP). The 2023 state budget estimates state revenues at IDR2,463.0 trillion and state expenditures at IDR3,061.2 trillion. Debt financing was projected to reach IDR696.3 trillion. The following macroeconomic assumptions, among others, were used as reference for the budget: (i) an economic growth of 5.3%, (ii) an inflation rate of 3.6%, (iii) a 10-year bond yield of 7.9%, (iv) an exchange rate of IDR14,800 per USD1.0, and (v) an Indonesia crude price per barrel of USD90.0.

## Republic of Korea

### The Government Announces 2023 Budget Proposal

On 30 August, the Government of the Republic of Korea announced its 2023 budget proposal totaling KRW639 trillion. This represented a 5.2% increase from the original 2022 budget, which is less than the average yearly increase of 8.7% over the last 5 years. The proposed 2023 budget is also 5.9% less than the 2022 final budget, which includes the supplementary budget. The smaller annual increase in the budget is in line with government efforts to reduce spending as part of its 2022–2026 fiscal management plan to improve fiscal sustainability. The proposed budget is projected to result in a 0.6% fiscal-deficit-to-GDP ratio, which is lower than the 2.5% ratio for 2022. Priorities in the budget include the expansion of protections for low-income and vulnerable households, support for the private-sector-led economy, and improvements to national safety and security.

### Fiscal Rules Introduced

In its 13 September emergency ministerial meeting on economic affairs, the Government of the Republic of Korea announced its plans to introduce rules to improve the government's fiscal soundness. This includes the use of the managed fiscal balance as a standard for fiscal rules instead of the consolidated fiscal balance. In addition, the managed fiscal balance shall have an upper limit of 3% of GDP, and it will be reduced to 2% when government debt exceeds 60% of GDP. However, this shall not be applied in the case of exceptional situations such as wars, national disasters, and economic downturns. The rules shall be established on a legal basis via inclusion of fiscal rule management standards in the National Finance Act and will be used in the design of the 2024 budget proposal.

## Malaysia

### Government of Malaysia Issues First Sustainability *Sukuk*

On 30 September, the Government of Malaysia raised funds through its inaugural Sustainability Government Investment Issues, worth MYR4.5 billion and with a tenor of 15 years. The issuance showed Malaysia's commitment to develop a sustainable economy. The sustainable bond served as a new benchmark bond in Malaysia's Islamic bond market. The proceeds will be used to fund the government's social and green projects under its Sustainable Development Goals Sukuk Framework.

## Philippines

### Bureau of the Treasury Releases Borrowing Program for October 2022

The Bureau of the Treasury intends to borrow PHP200 billion from local creditors in October by offering PHP60 billion worth of Treasury bills and PHP140 billion worth of Treasury bonds with tenors of 3, 6, 10, and 13 years. The borrowing program for October is the same as September's planned borrowing, which the Bureau of the Treasury failed to meet due to investors' demand for higher yield in anticipation of a continued rise in interest rates. However, the government remains confident that funding requirements for its various programs remain adequate against current market circumstances.

## Singapore

### Monetary Authority of Singapore Lays Out Vision for 2025

On 15 September, the Monetary Authority of Singapore launched its Financial Services Industry Transformation Map 2025, which details Singapore's plans to be the chief financial center in the region. Under its key strategy of digitalizing financial infrastructure, the Monetary Authority of Singapore aims to develop its bond market infrastructure by making the processes for listing, issuance, and settlement more efficient. This will allow investors to choose Singapore as their preferred destination for bond listing and issuance.

## Thailand

### Thai Cabinet Approves Public Debt Management Plan for Fiscal Year 2023

On 27 September, the Thai cabinet approved the public debt management plan for fiscal year 2023, which started on 1 October. The plan puts the ceiling for government borrowing for fiscal year 2023 at THB1.05 trillion, of which THB820.0 billion was allotted for new central government debt to offset the annual budget deficit, manage liquidity in the Treasury, and invest in infrastructure projects. The remaining THB233.0 billion was allocated for new debt for state enterprises and other government agencies to finance investments in transport infrastructure, power transmission systems, and other general operations. Under the new plan, the ratio of public debt-to-GDP will reach 60.4% by the end of fiscal year 2023, which is within the public debt ceiling of 70.0% of GDP.

### Public Debt Management Offices Plans to Issue THB130.0 Billion of Government Savings Bonds in Fiscal Year 2023

On 12 October, the Public Debt Management Office (PDMO) announced that it plans to sell THB130.0 billion of government savings bonds in fiscal year 2023. The PDMO assessed that there is ample liquidity in the Thai bond market for government bond issuance. In fiscal year 2023, the PDMO will focus on issuing medium-term bonds with maturities of 10–20 years in response to high market demand for such tenors. The government plans to borrow up to THB30.0 billion from international lenders such as the Asian Development Bank and the Japan International Cooperation Agency, and it will not issue USD-denominated bonds unless necessary.

## Viet Nam

### Government Releases Guidance on Offering and Trading Privately Issued Corporate Bonds

In September, the Government of Viet Nam promulgated Decree No. 65/2022/ND-CP (Decree 65) to amend the existing regulations on the offering and trading of privately issued bonds. Decree 65 aims to enhance transparency and sustainability in the bond market by tightening disclosure requirements and imposing more stringent conditions on bonds' private placements. It was developed to protect investors in several key areas, such as limiting the purpose of bond proceeds, implementing new requirements on the issuer's credit rating, and mandating additional disclosures by the issuers. Decree 65 also launches the centralized bond exchange system for bond registration and trading, which is expected to be operational by June 2023.

## State Bank of Vietnam Releases Guidance on Foreign Exchange Management for Foreign Borrowing and Foreign Debt Repayment

At the end of September, Circular No. 12/2022/TT-NHNN was issued by the State Bank of Vietnam to provide guidelines on foreign exchange administration relating to institutions' foreign borrowings and foreign debt repayments, which are not guaranteed by the government. The new circular focuses on public administrative reform, supplementing related processes and procedures, and improving the reporting mechanism to sustain enterprises' practical needs to borrow and pay off foreign debts and meet the State Bank of Vietnam's management objectives. The circular seeks to improve the legal framework for companies' borrowing and repayment of foreign loans, reflect the targets of public administrative reform through simplification and application of information technology in providing public services, and support companies to mobilize foreign financial resources for their business operations.

# Special Topics on Financial Markets

## Local Currency Bond Market Development and Exchange Rate Volatility

### Introduction

In 2022, accelerated monetary tightening in the United States (US) has led to currency depreciation and capital outflows in emerging markets.[7] This again highlights emerging markets' vulnerability to global shocks. Market liquidity is negatively affected as investors sell risky assets and shift funds to safe and liquid assets, which is known as flight-to-quality and flight-to-liquidity. A liquidity shortage, combined with structural issues in the market, could lead to a systemic financial crisis. For example, in the late 1990s, maturity and currency mismatches were widely documented as a key structural issue in financial markets that contributed to the 1997/98 Asian financial crisis. Eichengreen and Hausman (1999) claim that emerging markets become vulnerable to shocks because these economies have difficulty borrowing from abroad in their domestic currency or borrowing longer term. To mitigate financial fragility arising from these weaknesses, many Asian economies have put efforts into developing local currency (LCY) bond markets to channel LCY funding, especially longer-term tenors, to borrowers (Park, Shin, and Tian 2019). According to the International Monetary Fund (2016), LCY bond market development can prevent excessive cross-border capital flows, reduce excessive reliance on foreign capital, and reduce the currency mismatch problem on the balance sheet. There are studies linking LCY bond market development with financial stability by reducing foreign borrowing, providing a variety of funding maturities (especially long-term financing), and improving risk management in the banking sector (International Monetary Fund 2016; Jeanneau and Tovar 2008; Caballero, Farhi, and Gourinchas 2008; Park, Shin, and Tian 2019; Tian, Park, and Cagas 2021).

### Local Currency Bond Market Development in Emerging East Asia

The LCY bond market in emerging East Asia underwent rapid development during the past 2 decades. The size of the region's outstanding LCY bond market reached USD22.9 trillion at the end of June 2022, almost 27 times its size in 2000 (**Figure 26**). The market is dominated by government LCY bonds, which accounted for more than 60% of the region's bond market at the end of June 2022. The share of LCY bonds outstanding in the region's total bond market averaged about 90% over the past 2 decades.

After more than 20 years of development, emerging East Asia has made significant progress in channeling long-term funding into its LCY bond markets. The share of LCY bond issuance with tenors greater than 10 years increased from 6.9% in 2000 to 20.7% in the first half of 2022 (**Figure 27**). Tenors ranging from 5 years to

**Figure 26: Size of Local Currency Bonds in Select Emerging East Asian Markets**

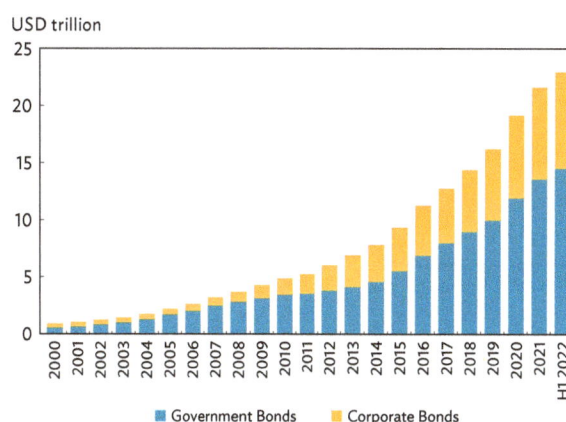

USD trillion

H1 = first half, USD = United States dollar.
Note: Emerging East Asia includes the People's Republic of China; Hong Kong, China; Indonesia; the Republic of Korea; Malaysia; the Philippines; Singapore; Thailand; and Viet Nam.
Sources: *AsianBondsOnline* and Bloomberg LP.

---

[7] This summary was written by Shu Tian (Senior Economist) and Mai Lin Villaruel (Economics Officer) based on Cheonkoo Kim, Jungsoo Park, Donghyun Park, and Shu Tian. "Local Currency Bond Market Development and Currency Stability during Market Turmoil." ADB Working Paper Series. Forthcoming.

**Figure 27: Maturity Profile of Bond Issuance in Select Emerging East Asian Local Currency Bond Markets**

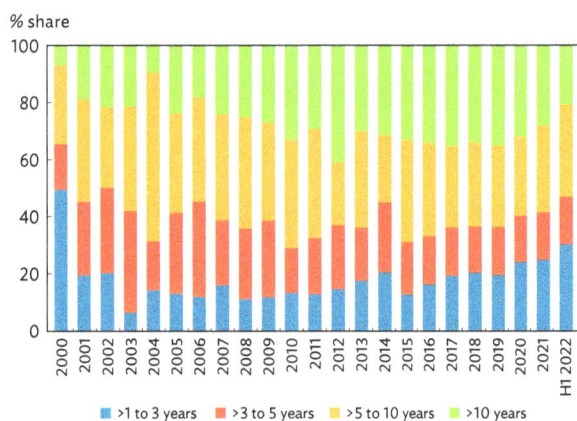

H1 = first half.
Note: Emerging East Asia includes the People's Republic of China; Hong Kong, China; Indonesia; the Republic of Korea; Malaysia; the Philippines; Singapore; Thailand; and Viet Nam.
Sources: *AsianBondsOnline* and Bloomberg LP.

10 years also increased from 27.6% in 2000 to 32.1% in the first half of 2022. On average, LCY bonds with tenors of 5 years or more accounted for 60.1% of the region's annual LCY bond issuance during the past 2 decades.

## Empirical Evidence: Local Currency Bond Market and Currency Stability during Market Turmoil

This study aims to examine whether LCY bond market development can contribute to financial stability during periods of market turmoil. In particular, the study focuses on the impact of the LCY bond market development in stabilizing exchange rate volatility during stress periods. Specifically, it examines whether a greater share of LCY bonds in the overall bond market and a greater share of long-term maturities have an additional stabilizing effect on exchange rate volatility during different types of global shocks, such as financial crises, the coronavirus disease (COVID-19) pandemic, and US monetary tightening.

Empirically, the study employs fixed-effects panel regressions using annual–economy panel data. The study covers 28 global economies with a total of 482 observations from 1989 to 2020.[8] The dependent

variable is the volatility of exchange rate changes, which is defined as the standard deviation of monthly exchange rate changes (against the USD) during a year. The key independent variables of interest are the size of the LCY bond market (outstanding LCY bonds) as a share of gross domestic product (GDP), the share of LCY bonds to total bonds, and the share of bonds with tenors of more than 10 years to total bonds. Following Park, Shin, and Tian (2019), the analysis controls common exchange rate volatility drivers such as inflation; the ratios of current account balance to GDP, foreign reserves to GDP, capital inflows to GDP, and portfolio flows to GDP; financial market development (including bank loans and stock market capitalization as shares of GDP); as well as market fixed effects to account for time-invariant market characteristics. To gauge the impact of LCY bond market development on exchange rate volatility during crisis, the study includes indicators for financial crises—including the Asian financial crisis, the global financial crisis, and the COVID-19 pandemic—as well as an interaction term between LCY bond market development variables and the crisis indicators in model specifications.

**Table 6** reports the estimated impacts of LCY bond market development on exchange rate volatility during the Asian financial crisis, the global financial crisis, and the COVID-19 pandemic. It is found that larger LCY bond markets experienced significantly lower exchange rate volatility during the two financial crises and the COVID-19 pandemic, as shown in columns 2 and 4, respectively. The volatility reduction effect is larger in Asian markets, as shown in column 3. In particular, a 1% larger LCY bond market as a share of GDP reduced exchange rate volatility by 0.00649 (0.31% of sample mean) during the financial crises and by 0.00795 (0.37% of sample mean) during the pandemic. In addition, a 1% larger LCY bond market as a share of GDP contributed to 0.0152 less exchange rate volatility (0.716% of sample mean) in Asian markets.

**Table 7** reports the impacts of bond market structure on exchange rate volatility. This analysis focuses on the role of LCY bonds and long-term bonds. Evidence shows that economies with a larger share of LCY and longer-term bonds in their bond market experienced less exchange rate volatility, especially during a crisis.

---

8   The 28 global economies included in the sample are Australia; Brazil; Canada; the People's Republic of China; Colombia; Croatia; Denmark; Hong Kong, China; Hungary; India; Indonesia; Israel; Japan; the Republic of Korea; Malaysia; Mexico; New Zealand; Norway; Pakistan; Peru; the Philippines; the Russian Federation; Singapore; South Africa; Sweden; Switzerland; Thailand; and the Republic of Türkiye.

**Table 6: Local Currency Bond Market Development and Exchange Rate Volatility during Periods of Financial Uncertainty**

| Variables | 1 | 2 | 3 | 4 |
|---|---|---|---|---|
| *LCY bonds as share of GDP* | −0.226 (−0.745) | −0.100 (−0.340) | −0.165 (−0.515) | −0.028 (−0.095) |
| *LCY bonds as share of GDP * financial crisis* | | −0.649** (−2.309) | 0.781 −1.174 | |
| *LCY bonds as share of GDP * financial crisis * Asia* | | | −1.520*** (−2.842) | |
| *LCY bonds as share of GDP * COVID-19* | | | | −0.795* (−1.918) |
| Observations | 482 | 482 | 482 | 482 |
| R-squared | 0.257 | 0.265 | 0.287 | 0.157 |
| Number of economies | 28 | 28 | 28 | 28 |
| Control variables | YES | YES | YES | YES |
| Market fixed effects | YES | YES | YES | YES |

COVID-19 = coronavirus disease, GDP = gross domestic product, LCY = local currency.
Note: * indicate statistical significance at the 10% level, ** at 5%, and *** at 1%. The numbers in parentheses represent robust t-statistics.
Source: Authors' calculations.

**Table 7: Impact of Local Currency Bond Market Structure on Exchange Rate Volatility**

| Variables | 1 | 2 | 3 | 4 | 5 |
|---|---|---|---|---|---|
| *Share of local currency bonds* | −1.942** (−2.317) | | −1.737* (−1.873) | −1.948** (−2.317) | −1.747* (−1.929) |
| *Share of longer tenor (>10 years)* | | −2.607** (−2.558) | −2.534** (−2.597) | | −2.481** (−2.543) |
| *LCY bonds as share of GDP * financial crisis* | | | | −0.608** (−2.232) | −0.554* (−1.994) |
| *Financial crisis* | 1.335*** −5.353 | 1.305*** −5.313 | 1.319*** −5.45 | 1.724*** −5.162 | 1.674*** −5.011 |
| Observations | 468 | 468 | 468 | 468 | 468 |
| R-squared | 0.287 | 0.313 | 0.321 | 0.295 | 0.328 |
| Number of economies | 28 | 28 | 28 | 28 | 28 |
| Control variables | YES | YES | YES | YES | YES |
| Market fixed effects | YES | YES | YES | YES | YES |

GDP = gross domestic product, LCY = local currency.
Note: * indicate statistical significance at the 10% level, ** at 5%, and *** at 1%. The numbers in parentheses represent robust t-statistics.
Source: Authors' calculations.

Specifically, a 1% larger LCY bond market as a share of the total bond market reduced exchange rate volatility by 0.019 (0.895% of sample mean), and 1% more long-term bonds (tenors of 10 years or above) as a share of the total bond market is associated with 0.026 less exchange rate volatility (1.224% of sample mean). During financial crises, a 1% larger LCY bond market as a share of the total bond market is associated with 0.006 less exchange rate volatility, as shown in column 4.

As an important source of global shocks, US monetary policy has a significant impact on global exchange rates. **Table 8** examines whether LCY bond market development contributed to exchange rate stability in periods when US monetary policy tightening occurred. Following Bu, Rogers, and Wu (2021) in measuring US monetary policy shock data series, the monthly frequency of monetary policy shocks for each year is aggregated to derive an annual series to match the dataset. The variable (US monetary tightening) takes a value of one for a period with tightening US monetary policy and zero, otherwise. The results in Table 8 show that LCY bond market development reduces exchange rate volatility during periods with US monetary policy tightening. On average, exchange rate volatility is 0.002 lower in economies with larger LCY bond markets during

**Table 8: Local Currency Bond Market Development and Exchange Rate Volatility in Response to United States Monetary Policy Shocks**

| Variables | 1 | 2 | 3 |
|---|---|---|---|
| LCY bonds as share of GDP * US monetary tightening | −0.231* (−1.875) | −0.202* (−1.832) | −0.225* (−1.942) |
| LCY bonds as share of GDP * US monetary tightening * Asia | | −0.227 (−1.167) | |
| LCY bonds as share of GDP * US monetary tightening * emerging market | | | −0.257 (−1.087) |
| Observations | 455 | 455 | 455 |
| R-squared | 0.158 | 0.159 | 0.159 |
| Number of economies | 28 | 28 | 28 |
| Control variables | YES | YES | YES |
| Market fixed effects | YES | YES | YES |

GDP = gross domestic product, LCY = local currency, US = United States.
Note: * indicate statistical significance at the 10% level, ** at 5%, and *** at 1%. The numbers in parentheses represent robust t-statistics.
Sources: Authors' calculations.

periods of US monetary tightening relative to smaller LCY bond markets. Such a currency stabilizing effect is more general for all markets, and is not only relevant in Asian and emerging markets, as shown in columns 2 and 3, respectively.

## Conclusion

This study provides empirical evidence to show that LCY bond market development contributes to financial stability during periods of global market turmoil. A larger LCY bond market was associated with less exchange rate volatility during recent financial crises, the COVID-19 pandemic, and US monetary policy shocks. A higher share of LCY bonds in the total bond market and a higher share of long-term bonds in the bond market are also generally related to less exchange rate volatility, with an extra stabilizing impact during financial crises. This evidence joins existing literature to show that LCY bond markets help stabilize the domestic currency during stress periods. LCY bond markets deliver such benefits by addressing the well-known "original sin in emerging market borrowing" (Eichengreen and Hausman 1999), with LCY funding and longer-tenor borrowings cushioning liquidity drains when investors sell risky assets amid a flight-to-safety and -liquidity.

An LCY bond market is only one of the factors that contributes to financial stability by fixing structural issues in the financial market. Stronger economic fundamentals, including factors such as sufficient reserves, a strong

current account performance, a sound fiscal balance, and modest inflation and domestic interest rates, also play an important role. Emerging markets should continue to broaden the investor base in their bond markets to diversify demand for different bond maturities and risk appetite, and to enhance transparency and institutional quality in financial markets to make it more accessible to global investors. Improved liquidity and enhanced hedging tools are also important factors to attract a well-diversified investor base.

## References

Bu, Chunya, John Rogers, and Wenbin Wu. 2021 "A Unified Measure of Fed Monetary Policy Shocks." *Journal of Monetary Economics* 118 (2021): 331–349.

Caballero, Ricardo J., Emmanuel Farhi, and Pierre-Olivier Gourinchas. 2008. "Financial Crash, Commodity Prices, and Global Imbalances." *Brookings Papers on Economic Activity* 200 (2008): 1–55.

Eichengreen, Barry, and Ricardo Hausmann. 1999. "Exchange Rates and Financial Fragility." NBER Working Papers 7418.

International Monetary Fund. 2016. "Development of Local Currency Bond Markets: Overview of Recent Development and Key Themes." Staff Note for the G20.

Jeanneau, Serge, and Camilo E. Tovar. 2008. "Latin America's Local Currency Bond Markets: An Overview." In Bank for International Settlements (ed.), *New Financing Trends in Latin America: A Bumpy Road towards Stability*, 46–64.

Park, Donghyun, Kwanho Shin, and Shu Tian. 2019. "Do Local Currency Bond Markets Enhance Financial Stability? Some Empirical Evidence." *Emerging Markets Finance and Trade* 57 (2): 562–90.

Tian, Shu, Donghyun Park, and Marie Anne Cagas. 2021. "Bond Market Development and Bank Stability: Evidence from Emerging Markets." *Research in International Business and Finance* 58 (2021): 101498.

## Does Regional Trade Integration Automatically Foster Regional Financial Integration? The Case of Regional Comprehensive Economic Partnership

Well before the outbreak of the coronavirus disease (COVID-19) pandemic in early 2020, the world economy witnessed a slowdown in the momentum of economic globalization.[9] The seemingly unstoppable expansion of global trade and cross-border capital flows that drove global economic growth and prosperity in the postwar period have shown signs of decelerating since 2010. *The Economist* even coined the term "slowbalisation" for the noticeably slower pace of globalization that had been preceded by a golden age of globalization, which spanned from 1990 to 2010. Structural factors—such as the cost of transportation no longer falling and the growing self-reliance of the People's Republic of China's (PRC) manufacturing sector and, hence, reduced demand for imports—underlie the trends behind slowbalisation. The United States (US)–PRC trade conflict, which pitted the world's two biggest economies against one another, further dampened globalization. Then, the pandemic alerted multinational corporations, whose global supply chains were a key engine of globalization, to the risks of long supply chains. Specifically, production disruption in any one location of a long supply chain can disrupt the entire production process.

One key consequence of the deceleration of economic globalization in recent years has been the deepening of regional economic integration. In response to the high risks of distance and multistage supply chains, some firms are turning to reshoring, or the shifting of production from abroad back to the home economy. But other firms are moving production from distant foreign locations to nearby foreign locations. Generally, slowbalisation is leading to closer economic links within regions. This is especially evident in Asia, where greater intra-regional trade has gained momentum in recent years. In contrast to western Europe, where intra-regional trade has dominated trade for a long time, intra-Asian trade is a relatively recent phenomenon. Intra-Asian trade is by far the most advanced among East Asian and Southeast Asian economies, which collectively form what is referred to as "Factory Asia." In the past, Factory Asia produced manufactured goods that were exported to rich consumers in the US and other high-income economies. However, decades of world-topping economic growth elevated Asia's general living standards many times over and produced a large middle class that increasingly consumes what the region produces.

The transformation of Factory Asia into "Consumer Asia" is a powerful driver of greater intra-regional trade among Asian economies, especially East and Southeast Asian economies. The post-2010 trend toward deglobalization and regionalization will add further impetus to intra-regional trade integration, as will the post-COVID-19 shift away from global supply chains and toward regional supply chains. Rising trade protectionism and economic nationalism in advanced economies is yet another key driver of intra-Asian trade integration. While the de facto integration of Asian economies has proceeded full-steam, institutional integration has lagged behind. However, in this connection, one relatively unnoticed but potentially significant recent development was the formation of the Regional Comprehensive Economic Partnership (RCEP) free trade agreement, which came into effect on 1 January 2022. RCEP members include Australia, Brunei Darussalam, Cambodia, the PRC, Indonesia, Japan, the Republic of Korea, the Lao People's Democratic Republic, Malaysia, New Zealand, the Philippines, Singapore, Thailand, and

[9] This write-up was prepared by Donghyun Park (economic advisor), Shu Tian (senior economist), and Gemma Estrada (senior economics officer) of the Economic Research and Regional Cooperation Department of the Asian Development Bank based on Hyun-Hoon Lee, Danbee Park, Donghyun Park, and Shu Tian. 2022. "RCEP's Financial Integration Before and After the Global Financial Crisis: An Empirical Analysis." *The Journal of International Trade & Economic Development*. DOI: 10.1080/09638199.2022.2115106.

Viet Nam. RCEP, thus, encompasses the member economies of the Association of Southeast Asian Nations (ASEAN) plus all major economies of Asia and the Pacific except India. The total population of RCEP members is about 2.3 billion, representing 30% of the global population. The free trade agreement's share of global output is around 30.7% (**Table 9**).

RCEP is significant because it is the first regional trade bloc that covers all of East Asia and Southeast Asia. The free trade agreement also includes Australia and New Zealand, which have close trade links with and are geographically close to the Asia and Pacific region. In addition to being a globally significant economic force, RCEP is a powerful force in global trade. The group collectively accounted for 30.6% of total global exports and 26.5% of total global imports in 2021 (**Table 10**). Furthermore, as noted earlier, as a result of rapid economic growth that boosted purchasing power, the region's economies are increasingly exporting more to each other than to rest of the world. In fact, the intra-RCEP share of RCEP members' exports reached 50.4% in 2019. In contrast to such rapid de facto integration, institutional integration has remained

largely just a patchwork of bilateral deals such as the ASEAN–China Free Trade Area. In this context, the formation of RCEP is a significant development in the institutional integration of Asian economies.

Trade integration is only one dimension of economic integration, although a highly significant dimension. Another major dimension is financial integration, or the integration of the financial markets of member economies. Although RCEP economies show a high level of trade integration, their financial integration is limited. The financial markets of RCEP economies are more integrated with those of the US and other advanced economies than with each other. In light of the efforts of East and Southeast Asian economies to reduce their heavy dependence on US financial markets, as epitomized by the Chiang Mai Initiative and its multilateralization, it is worthwhile to empirically examine whether intra-regional financial integration has increased over time. Notably, the membership of the Chiang Mai Initiative is almost identical to that of RCEP except that the latter also includes Australia and New Zealand.

### Table 9: RCEP Members' GDP and GDP per Capita, 2021

| Economy | GDP (USD billion) | GDP per Capita (USD) |
|---|---|---|
| Australia | 1,542.66 | 59,934.13 |
| Brunei Darussalam | 14.01 | 31,722.66 |
| Cambodia | 26.96 | 1,590.96 |
| China, People's Republic of | 17,734.06 | 12,556.33 |
| Indonesia | 1,186.09 | 4,291.81 |
| Japan | 4,937.42 | 39,285.16 |
| Korea, Republic of | 1,798.53 | 34,757.72 |
| Lao PDR | 18.83 | 2,551.33 |
| Malaysia | 372.70 | 11,371.10 |
| New Zealand | 249.99 | 48,801.69 |
| Philippines | 394.09 | 3,548.83 |
| Singapore | 396.99 | 72,794.00 |
| Thailand | 505.98 | 7,233.39 |
| Viet Nam | 362.64 | 3,694.02 |
| **RCEP Total** | **29,540.95** | |
| **World Total** | **96,100.09** | |
| **RCEP's Share in World (%)** | **30.74** | |

GDP = gross domestic product, Lao PDR = Lao People's Democratic Republic, RCEP = Regional Comprehensive Economic Partnership, USD = United States dollar.
Source: World Bank. World Development Indicators. https://databank.worldbank.org/reports.aspx?source=world-development-indicators (accessed 7 October 2022).

### Table 10: RCEP Members' Merchandise Exports and Imports, 2021

| Economy | Merchandise Exports (USD billion) | Merchandise Imports (USD billion) |
|---|---|---|
| Australia | 343.59 | 261.26 |
| Brunei Darussalam | 11.07 | 8.28 |
| Cambodia | 17.97 | 28.03 |
| China, People's Republic of | 3,363.96 | 2,687.53 |
| Indonesia | 229.85 | 196.04 |
| Japan | 756.03 | 768.98 |
| Korea, Republic of | 644.40 | 615.09 |
| Lao PDR | 7.62 | 6.53 |
| Malaysia | 299.03 | 237.98 |
| New Zealand | 44.87 | 49.46 |
| Philippines | 74.61 | 123.88 |
| Singapore | 457.36 | 406.23 |
| Thailand | 271.17 | 267.60 |
| Viet Nam | 335.93 | 331.58 |
| **RCEP Total** | **6,857.46** | **5,988.48** |
| **World Total** | **22,393.05** | **22,592.28** |
| **RCEP's Share in World (%)** | **30.62** | **26.51** |

Lao PDR = Lao People's Democratic Republic, RCEP = Regional Comprehensive Economic Partnership, USD = United States dollar.
Source: World Bank. World Development Indicators. https://databank.worldbank.org/reports.aspx?source=world-development-indicators (accessed 7 October 2022).

Furthermore, there are conceptual reasons that suggest trade integration promotes financial integration. Most immediately, as the firms of two economies trade more with each other, the banks, insurers, and other financial institutions that facilitate trade will become more involved with their counterparts in the other economy. But more fundamentally, closer trade links between two economies improve investor knowledge about the economic structure and investment opportunities of the other economy. That is, greater bilateral trade increases investors' information and familiarity about the other economy and, hence, their confidence in investing there. As noted above, trade integration within RCEP has already progressed to the extent that over half of RCEP economies' trade is with each other. Therefore, the high and growing level of intra-RCEP trade integration may lead to greater intra-RCEP financial integration.

In connection with this, Lee et al. (forthcoming) empirically examine the IMF's Coordinated Portfolio Investment Survey data on cross-border holdings of portfolio investment (equities and debt securities) from 2001 to 2019 to examine whether RCEP economies have in fact become more financially integrated in recent years. The evidence suggests that they have not. Lee et al. (forthcoming) find that intra-RCEP integration of financial markets is limited and did not increase even after the global financial crisis, which was an event that highlighted the risks of excessive dependence on US financial markets. In stark contrast to RCEP members, the intra-regional integration of euro area financial markets increased during the review period. Most significantly, the authors find that trade integration among RCEP economies does not promote their financial integration. That is, although RCEP economies are trading heavily with each other and that such trade is increasing over time, their financial transactions with each other are limited and not increasing over time. The evidence from the analysis indicates that deepening trade linkages among RCEP members will not automatically intensify their financial linkages.

Furthermore, the evidence suggests that even if economic regionalization in the post-COVID-19 period further expands intra-RCEP trade, this will not automatically promote intra-RCEP financial integration. The failure of financial integration to keep pace with trade integration is partly due to the fact that the USD-dominated global financial system drove the growth of intra-RCEP trade. Since trade integration does not automatically foster financial integration, financial integration cannot rely solely on de facto integration but also requires institutional integration. A good example of such institutional arrangements to foster financial integration in the region is the ASEAN+3 Bond Market Initiative, which comprises the 10 member economies of ASEAN plus the PRC, Japan, and the Republic of Korea.

# Market Summaries

## People's Republic of China

### Yield Movements

Between 31 August and 14 October, the People's Republic of China's (PRC) local currency (LCY) government bond yields rose for nearly all tenors (**Figure 1**). The rise, however, was marginal, with tenors of longer than 3 months rising between 0.2 and 8.0 basis points (bps). The spread of the 10-year over 2-year tenor rose slightly to 65 bps on 14 October from 59 bps on 31 August.

In contrast to other regional markets, the PRC's yield curve was only marginally changed during the review period, with many other emerging East Asian markets pressured by tightening monetary policy in the United States (US) and throughout the region. In contrast, external pressure on the PRC's yields was offset by persistent weakness in the domestic economy. The PRC's continued pandemic containment measures have led to concerns that they will continue to stifle the economy. However, there was some recovery in the third quarter (Q3) of 2022, with gross domestic product expanding 3.9% year-on-year (y-o-y) after a 0.4% y-o-y gain in the second quarter (Q2). All sectors grew, with secondary industry expanding the fastest at 5.2% y-o-y, followed by tertiary industry at 3.2% y-o-y and primary industry at 2.4% y-o-y. Economic growth, however, continued to fall below the full-year target of the government set at 5.5%. Inflation also continued to be muted in the PRC, with inflation easing to 2.1% y-o-y in October from 2.8% y-o-y in September and 2.5% y-o-y in August.

### Size and Composition

The LCY bond market in the PRC grew to a size of CNY125.8 trillion (USD17.7 trillion) at the end of September (**Table 1**). Growth decelerated to 2.2% quarter-on-quarter (q-o-q) in Q3 2022 from 3.5% q-o-q in Q2 2022. While weaknesses were noted in both the government and corporate bond segments, the biggest contributor to slowing growth was softness in the government bond sector. On a y-o-y basis, however,

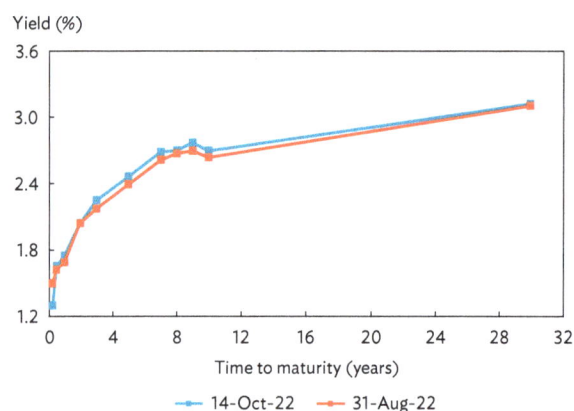

**Figure 1: The People's Republic of China's Benchmark Yield Curve—Local Currency Government Bonds**

Source: Based on data from Bloomberg LP.

bond market growth reached 13.5% in Q3 2022. The PRC remained the largest LCY bond market in emerging East Asia, accounting for 80.2% of the region's aggregate bond stock at the end of September.

**Government bonds.** The share of government bonds as a percentage of total LCY bonds outstanding slightly increased to 65.1% at the end of September from 64.8% at the end of June. Total government bonds outstanding reached CNY81.9 trillion, with growth slowing to 2.8% q-o-q in Q3 2022 from 4.3% q-o-q in Q2 2022 as local government bond issuance weakened following the massive issuance spree in previous months in order to meet annual bond quotas.

Local government bonds outstanding grew only 0.8% q-o-q in Q3 2022 after expanding 7.5% q-o-q in Q2 2022. The growth of Treasury and other government bonds rose to 4.9% q-o-q from 3.1% q-o-q in the same period, while policy bank bonds gained 3.8% q-o-q in Q3 2022, up from 0.5% q-o-q growth in Q2 2022.

**Corporate bonds.** The PRC's corporate bond market growth moderated to 1.2% q-o-q from 2.0% q-o-q in

Table 1: Size and Composition of the Local Currency Bond Market in the People's Republic of China

| | Outstanding Amount (billion) | | | | | | Growth Rates (%) | | | |
|---|---|---|---|---|---|---|---|---|---|---|
| | Q3 2021 | | Q2 2022 | | Q3 2022 | | Q3 2021 | | Q3 2022 | |
| | CNY | USD | CNY | USD | CNY | USD | q-o-q | y-o-y | q-o-q | y-o-y |
| Total | 110,784 | 17,190 | 123,050 | 18,368 | 125,779 | 17,676 | 3.9 | 12.8 | 2.2 | 13.5 |
| Government | 71,171 | 11,043 | 79,710 | 11,898 | 81,918 | 11,512 | 4.1 | 13.4 | 2.8 | 15.1 |
| Treasury Bonds and Other Government Bonds | 22,370 | 3,471 | 24,092 | 3,596 | 25,261 | 3,550 | 3.8 | 15.7 | 4.9 | 12.9 |
| Central Bank Bonds | 15 | 2 | 15 | 2 | 15 | 2 | 0.0 | 0.0 | 0.0 | 0.0 |
| Policy Bank Bonds | 19,253 | 2,987 | 20,213 | 3,017 | 20,984 | 2,949 | 3.2 | 10.1 | 3.8 | 9.0 |
| Local Government Bonds | 29,533 | 4,583 | 35,390 | 5,283 | 35,658 | 5,011 | 4.9 | 14.0 | 0.8 | 20.7 |
| Corporate | 39,613 | 6,146 | 43,340 | 6,469 | 43,861 | 6,164 | 3.7 | 11.8 | 1.2 | 10.7 |

CNY = Chinese yuan, q-o-q = quarter-on-quarter, Q2 = second quarter, Q3 = third quarter, USD = United States dollar, y-o-y = year-on-year.
Notes:
1. Other government bonds include savings bonds and local government bonds.
2. Bloomberg LP end-of-period local currency–USD rates are used.
3. Growth rates are calculated from local currency base and do not include currency effects.
Sources: CEIC Data Company and Bloomberg LP.

Q2 2022. Corporate bond issuers remained cautious over domestic market conditions. Corporate bonds outstanding reached CNY43.9 trillion at the end of September, comprising roughly 76.7% of emerging East Asia's corporate bond total.

Among the different categories of corporate bonds, listed corporate bonds comprise the largest share of the market, hitting CNY12.5 trillion at the end of September on growth of 1.9% q-o-q and 9.1% y-o-y (**Table 2**). The fastest growth in the LCY corporate bond market came from financial bonds, which expanded 3.8% q-o-q to CNY10.0 trillion at the end of September. Medium-term notes also continued to grow, rising 3.1% q-o-q. The remaining bond types either posted declines or only marginal growth rates during Q3 2022.

Overall corporate bond issuance gained 7.2% q-o-q in Q3 2022, as corporates largely refinanced existing maturities. The fastest issuance came from listed corporate bonds, which gained 16.6% q-o-q, and medium-term notes, which gained 11.4% q-o-q (**Figure 2**).

At the end of September, the top 30 issuers of corporate bonds in the PRC had an outstanding bond stock of CNY12.5 trillion, representing 28.6% of the corporate bond total (**Table 3**). State-owned China Railway continued to account for the largest amount of bonds outstanding at CNY3.2 trillion. Next was Agricultural Bank of China with bonds outstanding of CNY900.0 billion. The top 30 list comprised 14 state-owned firms and 23 listed firms.

The largest corporate bond issuances in the PRC during Q3 2022 are listed in **Table 4**. Three banks and one state-owned institution had the largest aggregate issuance amounts. Banks continued to be major issuers of bonds as they beefed up their capital and funding for lending activities by issuing perpetual and subordinated debt. The State Grid Corporation issued only 5-year bonds during the quarter. Among the issuances in the list, the shortest-dated tenor was a 5-year bond, and the longest-dated tenor was a perpetual bond.

## Investor Profile

**Government bonds.** At the end of September, banking institutions remained the largest investor group in the PRC's government bond market (**Figure 3**). The shares of bank holdings of Treasury bonds, policy bank bonds, and local government bonds stood at 86.4%, 65.3%, and 71.1%, respectively. However, all of these shares declined compared with the same month a year earlier except for policy bank bonds.

The PRC managed to attract net foreign bond inflows in July and August totaling USD0.8 billion. However, the inflows were marginal, especially compared to the USD15.8 billion of net outflows recorded in Q2 2022 as the US continued to tighten monetary policy, making the PRC's LCY bonds less attractive. In September, the PRC posted outflows of USD5.0 billion.

**Table 2: Corporate Bonds Outstanding in Key Categories**

| | Amount (CNY billion) | | | Growth Rate (%) | | | |
|---|---|---|---|---|---|---|---|
| | | | | Q3 2021 | | Q3 2022 | |
| | Q3 2021 | Q2 2022 | Q3 2022 | q-o-q | y-o-y | q-o-q | y-o-y |
| Financial Bonds | 8,448 | 9,671 | 10,038 | 1.1 | 24.2 | 3.8 | 18.8 |
| Enterprise Bonds | 3,897 | 3,961 | 3,991 | 1.0 | 3.3 | 0.8 | 2.4 |
| Listed Corporate Bonds | 11,464 | 12,282 | 12,511 | 1.0 | 27.4 | 1.9 | 9.1 |
| Commercial Paper | 2,249 | 2,840 | 2,613 | 1.0 | (20.4) | (8.0) | 16.2 |
| Medium-Term Notes | 7,693 | 8,549 | 8,811 | 1.0 | 5.4 | 3.1 | 14.5 |
| Asset-Backed Securities | 3,238 | 3,400 | 3,282 | 1.1 | 34.6 | (3.5) | 1.4 |

( ) = negative, CNY = Chinese yuan, q-o-q = quarter-on-quarter, Q2 = second quarter, Q3 = third quarter, y-o-y = year-on-year.
Source: CEIC Data Company.

**Figure 2: Corporate Bond Issuance in Key Sectors**

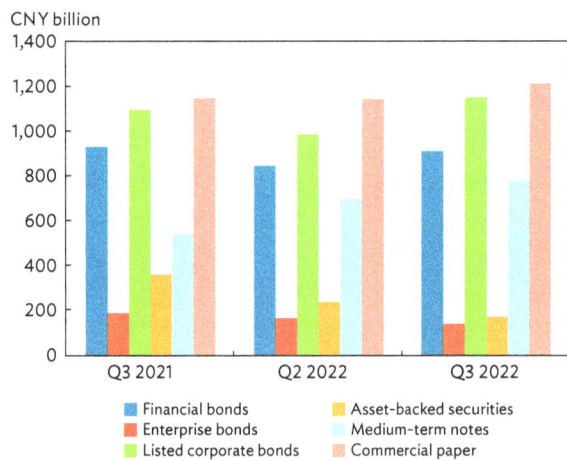

CNY = Chinese yuan, Q2 = second quarter, Q3 = third quarter.
Source: CEIC Data Company.

# Policy, Institutional, and Regulatory Developments

## People's Bank of China Eases Foreign Borrowing Limits

In October, the People's Bank of China raised the ratio for the cross-border borrowing of firms and banks from 1.00 to 1.25. The move will allow companies to issue more foreign debt.

**Table 3: Top 30 Issuers of Local Currency Corporate Bonds in the People's Republic of China**

| | Issuers | Outstanding Amount | | State-Owned | Listed Company | Type of Industry |
|---|---|---|---|---|---|---|
| | | LCY Bonds (CNY billion) | LCY Bonds (USD billion) | | | |
| 1. | China Railway | 3,223.5 | 452.99 | Yes | No | Transportation |
| 2. | Agricultural Bank of China | 900.0 | 126.48 | Yes | Yes | Banking |
| 3. | Industrial and Commercial Bank of China | 881.0 | 123.81 | Yes | Yes | Banking |
| 4. | Bank of China | 858.1 | 120.59 | Yes | Yes | Banking |
| 5. | China Construction Bank | 603.0 | 84.74 | Yes | No | Asset Management |
| 6. | Bank of Communications | 569.9 | 80.09 | Yes | Yes | Banking |
| 7. | Shanghai Pudong Development Bank | 522.2 | 73.38 | Yes | Yes | Banking |
| 8. | Industrial Bank | 407.6 | 57.28 | No | Yes | Banking |
| 9. | Central Huijin Investment | 373.0 | 52.42 | No | Yes | Banking |
| 10. | China Citic Bank | 355.0 | 49.89 | No | Yes | Banking |
| 11. | State Grid Corporation of China | 293.0 | 41.17 | No | Yes | Power |
| 12. | China Minsheng Bank | 280.3 | 39.38 | Yes | No | Energy |
| 13. | State Power Investment | 260.1 | 36.55 | Yes | No | Power |
| 14. | China Everbright Bank | 254.3 | 35.73 | No | Yes | Banking |
| 15. | Huaxia Bank | 250.0 | 35.13 | No | Yes | Banking |
| 16. | Postal Savings Bank of China | 240.0 | 33.73 | Yes | Yes | Banking |
| 17. | China Merchants Bank | 217.8 | 30.61 | Yes | Yes | Banking |
| 18. | Shaanxi Coal and Chemical Industry Group | 180.5 | 25.37 | Yes | No | Coal |
| 19. | Ping An Bank | 180.0 | 25.30 | No | Yes | Banking |
| 20. | China National Petroleum | 174.3 | 24.49 | No | Yes | Banking |
| 21. | China Merchants Securities | 173.6 | 24.39 | Yes | Yes | Brokerage |
| 22. | Tianjin Infrastructure Investment Group | 166.1 | 23.34 | No | No | Holding Company |
| 23. | China Southern Power Grid | 159.3 | 22.39 | No | Yes | Energy |
| 24. | Bank of Beijing | 155.9 | 21.91 | No | Yes | Banking |
| 25. | Huatai Securities | 152.5 | 21.42 | No | No | Brokerage |
| 26. | CITIC Securities | 149.8 | 21.05 | Yes | Yes | Brokerage |
| 27. | Shenwan Hongyuan Securities | 145.2 | 20.40 | No | Yes | Brokerage |
| 28. | China Galaxy Securities | 143.2 | 20.12 | No | Yes | Brokerage |
| 29. | Guotai Junan Securities | 139.2 | 19.56 | No | Yes | Brokerage |
| 30. | GF Securities | 136.8 | 19.22 | No | Yes | Brokerage |
| | **Total Top 30 LCY Corporate Issuers** | **12,545.1** | **1,762.94** | | | |
| | **Total LCY Corporate Bonds** | **43,861.36** | **6,163.8** | | | |
| | **Top 30 as % of Total LCY Corporate Bonds** | **28.6%** | **28.6%** | | | |

CNY = Chinese yuan, LCY = local currency, USD = United States dollar.
Notes:
1. Data as of 30 September 2022.
2. State-owned firms are defined as those in which the government has more than a 50% ownership stake.
Source: *AsianBondsOnline* calculations based on Bloomberg LP data.

**Table 4: Notable Local Currency Corporate Bond Issuances in the Third Quarter of 2022**

| Corporate Issuers | Coupon Rate (%) | Issued Amount (CNY billion) |
|---|---|---|
| Agricultural Bank of China | | |
| 10-year bond | 3.03 | 7.0 |
| 15-year bond | 3.34 | 2.8 |
| Perpetual bond | 3.17 | 4.3 |
| China Reform Holdings[a] | | |
| 5-year bond | 2.65 | 4.3 |
| 5-year bond | 2.80 | 2.8 |
| China Everbright Bank | | |
| 10-year bond | 3.10 | 5.8 |
| 15-year bond | 3.35 | 0.7 |
| Industrial and Commercial Bank | | |
| 10-year bond | 3.02 | 4.4 |
| 15-year bond | 3.32 | 1.5 |
| State Grid Corporation[a] | | |
| 5-year bond | 2.88 | 1.0 |
| 5-year bond | 3.04 | 1.0 |
| 5-year bond | 3.05 | 0.9 |
| 5-year bond | 2.88 | 0.9 |
| 5-year bond | 3.05 | 0.8 |
| 5-year bond | 2.92 | 0.7 |
| 5-year bond | 2.92 | 0.4 |
| 5-year bond | 3.05 | 0.2 |

CNY = Chinese yuan.
[a] Multiple issuance of the same tenor indicates issuance on different dates.
Source: Based on data from Bloomberg LP.

**Figure 3: Local Currency Treasury Bonds and Policy Bank Bonds Investor Profile**

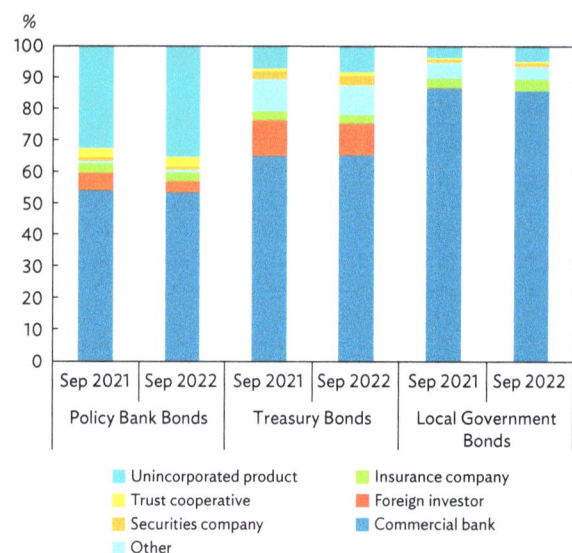

Source: CEIC Data Company.

# Hong Kong, China

## Yield Movements

Between 31 August and 14 October, Hong Kong, China's local currency (LCY) government bond yield curve shifted upward, with yields rising for all tenors (**Figure 1**). Yields rose an average of 80 basis points (bps) across the curve. Bonds with maturities between 1 year and 3 years posted the biggest yield gains, rising 110 bps on average. Yields for bonds with maturities of less than 1 year jumped an average of 69 bps, while yields for bonds with maturities of 10 years or longer rose 65 bps on average. The yield curve remained inverted during the review period. The negative spread between the 10-year and 2-year yields deepened from –19 bps on 31 August to –57 bps on 14 October.

The movements of Hong Kong, China's LCY bond yields during the review period tracked those of United States (US) Treasury yields, owing to the Hong Kong dollar's peg to the US dollar. US Treasury yields jumped an average of 89 bps across all tenors during the review period, with the 2-year Treasury yield posting the highest gain at 100 bps. The US Treasury yield curve remained inverted during the review period, with the negative spread between the 10-year and 2-year yields widening from –30 bps on 31 August to –48 bps on 14 October.

The rise in US Treasury yields was primarily due to the Federal Reserve's continuing aggressive monetary policy tightening to arrest mounting inflation. In its September policy rate meeting, the Federal Reserve increased the target range for its policy rate by 75 bps to a range of 3.00%–3.25%. From March to September, the Federal Reserve had raised its policy rate by a total of 300 bps. To maintain the Hong Kong dollar's peg to the US dollar, the Hong Kong Monetary Authority (HKMA) increased its base rate by 75 bps to 2.75% on 28 July and by another 75 bps to 3.50% on 22 September.[10] The relentless monetary policy tightening by the US and the consequent base rate adjustment by the HKMA continued to create upward pressure on yields at the shorter-end of the government bond yield curves of the US and Hong Kong, China, respectively. Investors

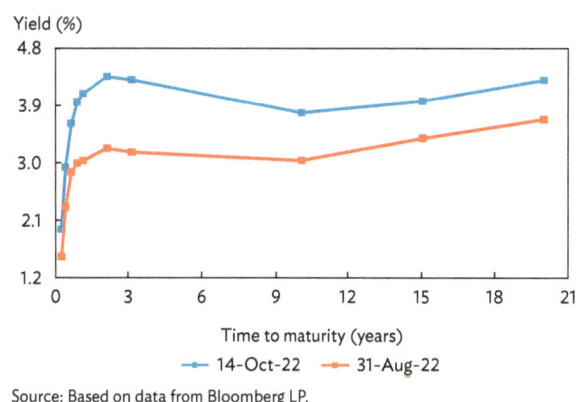

**Figure 1: Hong Kong, China's Benchmark Yield Curve—Exchange Fund Bills and Notes**

Source: Based on data from Bloomberg LP.

priced in the rate hikes as well as expectations that the Federal Reserve would maintain its hawkish monetary policy stance for an extended period.

The inverted yield curve in Hong Kong, China also reflected expectations of a prolonged economic downturn. Hong Kong, China has recorded 3 consecutive quarters of economic contractions in 2022: gross domestic product (GDP) plunged 4.5% year-on-year (y-o-y) in the third quarter (Q3) following contractions of 1.3% year-on-year (y-o-y) in the second quarter (Q2) and 3.9% y-o-y in the first quarter. The GDP decline in Q3 2022 was primarily due to sharp contractions in exports and investment expenditure. Merchandise exports fell 15.6% y-o-y in Q3 2022, following an 8.4% y-o-y drop in Q2 2022 amid weakened global demand and continued cross-border disruptions. Domestic fixed capital formation dropped 14.3% y-o-y in Q3 2022 due to tightened financial conditions brought about by rising interest rates. Hong Kong, China's economy continues to face downside risks from persistent global inflation, continued monetary policy tightening by global central banks, heightened geopolitical tensions, and the uncertain trajectory of the pandemic. In October, the Census and Statistics Department revised downward its full-year 2022 GDP growth forecast to –3.2% from its August projection of –0.5% to 0.5%.

---

[10] The Hong Kong dollar is pegged to a narrow band of between HKD7.75 and HKD7.85 versus the US dollar. The base rate is set at either 50 bps above the lower end of the prevailing target range of the US Federal Reserve rate or the average of the 5-day moving averages of the overnight and 1-month Hong Kong Interbank Offered Rate, whichever is higher.

Hong Kong, China's consumer price inflation remained relatively moderate compared with that of neighboring economies. Inflation jumped to 4.4% y-o-y in September from 1.9% y-o-y in August, mainly due to a low base as a waiver of public housing rentals subdued prices in September 2021. Inflation was relatively low in the prior months at 1.9% y-o-y in July and 1.8% y-o-y in June. In October, the Census and Statistics Department revised its full-year 2022 forecast for headline inflation to 1.9%, down from 2.1% as announced in August.

During the review period, the HKMA intervened multiple times in the currency market to defend the Hong Kong dollar's peg to the US dollar. As a result, the aggregate balance—a measure of liquidity in the local banking system—dropped to HKD106.6 billion on 14 October from HKD125.0 billion on 31 August.

## Size and Composition

Hong Kong, China's LCY bond market reached a size of HKD2,748.2 billion (USD350.1 billion) at the end of September after rising 4.9% quarter-on-quarter (q-o-q) and 13.2% y-o-y in Q3 2022 (**Table 1**). Growth accelerated from 2.9% q-o-q and 7.9% y-o-y in Q2 2022 primarily due to faster expansions in both the government and corporate bond segments. Growth in government bonds outstanding more than doubled to 3.7% q-o-q in Q3 2022 from 1.5% q-o-q in the previous quarter. Meanwhile, the stock of outstanding corporate bonds rose 6.2% q-o-q in Q3 2022, up from 4.4% q-o-q in the previous quarter. Government bonds comprised 52.1% of Hong Kong, China's LCY bond market, while

corporate bonds represented the remaining 47.9% at the end of September.

**Government bonds.** Outstanding LCY government bonds amounted to HKD1,432.8 billion at the end of September. Quarterly growth in outstanding government bonds was driven by robust growth in Hong Kong Special Administrative Region (HKSAR) bonds and Exchange Fund Bills (EFBs). Exchange Fund Notes (EFNs) continued to contract. On an annual basis, LCY government bonds outstanding rose 14.4% y-o-y in Q3 2022, up from 13.6% y-o-y growth in the prior quarter. At the end of September, LCY government bonds outstanding comprised 82.0% EFBs, 1.5% EFNs, and 16.5% HKSAR bonds.

Total issuance of new government bonds reached HKD1,001.4 billion in Q3 2022 after expanding 3.5% q-o-q and 14.6% y-o-y. Growth was supported by robust issuance of HKSAR bonds and EFBs, which rose 71.9% q-o-q and 1.5% q-o-q, respectively, during the review period.

**Exchange Fund Bills.** The stock of outstanding EFBs reached HKD1,174.3 billion at the end of September on growth of 0.6% q-o-q and 10.3% y-o-y. New EFBs issued in Q3 2022 totaled HKD961.2 billion. EFB issuance growth picked up, rising to 1.5% q-o-q in Q3 2022 from 1.1% q-o-q in the preceding quarter.

**Exchange Fund Notes.** Outstanding EFNs totaled HKD22.0 billion at the end of September, down from HKD22.6 billion at the end of June. The HKMA

**Table 1: Size and Composition of the Local Currency Bond Market in Hong Kong, China**

| | Outstanding Amount (billion) | | | | | | Growth Rate (%) | | | |
|---|---|---|---|---|---|---|---|---|---|---|
| | Q3 2021 | | Q2 2022 | | Q3 2022 | | Q3 2021 | | Q3 2022 | |
| | HKD | USD | HKD | USD | HKD | USD | q-o-q | y-o-y | q-o-q | y-o-y |
| Total | 2,429 | 312 | 2,619 | 334 | 2,748 | 350 | 0.1 | 6.1 | 4.9 | 13.2 |
| Government | 1,252 | 161 | 1,381 | 176 | 1,433 | 183 | 3.0 | 8.2 | 3.7 | 14.4 |
| Exchange Fund Bills | 1,064 | 137 | 1,168 | 149 | 1,174 | 150 | 1.9 | 2.1 | 0.6 | 10.3 |
| Exchange Fund Notes | 24 | 3 | 23 | 3 | 22 | 3 | 0.0 | (6.2) | (2.7) | (9.1) |
| HKSAR Bonds | 164 | 21 | 191 | 24 | 236 | 30 | 11.1 | 82.8 | 24.0 | 44.5 |
| Corporate | 1,176 | 151 | 1,238 | 158 | 1,315 | 168 | (2.9) | 4.1 | 6.2 | 11.8 |

( ) = negative, HKD = Hong Kong dollar, HKSAR = Hong Kong Special Administrative Region, q-o-q = quarter-on-quarter, Q2 = second quarter, Q3 = third quarter, USD = United States dollar, y-o-y = year-on-year.
Notes:
1. Bloomberg LP end-of-period local currency–USD rates are used.
2. Growth rates are calculated from local currency base and do not include currency effects.
Source: Hong Kong Monetary Authority.

issued HKD1.2 billion of 2-year EFNs in August with a record-high coupon of 2.84%.

**HKSAR bonds.** The outstanding stock of HKSAR bonds reached HKD236.5 billion at the end of September after expanding 24.0% q-o-q. HKSAR bond issuance totaled HKD49.0 billion in Q3 2022. Issuances under the Institutional Bond Programme included HKD1.5 billion of 10-year HKSAR bonds issued in July, HKD1.5 billion of 1-year floating rate notes indexed to the Hong Kong Overnight Index Average issued in August, and HKD1.0 billion of 15-year bonds issued in September. In September, the government issued HKD45.0 billion of 3-year Silver Bonds under its Retail Bond Issuance Programme. Due to strong demand, the issuance amount of the Silver Bonds, which are intended for senior citizens, was higher than the target issuance of HKD35.0 billion.

**Corporate bonds.** Hong Kong, China's LCY corporate bond market reached a size of HKD1,315.4 billion at the end of September. Growth accelerated to 6.2% q-o-q in Q3 2022 from 4.4% q-o-q in the previous quarter.

The outstanding LCY bonds of the top 30 nonbank issuers in Hong Kong, China totaled HKD311.2 billion at the end of September, representing 23.7% of the total LCY corporate bond market (**Table 2**). Hong Kong Mortgage Corporation remained the largest issuer, with an outstanding debt stock of HKD86.5 billion at the end of September. Sun Hung Kai & Co. and the Hong Kong and China Gas Company were the next largest issuers with outstanding debt stocks of HKD20.5 billion and HKD18.6 billion, respectively. Firms in the finance, real estate, and transportation sectors dominated the top 30 nonbank issuers list. Only four of the top 30 nonbank issuers were state-owned firms, while the majority were listed on the Hong Kong Stock Exchange.

Corporate bond issuance in Q3 2022 amounted to HKD241.6 billion. Issuance contracted 3.3% q-o-q in Q3 2022 amid rising borrowing costs and heightened uncertainties. Continued monetary policy tightening by the US Federal Reserve and the consequent base rate adjustments by the HKMA raised borrowing costs. Meanwhile, the extended economic downturn soured investor confidence, resulting in less corporate borrowing during the quarter.

**Table 3** shows notable nonbank corporate bond issuances in Q3 2022. Hong Kong Mortgage Corporation was the largest issuer with a total of HKD10.6 billion from 27 issuances of bonds with maturities ranging from 91 days to 3 years. The state-owned Airport Authority was the second-largest issuer in Q3 2022, with four issuances totaling HKD1.8 billion. The next largest issuers during the quarter were the Hong Kong and China Gas Company and MTR, which raised a total of HKD1.5 billion and HKD1.3 billion, respectively. The longest tenor issued in Q3 2022 was a 10-year bond with a 4.10% coupon issued by the Hong Kong and China Gas Company.

## Policy, Institutional, and Regulatory Developments

### Hong Kong Monetary Authority Announces Tentative Issuance for Hong Kong Special Administrative Region Government Bonds

On 30 September, the HKMA announced the tentative issuance schedule for HKSAR bonds under the Institutional Bond Issuance Programme for the period between October 2022 and March 2023. The issuance schedule included planned issuances of bonds with tenors ranging from 1 year to 20 years. Of note are two planned switch tenders. The first such switch tender will involve the issuance of a 3-year HKSAR bond in exchange for the early redemption of a 15-year HKSAR bond with an original maturity of March 2032. The other switch tender will involve the issuance of a 3-year bond in exchange for the early redemption of a 15-year bond with an original maturity of March 2036. Switch tender operations are intended to promote liquidity in the bond market by allowing market participants to switch bonds with different maturities through a competitive tender.

### Table 2: Top 30 Nonbank Corporate Issuers of Local Currency Corporate Bonds in Hong Kong, China

| | Issuers | Outstanding Amount | | State-Owned | Listed Company | Type of Industry |
|---|---|---|---|---|---|---|
| | | LCY Bonds (HKD billion) | LCY Bonds (USD billion) | | | |
| 1. | Hong Kong Mortgage Corporation | 86.5 | 11.0 | Yes | No | Finance |
| 2. | Sun Hung Kai & Co. | 20.5 | 2.6 | No | Yes | Finance |
| 3. | The Hong Kong and China Gas Company | 18.6 | 2.4 | No | Yes | Utilities |
| 4. | New World Development | 15.3 | 1.9 | No | Yes | Diversified |
| 5. | Airport Authority | 15.2 | 1.9 | Yes | No | Transportation |
| 6. | Henderson Land Development | 14.7 | 1.9 | No | Yes | Real Estate |
| 7. | Hang Lung Properties | 12.7 | 1.6 | No | Yes | Real Estate |
| 8. | Hongkong Land | 12.0 | 1.5 | No | No | Real Estate |
| 9. | Wharf Real Estate Investment Company | 11.2 | 1.4 | No | Yes | Finance |
| 10. | MTR | 10.7 | 1.4 | Yes | Yes | Transportation |
| 11. | Link Holdings | 9.3 | 1.2 | No | Yes | Finance |
| 12. | Cathay Pacific | 8.9 | 1.1 | No | Yes | Transportation |
| 13. | Swire Pacific | 8.7 | 1.1 | No | Yes | Diversified |
| 14. | CK Asset Holdings | 8.5 | 1.1 | No | Yes | Real Estate |
| 15. | Hongkong Electric | 8.5 | 1.1 | No | No | Utilities |
| 16. | AIA Group | 7.6 | 1.0 | No | Yes | Insurance |
| 17. | Swire Properties | 7.3 | 0.9 | No | Yes | Diversified |
| 18. | CLP Power Hong Kong Financing | 6.6 | 0.8 | No | No | Finance |
| 19. | Hysan Development Corporation | 5.9 | 0.8 | No | Yes | Real Estate |
| 20. | Lerthai Group | 3.0 | 0.4 | No | Yes | Real Estate |
| 21. | Haitong International | 2.8 | 0.4 | No | Yes | Finance |
| 22. | Wheelock and Company | 2.8 | 0.4 | No | Yes | Real Estate |
| 23. | Ev Dynamics Holdings | 2.4 | 0.3 | No | Yes | Diversified |
| 24. | South Shore Holdings | 2.2 | 0.3 | No | Yes | Industrial |
| 25. | Future Days | 2.2 | 0.3 | No | No | Transportation |
| 26. | IFC Development | 2.0 | 0.3 | No | No | Finance |
| 27. | Champion REIT | 1.7 | 0.2 | No | Yes | Real Estate |
| 28. | Asia Standard Hotel Group | 1.2 | 0.2 | No | Yes | Finance |
| 29. | Yuexiu REIT | 1.1 | 0.1 | No | Yes | Real Estate |
| 30. | Urban Renewal Authority | 1.1 | 0.1 | Yes | No | Industrial Services |
| | **Total Top 30 Nonbank LCY Corporate Issuers** | **311.2** | **39.6** | | | |
| | **Total LCY Corporate Bonds** | **1,315.4** | **167.6** | | | |
| | **Top 30 as % of Total LCY Corporate Bonds** | **23.7%** | **23.7%** | | | |

HKD = Hong Kong dollar, LCY = local currency, REIT = real estate investment trust, USD = United States dollar.
Notes:
1.  Data as of 30 September 2022.
2.  State-owned firms are defined as those in which the government has more than a 50% ownership stake.
Source: *AsianBondsOnline* calculations based on Bloomberg LP data.

**Table 3: Notable Local Currency Corporate Bond Issuances in the Third Quarter of 2022**

| Corporate Issuers | Coupon Rate (%) | Issued Amount (HKD million) | Corporate Issuers | Coupon Rate (%) | Issued Amount (HKD million) |
|---|---|---|---|---|---|
| Hong Kong Mortgage Corporation[a] | | | MTR[a] | | |
| 91-day bond | 0.00 | 1,000 | 2-year bond | 4.20 | 300 |
| 91-day bond | 0.00 | 1,000 | 2-year bond | 3.25 | 500 |
| 1-year bond | 3.40 | 900 | 3-year bond | 3.11 | 250 |
| 2-year bond | 3.00 | 804 | 3-year bond | 3.05 | 251 |
| 3-year bond | 3.09 | 300 | Henderson Land[a] | | |
| Airport Authority[a] | | | 2-year bond | 4.10 | 150 |
| 5-year bond | 3.20 | 335 | 2-year bond | 3.70 | 500 |
| 5-year bond | 3.20 | 365 | Wharf Real Estate Investment Company | | |
| 5-year bond | 3.20 | 574 | 3-year bond | 4.00 | 300 |
| 5-year bond | 3.30 | 575 | Cathay Pacific | | |
| The Hong Kong and China Gas Company[a] | | | 2-year bond | 5.00 | 200 |
| 2-year bond | 3.81 | 400 | | | |
| 3-year bond | 3.76 | 380 | | | |
| 3 year bond | 3.83 | 400 | | | |
| 10-year bond | 4.10 | 350 | | | |

HKD = Hong Kong dollar.
[a] Multiple issuance of the same tenor indicates issuance on different dates.
Source: Bloomberg LP.

# Indonesia

## Yield Movements

Between 31 August and 14 October, Indonesia's local currency (LCY) government bond yields edged up for all maturities except the 16-year maturity (**Figure 1**). Bond yields gained the most for maturities of 3 years or less, rising an average of 77 basis points (bps). Except for the 16-year bond, which shed a marginal 3 bps, yields for all tenors of 4 years or longer climbed an average of 29 bps during the review period. As yields rose much faster at the shorter-end than the longer-end of the curve, the spread between the 10-year and 2-year maturity narrowed from 139 bps on 31 August to 92 bps on 14 October.

The overall rise in yields was largely driven by the monetary policy tightening of Bank Indonesia. After keeping the policy rate steady at 3.50% since February 2021, the central bank raised the 7-day reverse repurchase rate by 25 bps on 23 August, which was followed by a 50 bps hike each on 22 September, 20 October, and 17 November. This lifted the 7-day reverse repurchase rate to 5.25%, the deposit facility rate to 4.50%, and the lending facility rate to 6.00%. Bank Indonesia had raised the policy rate by a cumulative 175 bps from August through November. The policy rate hikes were taken as a preemptive measure to help quell inflationary pressure and maintain the stability of the Indonesian rupiah amid uncertainties in global financial markets and the broad strengthening of the US dollar.

Consumer price inflation trended upward, rising to 6.0% year-on-year (y-o-y) in September from 4.7% y-o-y in August and 4.9% y-o-y in July, largely due to fuel price adjustments. While inflation moderated to 5.7% y-o-y in October, it remained above Bank Indonesia's target range of 2.0%-4.0% for 2022. Bank Indonesia expects inflation for the year to exceed the upper limit of its inflation target range.

Also contributing to the rise in yields was Indonesia's economic recovery, which continued to gain traction. Real gross domestic product (GDP) growth in the third quarter (Q3) of 2022 rose to 5.7% y-o-y from 5.4% y-o-y in the second quarter (Q2). Domestic consumption continued to support growth, expanding 5.4% y-o-y in Q3 2022, albeit slower than the 5.5% y-o-y growth in the earlier quarter. Gross fixed capital formation also grew

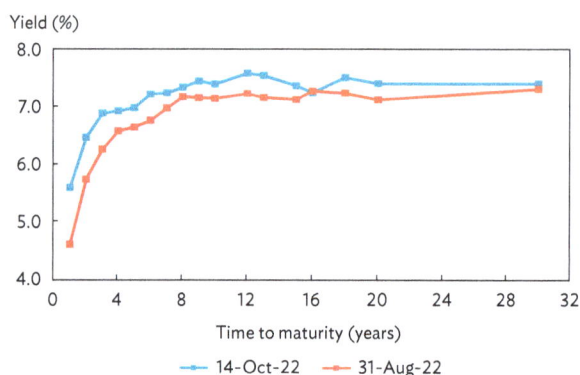

**Figure 1: Indonesia's Benchmark Yield Curve— Local Currency Government Bonds**

Yield (%)

Source: Based on data from Bloomberg LP.

5.0% y-o-y in Q3 2022. Exports continued to perform strongly, rising 21.6% y-o-y on increased demand from trading partners, and imports climbed 23.0% y-o-y. For the year as a whole, Bank Indonesia estimates GDP growth to lean toward the upper end of its target range of 4.5%–5.3%.

## Size and Composition

Indonesia's LCY bond market expanded to a size of IDR5,746.8 trillion (USD377.4 billion) at the end of September, buoyed by a rebound in issuance across all bond types during the quarter (**Table 1**). Growth of the bond market accelerated to 4.5% quarter-on-quarter (q-o-q) in Q3 2022, up from 0.3 q-o-q in Q2 2022. Indonesia was the second-fastest growing LCY bond market on a q-o-q basis in emerging East Asia in Q3 2022, next to Hong Kong, China (4.9% q-o-q). On an annual basis, the LCY bond market of Indonesia expanded 12.9% y-o-y in Q3 2022, up from 11.9% y-o-y in the prior quarter.

Indonesia's *sukuk* (Islamic bond) market remained the second-largest in emerging East Asia next to Malaysia's. The outstanding amount of *sukuk* climbed 7.1% q-o-q in Q3 2022, exceeding the 4.0% q-o-q growth of conventional bonds. This led to an increase in the share of *sukuk* in the total market to 18.7% at the end of September from 18.2% at the end of June. Conventional bonds continued to dominate the LCY bond market in Indonesia with a share of 81.3% at the end of Q3 2022.

**Table 1: Size and Composition of the Local Currency Bond Market in Indonesia**

| | Outstanding Amount (billion) | | | | | | Growth Rate (%) | | | |
|---|---|---|---|---|---|---|---|---|---|---|
| | Q3 2021 | | Q2 2022 | | Q3 2022 | | Q3 2021 | | Q3 2022 | |
| | IDR | USD | IDR | USD | IDR | USD | q-o-q | y-o-y | q-o-q | y-o-y |
| Total | 5,089,510 | 356 | 5,497,153 | 369 | 5,746,803 | 377 | 3.6 | 23.9 | 4.5 | 12.9 |
| Government | 4,667,501 | 326 | 5,057,678 | 339 | 5,289,292 | 347 | 4.0 | 27.3 | 4.6 | 13.3 |
| Central Govt. Bonds | 4,460,456 | 312 | 4,848,083 | 325 | 5,101,415 | 335 | 4.2 | 28.9 | 5.2 | 14.4 |
| of which: *Sukuk* | 834,323 | 58 | 874,110 | 59 | 961,562 | 63 | 12.7 | 35.1 | 10.0 | 15.3 |
| Nontradable Bonds | 146,334 | 10 | 144,435 | 10 | 141,668 | 9 | (1.3) | (12.7) | (1.9) | (3.2) |
| of which: *Sukuk* | 31,161 | 2 | 26,374 | 2 | 26,412 | 2 | (5.9) | (18.5) | 0.1 | (15.2) |
| Central Bank Bonds | 60,712 | 4 | 65,160 | 4 | 46,209 | 3 | 3.5 | 58.0 | (29.1) | (23.9) |
| of which: *Sukuk* | 60,712 | 4 | 65,160 | 4 | 46,209 | 3 | 3.5 | 58.0 | (29.1) | (23.9) |
| Corporate | 422,008 | 29 | 439,474 | 29 | 457,511 | 30 | (0.2) | (4.2) | 4.1 | 8.4 |
| of which: *Sukuk* | 36,143 | 3 | 37,273 | 3 | 39,660 | 3 | 14.1 | 16.9 | 6.4 | 9.7 |

( ) = negative, IDR = Indonesian rupiah, q-o-q = quarter-on-quarter, Q2 =second quarter, Q3 = third quarter, USD = United States dollar, y-o-y = year-on-year.
Notes:
1.  Bloomberg LP end-of-period local currency–USD rates are used.
2.  Growth rates are calculated from local currency base and do not include currency effects.
3.  *Sukuk* refers to Islamic bonds.
Sources: Bank Indonesia; Directorate General of Budget Financing and Risk Management, Ministry of Finance; Indonesia Stock Exchange; and Bloomberg LP.

**Government bonds.** At the end of September, the LCY government bond market expanded to a size of IDR5,289.3 trillion. Growth accelerated to 4.6% q-o-q and 13.3% y-o-y in Q3 2022 from 0.6% q-o-q and 12.7% y-o-y in the preceding quarter. Government bonds account for a dominant share (92.0%) of Indonesia's LCY bond market. This marked the largest share of government bonds to total bonds among regional peers.

**Central government bonds and nontradable bonds.**
A majority of government bonds are central government bonds, comprising tradable Treasury bills and bonds. The outstanding amount of central government bonds climbed to IDR5,101.4 trillion, as growth surged 5.2% q-o-q and 14.4% y-o-y in Q3 2022 from 0.4% q-o-q and 13.2% y-o-y in Q2 2022. In contrast, the nontradable bond stock contracted 1.9% q-o-q and 3.2% y-o-y to IDR141.7 trillion as maturities exceeded issuance.

In Q3 2022, issuance of central government bonds and nontradable bonds nearly doubled to reach IDR267.7 trillion on growth of 80.4% q-o-q. On an annual basis, central government and nontradable bond issuance growth moderated to 2.1% y-o-y. Issuances during the quarter were offered via regular Treasury bill and bond auctions (both for conventional and Islamic bonds), private placements, and bookbuilding. The greenshoe option was again tapped to raise funds in July as an auction fell short of the target amount. In addition, the government raised IDR27.0 trillion from the sale of *sukuk ritel* (Islamic retail bonds) in September.

**Central bank bonds.** The outstanding amount of central bank bonds contracted 29.1% q-o-q to reach IDR46.2 trillion at the end of September. In Q3 2022, issuance of Sukuk Bank Indonesia climbed 5.4% q-o-q, after contracting 12.5% q-o-q in Q2 2022, amid rising inflationary pressure. Issuances of Sukuk Bank Indonesia were concentrated in short-term maturities ranging from 7 days to 12 months.

**Corporate bonds.** The LCY corporate bond market of Indonesia expanded 4.1% q-o-q in Q3 2022 after contracting 2.3% q-o-q in the prior quarter. The total outstanding corporate bond stock rose to IDR457.5 trillion and accounted for 8.0% of the LCY bond total at the end of September, marking the lowest market share of corporate bonds in emerging East Asia.

The 30 largest corporate bond issuers in Indonesia accounted for an aggregate IDR315.0 trillion of outstanding bonds at the end of September, representing 68.9% of the corporate total (**Table 2**). The top 30 list comprised 16 state-owned firms, eight of which landed in the top 10. More than half of the firms on the list were also listed in the Indonesia Stock Exchange (17 firms). The top 30 list comprised firms from the banking and financial sectors and other highly capitalized industries such as energy, construction, telecommunications, and manufacturing.

Leading the list was state-owned energy firm Perusahaan Listrik Negara with outstanding bonds of

**Table 2: Top 30 Issuers of Local Currency Corporate Bonds in Indonesia**

| | Issuers | Outstanding Amount | | State-Owned | Listed Company | Type of Industry |
|---|---|---|---|---|---|---|
| | | LCY Bonds (IDR billion) | LCY Bonds (USD billion) | | | |
| 1. | Perusahaan Listrik Negara | 30,694 | 2.02 | Yes | No | Energy |
| 2. | Indah Kiat Pulp & Paper | 19,993 | 1.31 | No | Yes | Pulp and Paper Manufacturing |
| 3. | Bank Rakyat Indonesia | 18,849 | 1.24 | Yes | Yes | Banking |
| 4. | Indonesia Eximbank | 17,717 | 1.16 | Yes | No | Finance |
| 5. | Sarana Multi Infrastruktur | 14,806 | 0.97 | Yes | No | Finance |
| 6. | Pegadaian | 13,297 | 0.87 | Yes | No | Finance |
| 7. | Sarana Multigriya Finansial | 12,803 | 0.84 | Yes | No | Finance |
| 8. | Permodalan Nasional Madani | 12,614 | 0.83 | Yes | No | Finance |
| 9. | Merdeka Copper Gold | 12,318 | 0.81 | No | Yes | Mining |
| 10. | Bank Mandiri | 11,900 | 0.78 | Yes | Yes | Banking |
| 11. | Waskita Karya | 11,395 | 0.75 | Yes | Yes | Building Construction |
| 12. | Astra Sedaya Finance | 11,142 | 0.73 | No | No | Finance |
| 13. | Wijaya Karya | 10,000 | 0.66 | Yes | Yes | Building Construction |
| 14. | Pupuk Indonesia | 9,046 | 0.59 | Yes | No | Chemical Manufacturing |
| 15. | Tower Bersama Infrastructure | 8,663 | 0.57 | No | Yes | Telecommunications Infrastructure Provider |
| 16. | Chandra Asri Petrochemical | 8,500 | 0.56 | No | Yes | Petrochemicals |
| 17. | Bank Tabungan Negara | 8,182 | 0.54 | Yes | Yes | Banking |
| 18. | Hutama Karya | 8,148 | 0.54 | Yes | No | Nonbuilding Construction |
| 19. | Sinar Mas Agro Resources and Technology | 8,103 | 0.53 | No | Yes | Food |
| 20. | Bank Pan Indonesia | 7,802 | 0.51 | No | Yes | Banking |
| 21. | Lontar Papyrus Pulp & Paper Industry | 7,000 | 0.46 | No | No | Pulp and Paper Manufacturing |
| 22. | Medco Energi Internasional | 6,795 | 0.45 | No | Yes | Energy |
| 23. | Bank Pembangunan Daerah Jawa Barat Dan Banten | 6,413 | 0.42 | Yes | Yes | Banking |
| 24. | Adira Dinamika Multi Finance | 6,296 | 0.41 | No | Yes | Finance |
| 25. | Kereta Api Indonesia | 6,000 | 0.39 | No | No | Transportation and Logistics |
| 26. | Indosat | 5,803 | 0.38 | No | Yes | Telecommunications |
| 27. | OKI Pulp & Paper Mills | 5,485 | 0.36 | No | No | Pulp and Paper Manufacturing |
| 28. | Federal International Finance | 5,267 | 0.35 | No | No | Finance |
| 29. | Bank Negara Indonesia | 5,000 | 0.33 | Yes | Yes | Banking |
| 30. | Adhi Karya | 4,987 | 0.33 | Yes | Yes | Building Construction |
| | **Total Top 30 LCY Corporate Issuers** | **315,018** | **20.69** | | | |
| | **Total LCY Corporate Bonds** | **457,511** | **30.04** | | | |
| | **Top 30 as % of Total LCY Corporate Bonds** | **68.9%** | **68.9%** | | | |

IDR = Indonesian rupiah, LCY = local currency, USD = United States dollar.
Notes:
1.  Data as of 30 September 2022.
2.  State-owned firms are defined as those in which the government has more than a 50% ownership stake.
Source: *AsianBondsOnline* calculations based on Indonesia Stock Exchange data.

IDR30.7 trillion, which accounted for a 6.7% share of the total corporate bond stock at the end of September. Taking over the second spot was manufacturing firm Indah Kiat Pulp & Paper with IDR20.0 trillion of bonds for a 4.4% share. State-owned Bank Rakyat Indonesia climbed to the third spot with outstanding bonds of IDR18.8 trillion and a 4.1% share of the corporate total. State-owned financing firm Indonesia Eximbank dropped to the fourth spot (previously in the second spot) at a share of 3.9%, while state-owned financing firm Sarana Multi Infrastruktur held on to the fifth spot for a 3.2% share. All other corporate issuers accounted for a share of 2.9% or less of the corporate bond total at the end of September.

Indonesia's corporate bond segment saw robust issuance activities in Q3 2022, rebounding from the contraction in the prior quarter. Total corporate bond sales nearly doubled to IDR55.8 trillion in Q3 2022, rising 83.3% q-o-q and 71.0% y-o-y. Firms rushed to raise funds from the bond market while rates were still low. Indonesia was among the last few markets in the region to tighten its policy rate in August.

A total of 37 firms issued bonds during the quarter, adding 111 new corporate bond series to the outstanding corporate stock. Of these new bonds, 27 series were structured as *sukuk* including two series of *sukuk wakalah* (Islamic bonds in which the bondholder nominates another party to act on the bondholder's behalf). A majority of the corporate *sukuk* (15 series) issued during the quarter were structured as *sukuk ijarah* (Islamic bonds backed by lease agreements), while there were 10 series of *sukuk mudharabah* (Islamic bonds backed by a profit-sharing scheme from a business venture or partnership).

In terms of maturity, corporate bonds issued during the quarter were largely concentrated in short- to medium-dated tenors. There were 39 series of 3-year bonds, 31 series of 367/370-day bonds, and 30 series of 5-year bonds. The longest dated bonds issued in Q3 2022 were for 10 years, issued by Chandra Asri Petrochemical in August and XL Axiata's conventional and *sukuk ijarah* issues in September.

**Table 3** presents five of the largest corporate bond issuances during the quarter. The largest issuance for Q3 2022 came from state-owned Bank Rakyat Indonesia, which raised a total of IDR5.0 trillion from a triple-tranche offering of conventional bonds in July. Next was Merdeka Copper Gold with aggregate bond issuance of IDR4.0 trillion in September, also in three tranches of conventional bonds.

**Table 3: Notable Local Currency Corporate Bond Issuances in the Third Quarter of 2022**

| Corporate Issuers | Coupon Rate (%) | Issued Amount (IDR billion) | Corporate Issuers | Coupon Rate (%) | Issued Amount (IDR billion) |
|---|---|---|---|---|---|
| Bank Rakyat Indonesia | | | Pegadaian | | |
| 370-day bond | 3.70 | 2,500 | 370-day bond | 3.95 | 1,601 |
| 3-year bond | 5.75 | 2,000 | 370-day *sukuk mudharabah* | 3.95 | 878 |
| 5-year bond | 6.45 | 500 | 3-year bond | 5.75 | 276 |
| Merdeka Copper Gold | | | 3-year *sukuk mudharabah* | 5.75 | 245 |
| 367-day bond | 5.50 | 1,473 | XL Axiata | | |
| 3-year bond | 8.25 | 1,729 | 3-year bond | 6.75 | 735 |
| 5-year bond | 9.50 | 798 | 3-year *sukuk ijarah* | 6.75 | 681 |
| Medco Energi Internasional | | | 5-year bond | 7.40 | 412 |
| 2.5 year bond | 7.00 | 1,892 | 5-year *sukuk ijarah* | 7.40 | 421 |
| 5-year bond | 8.10 | 521 | 7-year bond | 7.90 | 178 |
| 7-year bond | 9.00 | 586 | 7-year *sukuk ijarah* | 7.90 | 135 |
| | | | 10-year bond | 8.25 | 175 |
| | | | 10-year *sukuk ijarah* | 8.25 | 263 |

IDR = Indonesian rupiah.
Notes:
1. *Sukuk mudharabah* are Islamic bonds backed by a profit-sharing scheme from a business venture or partnership.
2. *Sukuk ijarah* are Islamic bonds backed by lease agreement.
Source: Indonesia Stock Exchange.

## Investor Profiles

Amid a dimming economic outlook and weakening financial conditions that soured investment sentiments, Indonesia continued to experience net foreign outflows from its bond market in Q3 2022. Aggressive monetary policy tightening by the United States (US) Federal Reserve and the broad strengthening of the US dollar made emerging market assets less attractive. Offshore investors continued to shy away from the Indonesian bond market, with net foreign outflows reaching USD3.3 billion in Q3 2022. As a result, the foreign holdings share further declined to 14.3% at the end of September from 21.6% a year earlier (**Figure 2**). Foreign ownership of IDR-denominated bonds substantially declined by 24.1% y-o-y to IDR730.3 trillion at the end of September.

In terms of maturity, offshore investor holdings of bonds remained largely concentrated in longer-dated tenors. About 63.8% of nonresident investments in bonds were in maturities of over 5 years or longer at the end of September (**Figure 3**). This, however, was down from the 68.4% share recorded at the end of December 2021, but was slightly up from the 63.1% at the end of June 2022. Offshore holdings of bonds for maturities of over 2 years to 5 years slipped to a 22.3% share at the end of September from 23.8% at the end of December 2021. In contrast, foreign holdings of bonds with maturities of

2 years or less continued to rise, climbing to a 13.9% share of nonresident bond holdings at the end of September. This reflected investor preference for shorter-dated maturities amid uncertainties over the global and regional outlooks.

Domestic investors were active players in the Indonesian bond market, with banking institutions accounting for the largest holdings at a share of 31.4% at the end

**Figure 3: Foreign Holdings of Local Currency Central Government Bonds by Maturity**

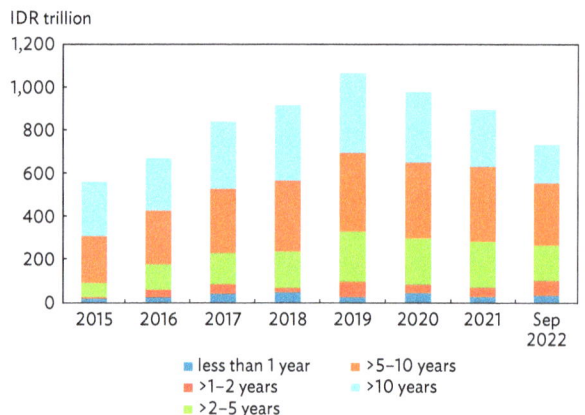

IDR = Indonesian rupiah.
Source: Directorate General of Budget Financing and Risk Management, Ministry of Finance.

**Figure 2: Local Currency Central Government Bonds Investor Profile**

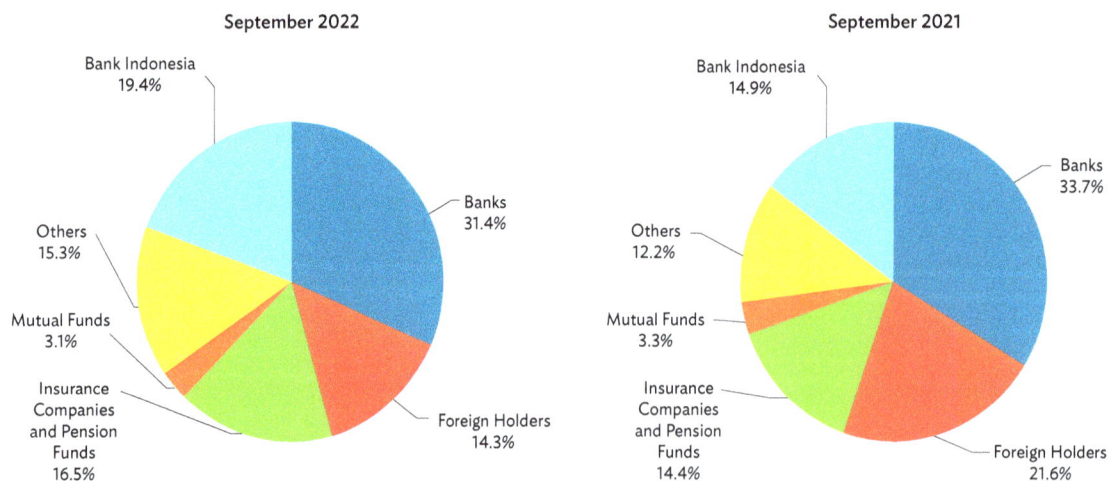

September 2022

- Bank Indonesia 19.4%
- Banks 31.4%
- Foreign Holders 14.3%
- Insurance Companies and Pension Funds 16.5%
- Mutual Funds 3.1%
- Others 15.3%

September 2021

- Bank Indonesia 14.9%
- Banks 33.7%
- Foreign Holders 21.6%
- Insurance Companies and Pension Funds 14.4%
- Mutual Funds 3.3%
- Others 12.2%

Source: Directorate General of Budget Financing and Risk Management, Ministry of Finance.

of September. This was slightly lower compared with their 33.7% share a year earlier. Next largest were the holdings of the central bank, as its burden-sharing agreement with the government that was set in place during the pandemic allowed it to purchase bonds to help stabilize bond prices and support government financing. Bank Indonesia's holdings of government bonds rose sharply to 19.4% from 14.9% a year earlier. For the period 1 January to 15 November, Bank Indonesia purchased a total of IDR142.4 trillion of government bonds. Insurance institutions also increased their holdings of government bonds, accounting for a 16.5% share in September, up from 14.4% a year earlier.

Other investor groups, largely comprising individuals and corporations, saw their bond holdings increase to 15.3% of government bond holdings at the end of September from 12.2% a year earlier. In contrast, mutual funds saw a slight dip in their holdings of governments bonds to a share of 3.1% in September from 3.3% a year earlier.

## Policy, Institutional, and Regulatory Developments

### Bank Indonesia and Bank Negara Malaysia Renew Local Currency Bilateral Swap Agreement

On 23 September, Bank Indonesia and Bank Negara Malaysia agreed to renew their LCY bilateral swap agreement, which both parties initially entered into in 2019. The bilateral agreement comprised up to an equivalent of MYR8.0 billion or IDR28.0 trillion in local currency that will be used for bilateral transactions between Indonesia and Malaysia. The new agreement will be effective for a period of 3 years.

### Indonesian Parliament Approves the 2023 State Budget

In September, the Indonesian Parliament approved the government's proposed budget for 2023, setting the deficit at IDR598.2 trillion or the equivalent of 2.8% of GDP. The 2023 state budget estimates state revenues at IDR2,463.0 trillion and state expenditures at IDR3,061.2 trillion. Debt financing was projected to reach IDR696.3 trillion. The following macroeconomic assumptions, among others, were used as reference for the budget: (i) an economic growth of 5.3%, (ii) an inflation rate of 3.6%, (iii) a 10-year bond yield of 7.9%, (iv) an exchange rate of IDR14,800 per USD1.0, and (v) an Indonesia crude price per barrel of USD90.0.

# Republic of Korea

## Yield Movements

The Republic of Korea's LCY government bond yield curve shifted upward between 31 August and 14 October (**Figure 1**). Yields for the 3-month and 6-month tenors rose 44 basis points (bps) on average, while the 1-year tenor rose 28 bps. Yields for tenors between 2-year and 10-year rose 47 bps on average, with the 3-year tenor posting the biggest increase of 52 bps. Meanwhile, yields for 20-year to 50-year tenors rose 44 bps on average. The spread between the 10-year and 2-year tenors remained almost negligible at 1 bp on 14 October, little changed from 2 bps on 31 August.

Yields rose sharply across the curve during the review period, tracking the rise in United States (US) Treasury yields, on expectations of further rate hikes by both the US Federal Reserve and the Bank of Korea. Following speculation of a possible slowdown in its aggressive monetary tightening, Chair Jerome Powell, in his Jackson Hole speech in late August, sent a clear signal that the Federal Reserve had no intentions of slowing the pace of rate hikes in the near term. He also reiterated the Federal Reserve's commitment to fight high inflation even as the US economy slows. Subsequently, at its 20–21 September meeting, the Federal Reserve raised the federal funds rate target range by 75 bps to between 3.00% and 3.25%, while also lowering its gross domestic product (GDP) growth forecast and raising its inflation forecast.

On the domestic front, the Bank of Korea, in its 12 October monetary policy meeting, raised the base rate by another 50 bps to 3.0%, following a 25 bps rate hike in August. This brought total policy rate hikes year-to-date to 200 bps. The Bank of Korea continued with its monetary policy tightening stance, despite a slowdown in inflation, as inflationary pressure remained high and in order to provide support to the foreign exchange market. Inflation peaked at 6.3% year-on-year (y-o-y) in July before easing to 5.7% y-o-y in August and 5.6% y-o-y in September, and slightly inching up to 5.7% y-o-y in October. Meanwhile, the Korean won fell sharply during the review period, reaching a more-than-a-decade low of KRW1,440.2 to USD1.0 on 28 September, and falling 16.8% year-to-date as of 14 October to

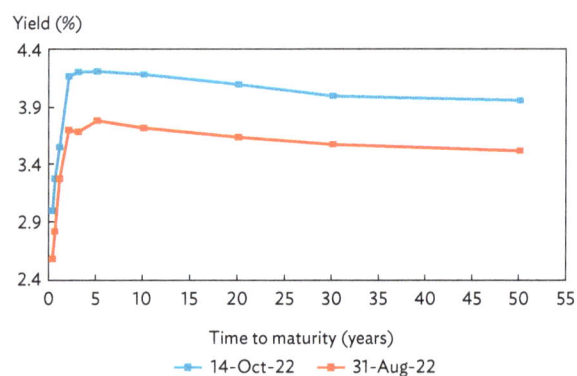

**Figure 1: The Republic of Korea's Benchmark Yield Curve—Local Currency Government Bonds**

Source: Based on data from Bloomberg LP.

KRW1,429.0 per USD1.0. This was largely due to the continued strengthening of the US dollar and concerns of an economic slowdown in the People's Republic of China, which is one of the Republic of Korea's major trading partners. The Bank of Korea has been actively intervening in the foreign exchange market to support the Korean won, with its foreign exchange reserves posting a large monthly drop of USD19.7 billion in September to USD416.8 billion at the end of the month. In efforts to stabilize the sharp rise in domestic yields, the Bank of Korea purchased KRW3.0 billion worth of government bonds on 29 September.

The Republic of Korea's economic growth inched up to 3.1% y-o-y in the third quarter (Q3) of 2022 from 2.9% y-o-y in the second quarter (Q2) of 2022, remaining above the Bank of Korea's 2.6% full-year growth forecast for 2022. The higher growth was primarily driven by the rebound in gross fixed capital formation, which expanded 1.0% q-o-q in Q3 2022 following a 2.9% y-o-y contraction in Q2 2022. Private consumption also posted higher growth of 5.9% y-o-y in Q3 2022 from 3.9% y-o-y in the previous quarter. Meanwhile, public consumption growth slowed to 2.4% y-o-y from 3.7% during the same period. Export growth held steady on an annual basis at 4.6% y-o-y in Q3 2022. However, on a quarter-on-quarter (q-o-q) basis, GDP growth slowed to 0.3% q-o-q in Q3 2022 from 0.7% q-o-q in the previous quarter.

Foreign investors returned to the Republic of Korea's LCY bond market in July, registering net foreign inflows of KRW3,561 billion following net outflows of KRW934 million in June. The reversal can be attributed to expectations at the time of a pending slowdown in the Federal Reserve's policy tightening. However, the impact was only temporary as the Federal Reserve, in the release of the minutes of its July Federal Open Market Committee meeting and Chair Jerome Powell's subsequent Jackson Hole speech in August, clarified that it would continue with its aggressive monetary tightening. Narrowing yield premiums between Korean bonds and US Treasuries, with periods of reversals, and the sharp depreciation of the Korean won drove foreign fund outflows of KRW1,852 billion and KRW980 billion from the LCY bond market in August and September, respectively.

## Size and Composition

The Republic of Korea's LCY bond market grew 1.3% q-o-q to reach KRW2,964.4 trillion (USD2.1 trillion) at the end of September, which was slightly higher than the 1.0% q-o-q growth posted in the previous quarter (**Table 1**). On an annual basis, growth slowed to 5.9% y-o-y from 6.1% y-o-y in Q3 2021.

**Government bonds.** The Republic of Korea's LCY government bond market reached a size of KRW1,264.0 trillion at the end of September, posting 1.8% q-o-q growth in Q3 2022, up slightly from 1.6% q-o-q in Q2 2022. Growth was largely driven by

the 2.1% q-o-q rise in the stock of central government bonds in Q3 2022 to KRW933.1 trillion; however, this was a slowdown from the 3.4% q-o-q growth in the previous quarter. Bonds of government-owned entities also posted growth of 3.0% q-o-q, up from 1.9% q-o-q in Q2 2022. Meanwhile, the stock of Monetary Stabilization Bonds issued by the Bank of Korea fell 2.3% q-o-q in Q3 2022.

Issuance of government bonds fell 15.5% q-o-q to KRW86.9 trillion in Q3 2022, driven by the 37.3% q-o-q drop in the issuance of central government bonds. This was due to a high issuance volume in Q2 2022 in line with the government's debt frontloading policy in the first half of the year. Meanwhile, issuance of bonds by government-owned entities and central bank bonds rose 10.7% q-o-q and 11.7% q-o-q, respectively, in Q3 2022.

**Corporate bonds.** The Republic of Korea's LCY corporate bond market inched up 1.0% q-o-q to KRW1,700.4 trillion at the end of September, slightly higher than the 0.5% q-o-q growth posted in the previous quarter. **Table 2** lists the top 30 LCY corporate bond issuers in the Republic of Korea, which had an aggregate outstanding bond stock of KRW1,015.4 trillion and accounted for 59.7% of the total LCY corporate bond market. Financial institutions, particularly banks and securities firms, comprised 63.0% of the top 30 list. Korea Housing Finance Corporation, a government-related institution providing financial assistance for social housing, remained the largest corporate issuer in the market with total bonds outstanding of

**Table 1: Size and Composition of the Local Currency Bond Market in the Republic of Korea**

| | Outstanding Amount (billion) | | | | | | Growth Rate (%) | | | |
| | Q3 2021 | | Q2 2022 | | Q3 2022 | | Q3 2021 | | Q3 2022 | |
| | KRW | USD | KRW | USD | KRW | USD | q-o-q | y-o-y | q-o-q | y-o-y |
|---|---|---|---|---|---|---|---|---|---|---|
| Total | 2,799,920 | 2,365 | 2,925,746 | 2,253 | 2,964,362 | 2,071 | 1.6 | 7.6 | 1.3 | 5.9 |
| Government | 1,179,746 | 996 | 1,241,968 | 956 | 1,263,967 | 883 | 1.9 | 10.4 | 1.8 | 7.1 |
| Central Government Bonds | 831,745 | 703 | 914,183 | 704 | 933,074 | 652 | 3.0 | 17.5 | 2.1 | 12.2 |
| Central Bank Bonds | 151,050 | 128 | 125,910 | 97 | 123,020 | 86 | (2.1) | (9.4) | (2.3) | (18.6) |
| Others | 196,951 | 166 | 201,875 | 155 | 207,874 | 145 | 0.3 | 1.2 | 3.0 | 5.5 |
| Corporate | 1,620,174 | 1,369 | 1,683,778 | 1,296 | 1,700,395 | 1,188 | 1.4 | 5.7 | 1.0 | 5.0 |

( ) = negative, KRW = Korean won, q-o-q = quarter-on-quarter, Q2 = second quarter, Q3 = third quarter, USD = United States dollar, y-o-y = year-on-year.
Notes:
1. Bloomberg LP end-of-period local currency–USD rates are used.
2. Growth rates are calculated from local currency base and do not include currency effects.
3. "Others" comprise Korea Development Bank Bonds, National Housing Bonds, and Seoul Metro Bonds.
4. Corporate bonds include equity-linked securities and derivatives-linked securities.
Sources: The Bank of Korea and KG Zeroin Corporation.

**Table 2: Top 30 Issuers of Local Currency Corporate Bonds in the Republic of Korea**

| | | Outstanding Amount | | State-Owned | Listed on | | Type of Industry |
|---|---|---|---|---|---|---|---|
| | Issuers | LCY Bonds (KRW billion) | LCY Bonds (USD billion) | | KOSPI | KOSDAQ | |
| 1. | Korea Housing Finance Corporation | 152,099 | 106.3 | Yes | No | No | Housing Finance |
| 2. | Industrial Bank of Korea | 74,500 | 52.1 | Yes | Yes | No | Banking |
| 3. | Meritz Securities | 61,783 | 43.2 | No | Yes | No | Securities |
| 4. | Korea Electric Power Corporation | 52,380 | 36.6 | Yes | Yes | No | Electricity, Energy, and Power |
| 5. | Korea Investment and Securities | 50,247 | 35.1 | No | No | No | Securities |
| 6. | Hana Securities | 48,288 | 33.7 | No | No | No | Securities |
| 7. | Shinhan Investment Corporation | 46,635 | 32.6 | No | No | No | Securities |
| 8. | Mirae Asset Securities | 46,565 | 32.5 | No | Yes | No | Securities |
| 9. | KB Securities | 43,129 | 30.1 | No | No | No | Securities |
| 10. | NH Investment & Securities | 34,502 | 24.1 | Yes | Yes | No | Securities |
| 11. | Korea Land & Housing Corporation | 32,421 | 22.7 | Yes | No | No | Real Estate |
| 12. | Shinhan Bank | 31,795 | 22.2 | No | No | No | Banking |
| 13. | The Export-Import Bank of Korea | 28,280 | 19.8 | Yes | No | No | Banking |
| 14. | Korea Expressway | 27,600 | 19.3 | Yes | No | No | Transport Infrastructure |
| 15. | Woori Bank | 25,170 | 17.6 | Yes | Yes | No | Banking |
| 16. | KEB Hana Bank | 24,611 | 17.2 | No | No | No | Banking |
| 17. | Samsung Securities | 23,793 | 16.6 | No | Yes | No | Securities |
| 18. | Kookmin Bank | 22,484 | 15.7 | No | No | No | Banking |
| 19. | NongHyup Bank | 21,290 | 14.9 | Yes | No | No | Banking |
| 20. | Korea SMEs and Startups Agency | 21,178 | 14.8 | Yes | No | No | SME Development |
| 21. | Korea National Railway | 19,060 | 13.3 | Yes | No | No | Transport Infrastructure |
| 22. | Shinhan Card | 17,100 | 11.9 | No | No | No | Credit Card |
| 23. | Hyundai Capital Services | 15,930 | 11.1 | No | No | No | Consumer Finance |
| 24. | Shinyoung Securities | 15,783 | 11.0 | No | Yes | No | Securities |
| 25. | KB Kookmin Bank Card | 14,515 | 10.1 | No | No | No | Consumer Finance |
| 26. | Standard Chartered Bank Korea | 14,070 | 9.8 | No | No | No | Banking |
| 27. | Hanwha Investment and Securities | 13,991 | 9.8 | No | No | No | Securities |
| 28. | NongHyup | 12,670 | 8.9 | Yes | No | No | Banking |
| 29. | Samsung Card Co. | 11,848 | 8.3 | No | Yes | No | Credit Card |
| 30. | Korea Railroad Corporation | 11,720 | 8.2 | Yes | No | No | Transport Infrastructure |
| | **Total Top 30 LCY Corporate Issuers** | **1,015,435** | **709.5** | | | | |
| | **Total LCY Corporate Bonds** | **1,700,395** | **1,188.1** | | | | |
| | **Top 30 as % of Total LCY Corporate Bonds** | **59.7%** | **59.7%** | | | | |

KOSDAQ = Korean Securities Dealers Automated Quotations, KOSPI = Korea Composite Stock Price Index, KRW = Korean won, LCY = local currency, SMEs = small and medium-sized enterprises, USD = United States dollar.
Notes:
1. Data as of 30 September 2022.
2. State-owned firms are defined as those in which the government has more than a 50% ownership stake.
3. Corporate bonds include equity-linked securities and derivatives-linked securities.
Sources: *AsianBondsOnline* calculations based on Bloomberg LP and KG Zeroin Corporation data.

KRW152.1 trillion at the end of Q3 2022. The Industrial Bank of Korea and Korea Investment and Securities were the next largest issuers at KRW74.5 trillion and KRW61.8 trillion, respectively.

**Table 3: Notable Local Currency Corporate Bond Issuances in the Third Quarter of 2022**

| Corporate Issuers | Coupon Rate (%) | Issued Amount (KRW billion) |
|---|---|---|
| Industrial Bank of Korea[a] | | |
| 2-month bond | – | 720 |
| 2.5-month bond | – | 710 |
| 6-month bond | 3.02 | 620 |
| 1-year bond | 4.03 | 660 |
| 1-year bond | – | 630 |
| 1-year bond | – | 610 |
| Kookmin Bank[a] | | |
| 1-year bond | 3.58 | 920 |
| 1-year bond | 3.65 | 900 |
| 1-year bond | 3.68 | 600 |
| Shinhan Bank[a] | | |
| 6-month bond | 3.60 | 560 |
| 1-year bond | 3.86 | 510 |
| 1.5-year bond | 3.60 | 650 |
| 1.5-year bond | 3.90 | 600 |
| KDIC Special Account Bond | | |
| 3-year bond | 3.70 | 720 |
| NongHyup Bank | | |
| 3-year bond | 4.04 | 650 |

– = not available, KRW = Korean won.
[a] Multiple issuance of the same tenor indicates issuance on different dates.
Source: Based on data from Bloomberg LP.

The marginal growth in the Republic of Korea's LCY corporate bond market was driven by the 2.4% q-o-q growth in issuance, which was slower than the 7.1% q-o-q increase in Q2 2022. Issuance remained relatively low in Q3 2022 due to continued yield volatility in the market. **Table 3** lists the notable corporate bond issuances in Q3 2022, including those from financial firms such as Industrial Bank of Korea, Kookmin Bank, and Shinhan Bank.

## Investor Profile

**Government Bonds.** Insurance companies and pension funds remained the largest investor group in the Republic of Korea's LCY government bond market at the end of June (**Figure 2**). However, this group also posted the largest decline in terms of market share, falling to 31.7% from 34.1% a year earlier. Banks were the second-largest investor group with a share of 22.3%, up from 19.1% in Q2 2021. The share of foreign investors' holdings also posted a large increase from 15.4% to 18.4% during the same period due to foreign net inflows in the LCY government bond market during most of the review period. Meanwhile, the shares of the general government and other financial institutions declined in between June 2021 and June 2022.

**Corporate bonds.** Other financial institutions held the largest share of the Republic of Korea's LCY corporate bonds at the end of June, with their share rising to 41.8% from 40.2% a year earlier (**Figure 3**).

**Figure 2: Local Currency Government Bonds Investor Profile**

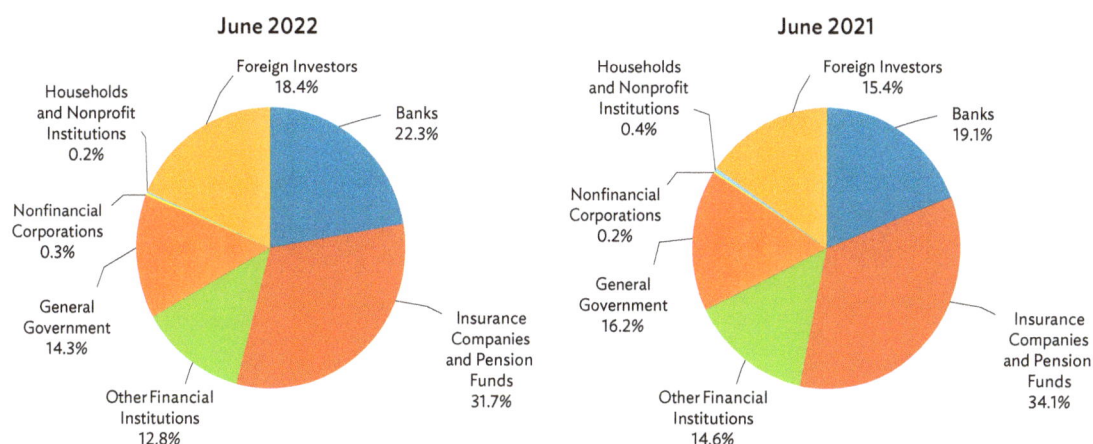

June 2022

Foreign Investors 18.4%
Banks 22.3%
Households and Nonprofit Institutions 0.2%
Nonfinancial Corporations 0.3%
General Government 14.3%
Other Financial Institutions 12.8%
Insurance Companies and Pension Funds 31.7%

June 2021

Foreign Investors 15.4%
Banks 19.1%
Households and Nonprofit Institutions 0.4%
Nonfinancial Corporations 0.2%
General Government 16.2%
Other Financial Institutions 14.6%
Insurance Companies and Pension Funds 34.1%

Source: *AsianBondsOnline* and The Bank of Korea.

**Figure 3: Local Currency Corporate Bonds Investor Profile**

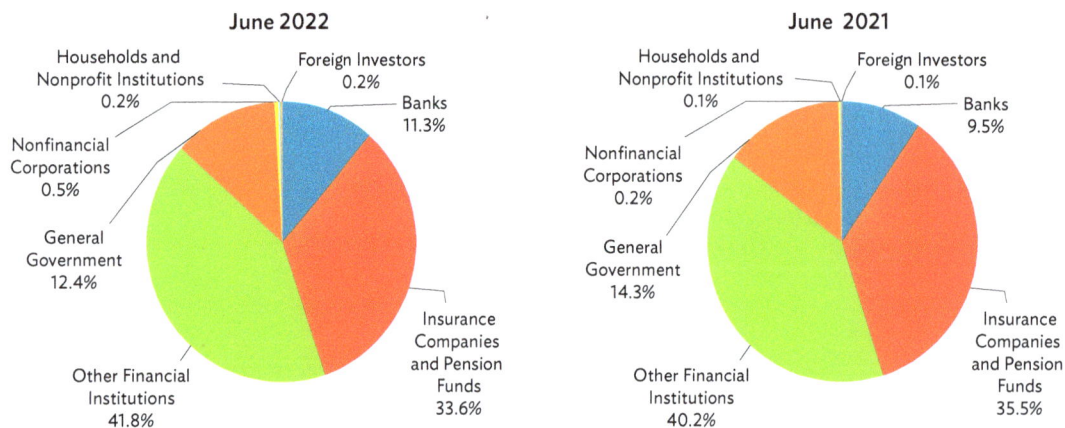

June 2022

Households and Nonprofit Institutions 0.2%
Foreign Investors 0.2%
Banks 11.3%
Nonfinancial Corporations 0.5%
General Government 12.4%
Insurance Companies and Pension Funds 33.6%
Other Financial Institutions 41.8%

June 2021

Households and Nonprofit Institutions 0.1%
Foreign Investors 0.1%
Banks 9.5%
Nonfinancial Corporations 0.2%
General Government 14.3%
Insurance Companies and Pension Funds 35.5%
Other Financial Institutions 40.2%

Source: *AsianBondsOnline* and The Bank of Korea.

Meanwhile, the shares of insurance companies and pension funds and the general government fell at the end of June to 33.6% and 12.4%, respectively, from 35.5% and 14.3% a year earlier. The share of foreign holders continued to remain negligible.

**Foreign fund flows.** Net foreign flows into the Republic of Korea's LCY bond market turned positive in July, posting KRW3,561 billion following net outflows of KRW0.9 billion in June (**Figure 4**). This was largely due to expectations of a slowdown in monetary policy tightening by the Federal Reserve. However, the Republic of Korea registered net foreign outflows of KRW1.9 billion in August as US Treasury yields rose

once again following the release of the minutes of the July Federal Open Market Committee meeting in which the Federal Reserve highlighted its resolve in fighting high inflation via aggressive monetary policy tightening. Chair Jerome Powell's Jackson Hole speech in late August confirmed this sentiment. Subsequently, the Federal Reserve raised the federal funds rate target range by an additional 75 bps in September. This move resulted in KRW980 billion of net foreign outflows from the Republic of Korea's LCY bond market in September. The foreign sell-off during Q3 2022 was most significant in bonds with remaining maturities of less than 1 year (**Figure 5**).

**Figure 4: Net Foreign Investment in Local Currency Bonds in the Republic of Korea**

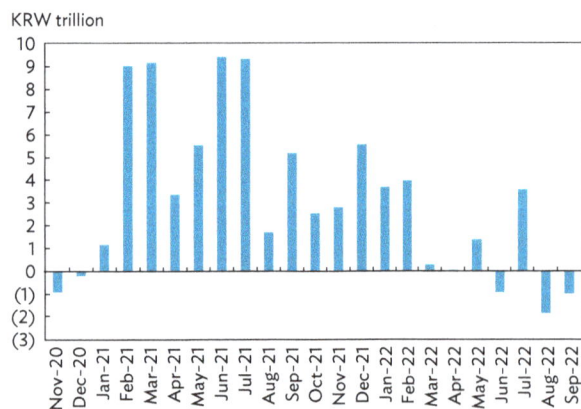

KRW trillion

( ) = negative, KRW = Korean won.
Source: Financial Supervisory Service.

**Figure 5: Net Foreign Investment in Local Currency Bonds in the Republic of Korea by Remaining Maturity**

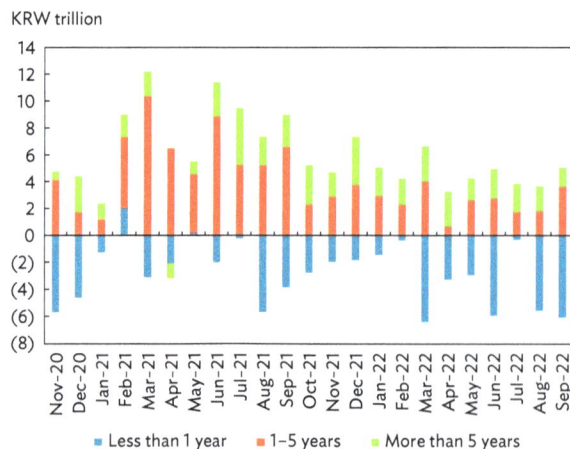

KRW trillion

■ Less than 1 year   ■ 1–5 years   ■ More than 5 years

( ) = negative, KRW = Korean won.
Source: Financial Supervisory Service.

## Ratings Update

On 28 September, Fitch Ratings affirmed the Republic of Korea's sovereign credit ratings of AA– with a stable outlook. The rating agency cited the Republic of Korea's robust external finances, resilient macroeconomic performance, and dynamic export sector as some of the reasons behind the rating affirmation. It also highlighted the Republic of Korea's sufficient fiscal space to accommodate the government's rising debt-to-GDP ratio in the near term, following the recently announced consolidation plans. The rating agency forecast that GDP growth would slow to 2.6% in 2022 amid a slowdown in global growth as well as in domestic exports and facilities investment.

## Policy, Institutional, and Regulatory Developments

### The Government Announces 2023 Budget Proposal

On 30 August, the Government of the Republic of Korea announced its 2023 budget proposal totaling KRW639 trillion. This represented a 5.2% increase from the original 2022 budget, which is less than the average yearly increase of 8.7% over the last 5 years. The proposed 2023 budget is also 5.9% less than the 2022 final budget, which includes the supplementary budget. The smaller annual increase in the budget is in line with government efforts to reduce spending as part of its 2022–2026 fiscal management plan to improve fiscal sustainability. The proposed budget is projected to result in a 0.6% fiscal-deficit-to-GDP ratio, which is lower than the 2.5% ratio for 2022. Priorities in the budget include the expansion of protections for low-income and vulnerable households, support for the private-sector-led economy, and improvements to national safety and security.

### Fiscal Rules Introduced

In its 13 September emergency ministerial meeting on economic affairs, the Government of the Republic of Korea announced its plans to introduce rules to improve the government's fiscal soundness. This includes the use of the managed fiscal balance as a standard for fiscal rules instead of the consolidated fiscal balance. In addition, the managed fiscal balance shall have an upper limit of 3% of GDP, and it will be reduced to 2% when government debt exceeds 60% of GDP. However, this shall not be applied in the case of exceptional situations such as wars, national disasters, and economic downturns. The rules shall be established on a legal basis via inclusion of fiscal rule management standards in the National Finance Act and will be used in the design of the 2024 budget proposal.

# Malaysia

## Yield Movements

Malaysia's local currency (LCY) government bond yield curve moved upward for all tenors between 31 August and 14 October (**Figure 1**). Yields of short-term bonds (from 1 month to 1 year) jumped an average of 19 basis points (bps), while yields of longer-term, fixed-income securities (2–30 years) soared an average of 45 bps. The yield spread between the 10-year and 2-year government bonds expanded from 70 bps to 78 bps during the review period.

Yields of government securities went up as Bank Negara Malaysia (BNM) raised its overnight policy rate in September to combat inflationary pressure. Investors also sold Malaysian fixed-income securities as the yields on United States (US) Treasuries became more attractive due to the series of interest rate hikes by the Federal Reserve.

On 8 September, BNM's Monetary Policy Committee hiked its overnight policy rate to 2.50% from 2.25%. The increase was meant to temper rising inflation as the economy of Malaysia continued to reopen, with demand-driven inflationary pressure creating a high-cost environment. BNM's decision also factored in its expectation that central banks around the world would continue adjusting their monetary policies to combat inflation. On 3 November, BNM raised the policy rate by another 25 bps.

Prices of basic goods and services in Malaysia remained elevated during the third quarter (Q3) of 2022. Consumer price inflation logged 4.4% year-on-year (y-o-y) in July, accelerating to 4.7% y-o-y in August before slightly slowing to 4.5% y-o-y in September. Average inflation for the first 9 months of 2022 was 3.3% y-o-y, higher than the upper limit of the central bank's inflation forecast of between 2.2% and 3.2% for full-year 2022.

Malaysia's gross domestic product jumped 14.2% y-o-y in Q3 2022, an extension of the 8.9% y-o-y growth recorded in the second quarter (Q2) of 2022 due to improved performance across all sectors of the economy. In the first 3 quarters of 2022, economic growth in Malaysia averaged 9.4% y-o-y, exceeding BNM's expected growth rate of 5.3%–6.3% for full-year 2022.

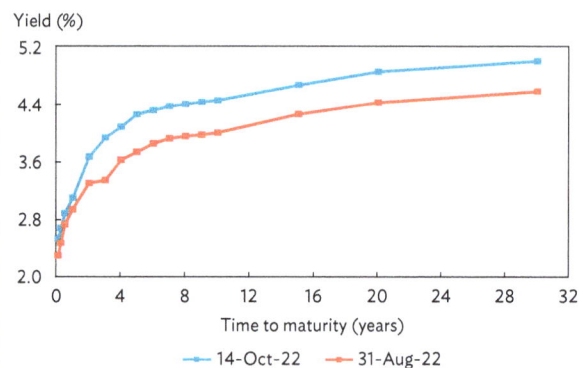

**Figure 1: Malaysia's Benchmark Yield Curve— Local Currency Government Bonds**

Source: Based on data from Bloomberg LP.

## Size and Composition

The LCY bond market of Malaysia expanded 2.6% quarter-on-quarter (q-o-q) in Q3 2022, reaching a size of MYR1,853.0 billion (USD399.6 billion) at the end of September (**Table 1**). This growth was faster than the 2.3% q-o-q increase recorded in the prior quarter. On an annual basis, Malaysia's bond market rose 7.8% y-o-y, accelerating from the 6.6% y-o-y expansion in Q2 2022. The growth was due to increases in both outstanding government and corporate bonds, which comprised 56.6% and 43.4%, respectively, of total outstanding bonds at the end of the review period. Total outstanding *sukuk* (Islamic bonds) grew 3.9% q-o-q in Q3 2022, extending the 1.5% q-o-q expansion logged in Q2 2022. This growth was spurred by expanding stocks of both government and corporate *sukuk*.

Issuance of LCY bonds in Q3 2022 grew 7.2% q-o-q on increased issuance of government bonds. However, this was slower than the 35.5% q-o-q growth registered in the previous quarter.

**Government bonds.** The LCY government bond market of Malaysia rose 3.2% q-o-q in Q3 2022, a deceleration from the expansion of 4.1% q-o-q recorded in Q2 2022. The growth was due to a 3.9% q-o-q rise in central government bonds outstanding, which comprised 98.7% of total government bonds outstanding at the end of September. Outstanding BNM bills at the end of Q3 2022 were more than four times the amount in the previous

**Table 1: Size and Composition of the Local Currency Bond Market in Malaysia**

| | Outstanding Amount (billion) | | | | | | Growth Rate (%) | | | |
| | Q3 2021 | | Q2 2022 | | Q3 2022 | | Q3 2021 | | Q3 2022 | |
| | MYR | USD | MYR | USD | MYR | USD | q-o-q | y-o-y | q-o-q | y-o-y |
|---|---|---|---|---|---|---|---|---|---|---|
| Total | 1,719 | 411 | 1,805 | 410 | 1,853 | 400 | 1.5 | 8.5 | 2.6 | 7.8 |
| Government | 938 | 224 | 1,016 | 230 | 1,049 | 226 | 1.5 | 10.6 | 3.2 | 11.8 |
| Central Government Bonds | 914 | 218 | 997 | 226 | 1,035 | 223 | 1.6 | 11.5 | 3.9 | 13.3 |
| of which: *Sukuk* | 435 | 104 | 470 | 107 | 507 | 109 | 4.8 | 15.2 | 7.9 | 16.7 |
| Central Bank Bills | 0 | 0 | 0.9 | 0.2 | 4 | 0.9 | – | (100.0) | 388.2 | – |
| of which: *Sukuk* | 0 | 0 | 0.2 | 0.05 | 1 | 0.2 | – | – | 400.0 | – |
| Sukuk Perumahan Kerajaan | 24 | 6 | 18 | 4 | 9 | 2 | 0.0 | 0.0 | (49.7) | (62.2) |
| Corporate | 780 | 186 | 790 | 179 | 804 | 173 | 1.4 | 6.1 | 1.9 | 3.1 |
| of which: *Sukuk* | 638 | 152 | 651 | 148 | 666 | 144 | 1.9 | 7.8 | 2.3 | 4.4 |

( ) = negative, – = not applicable, MYR = Malaysian ringgit, q-o-q = quarter-on-quarter, Q2 = second quarter, Q3 = third quarter, USD = United States dollar, y-o-y = year-on-year.
Notes:
1. Bloomberg LP end-of-period local currency–USD rates are used.
2. Growth rates are calculated from local currency base and do not include currency effects.
3. *Sukuk* refers to Islamic bonds.
4. Sukuk Perumahan Kerajaan are Islamic bonds issued by the Government of Malaysia to refinance funding for housing loans to government employees and to extend new housing loans.
Sources: Bank Negara Malaysia Fully Automated System for Issuing/Tendering and Bloomberg LP.

quarter. The amount of outstanding Sukuk Perumahan Kerajaan at the end of September was about half of the amount in the previous quarter.

Issuance of LCY government bonds in Q3 2022 expanded 12.4% q-o-q, spurred by increased issuance of Treasury and central bank bills. Malaysian Government Securities (conventional bonds) issuance decreased from the prior quarter, while issuance of Government Investment Issues (Islamic bonds) rose in Q3 2022. The increased Islamic bond issuance was supported by the Government of Malaysia's September issuance of its inaugural sustainability *sukuk* worth MYR4.5 billion.

**Corporate bonds.** LCY corporate bonds outstanding increased 1.9% q-o-q in Q3 2022, extending the marginal growth of 0.1% q-o-q recorded in Q2 2022. Outstanding corporate *sukuk* rose 2.3% q-o-q at the end of September, which was faster than the 0.2% q-o-q growth in the prior quarter.

Malaysia's 30 largest corporate bond issuers had a combined MYR476.3 billion worth of outstanding LCY corporate bonds at the end of Q3 2022. This was equivalent to a share of 59.2% of total corporate bonds outstanding (**Table 2**). Government-owned company DanaInfra Nasional continued to have the largest amount of outstanding corporate bonds at the end of September at MYR80.9 billion. In terms of sector, the largest

share comprised financial institutions (50.4%) with MYR239.8 billion worth of corporate bonds outstanding at the end of Q3 2022.

Issuance of LCY corporate bonds in Q3 2022 declined 0.7% q-o-q, a reversal from the 38.3% q-o-q growth logged in the prior quarter. Corporate entities refrained from issuing fixed-income securities as it became more expensive to raise funds through corporate bonds due to the high-interest-rate environment brought about by the central bank's rate hikes.

In Q3 2022, Lembaga Pembiayaan Perumahan Sektor Awam (Public Sector Home Financing Board) and Sarawak Petchem each issued MYR4.0 billion worth of bonds (**Table 3**). The Public Sector Home Financing Board issued nine Islamic medium-term notes (MTNs) in August, with tenors ranging from 3 years to 30 years. In July, Sarawak Petchem, a state-owned oil and gas company, issued 13 Islamic MTNs with tenors from 3 years to 15 years. Proceeds from the issuance will be used to fund the Sarawak Methanol Project. National mortgage company Cagamas issued MYR3.7 billion worth of conventional and Islamic MTNs in Q3 2022. Most notable of which was the issuance in July of a 1-year floating-rate MTN, the first bond in Malaysia to be priced using the Malaysia Overnight Rate, Malaysia's new alternative reference rate.

## Table 2: Top 30 Issuers of Local Currency Corporate Bonds in Malaysia

| | Issuers | Outstanding Amount | | State-Owned | Listed Company | Type of Industry |
|---|---|---|---|---|---|---|
| | | LCY Bonds (MYR billion) | LCY Bonds (USD billion) | | | |
| 1. | DanaInfra Nasional | 80.9 | 17.5 | Yes | No | Finance |
| 2. | Lembaga Pembiayaan Perumahan Sektor Awam | 40.3 | 8.7 | Yes | No | Property and Real Estate |
| 3. | Prasarana | 40.2 | 8.7 | Yes | No | Transport, Storage, and Communications |
| 4. | Cagamas | 32.9 | 7.1 | Yes | No | Finance |
| 5. | Project Lebuhraya Usahasama | 28.2 | 6.1 | No | No | Transport, Storage, and Communications |
| 6. | Urusharta Jamaah | 27.3 | 5.9 | Yes | No | Finance |
| 7. | Perbadanan Tabung Pendidikan Tinggi Nasional | 21.1 | 4.5 | Yes | No | Finance |
| 8. | Pengurusan Air | 19.0 | 4.1 | Yes | No | Energy, Gas, and Water |
| 9. | Tenaga Nasional | 17.0 | 3.7 | No | Yes | Energy, Gas, and Water |
| 10. | CIMB Group Holdings | 15.0 | 3.2 | Yes | No | Finance |
| 11. | Maybank Islamic | 13.0 | 2.8 | No | Yes | Banking |
| 12. | Malayan Banking | 12.6 | 2.7 | No | Yes | Banking |
| 13. | CIMB Bank | 12.1 | 2.6 | Yes | No | Finance |
| 14. | Sarawak Energy | 10.8 | 2.3 | Yes | No | Energy, Gas, and Water |
| 15. | Danum Capital | 10.1 | 2.2 | No | No | Finance |
| 16. | Danga Capital | 10.0 | 2.2 | Yes | No | Finance |
| 17. | Khazanah | 9.4 | 2.0 | Yes | No | Finance |
| 18. | Jimah East Power | 8.7 | 1.9 | Yes | No | Energy, Gas, and Water |
| 19. | Malaysia Rail Link | 7.9 | 1.7 | Yes | No | Construction |
| 20. | Public Bank | 6.9 | 1.5 | No | No | Banking |
| 21. | Sapura TMC | 6.4 | 1.4 | No | No | Finance |
| 22. | Kuala Lumpur Kepong | 5.6 | 1.2 | No | Yes | Energy, Gas, and Water |
| 23. | YTL Power International | 5.5 | 1.2 | No | Yes | Energy, Gas, and Water |
| 24. | Bank Pembangunan Malaysia | 5.5 | 1.2 | Yes | No | Banking |
| 25. | Turus Pesawat | 5.3 | 1.1 | Yes | No | Transport, Storage, and Communications |
| 26. | Bakun Hydro Power Generation | 5.1 | 1.1 | No | No | Energy, Gas, and Water |
| 27. | 1Malaysia Development | 5.0 | 1.1 | Yes | No | Finance |
| 28. | EDRA Energy | 4.9 | 1.1 | No | Yes | Energy, Gas, and Water |
| 29. | Infracap Resources | 4.9 | 1.0 | Yes | No | Finance |
| 30. | PNB Merdeka Ventures | 4.8 | 1.0 | No | No | Finance |
| | **Total Top 30 LCY Corporate Issuers** | **476.3** | **102.7** | | | |
| | **Total LCY Corporate Bonds** | **804.2** | **173.4** | | | |
| | **Top 30 as % of Total LCY Corporate Bonds** | **59.2%** | **59.2%** | | | |

LCY = local currency, MYR = Malaysian ringgit, USD = United States dollar.
Notes:
1.  Data as of 30 September 2022.
2.  State-owned firms are defined as those in which the government has more than a 50% ownership stake.
Source: *AsianBondsOnline* calculations based on Bank Negara Malaysia Fully Automated System for Issuing/Tendering data.

**Table 3: Notable Local Currency Corporate Bond Issuances in the Third Quarter of 2022**

| Corporate Issuers | Coupon Rate (%) | Issued Amount (MYR million) | Corporate Issuers | Coupon Rate (%) | Issued Amount (MYR million) |
|---|---|---|---|---|---|
| Lembaga Pembiayaan Perumahan Sektor Awam | | | 13-year Islamic MTN | 5.34 | 275 |
| 3-year Islamic MTN | 3.69 | 385 | 14-year Islamic MTN | 5.42 | 280 |
| 4-year Islamic MTN | 3.90 | 675 | 15-year Islamic MTN | 5.50 | 350 |
| 5-year Islamic MTN | 3.94 | 100 | Cagamas[a] | | |
| 7-year Islamic MTN | 4.12 | 480 | 1-year Islamic MTN | 3.45 | 25 |
| 8-year Islamic MTN | 4.16 | 400 | 1-year MTN | Floating | 200 |
| 10-year Islamic MTN | 4.20 | 910 | 1-year MTN | 3.45 | 85 |
| 12-year Islamic MTN | 4.28 | 300 | 1-year Islamic MTN | 3.41 | 560 |
| 16-year Islamic MTN | 4.46 | 300 | 1-year MTN | 3.49 | 30 |
| 30-year Islamic MTN | 4.81 | 450 | 2-year Islamic MTN | 3.75 | 285 |
| Sarawak Petchem | | | 2-year Islamic MTN | 3.77 | 115 |
| 3-year Islamic MTN | 4.38 | 190 | 2-year MTN | 3.75 | 110 |
| 4-year Islamic MTN | 4.71 | 200 | 2-year MTN | 3.76 | 205 |
| 5-year Islamic MTN | 4.83 | 305 | 2-year MTN | 3.74 | 45 |
| 6-year Islamic MTN | 5.01 | 400 | 2-year MTN | 3.89 | 40 |
| 7-year Islamic MTN | 5.05 | 415 | 3-year MTN | 3.85 | 250 |
| 8-year Islamic MTN | 5.09 | 350 | 3-year Islamic MTN | 3.93 | 100 |
| 9-year Islamic MTN | 5.11 | 325 | 3-year MTN | 3.93 | 390 |
| 10-year Islamic MTN | 5.11 | 400 | 3-year MTN | 4.00 | 30 |
| 11-year Islamic MTN | 5.19 | 250 | 5-year MTN | 4.25 | 1,000 |
| 12-year Islamic MTN | 5.27 | 260 | 5-year MTN | 4.18 | 200 |

MTN = medium-term note, MYR = Malaysian ringgit.
[a] Multiple issuance of the same tenor indicates issuance on different dates.
Source: Bank Negara Malaysia Bond Info Hub.

## Investor Profile

Capital amounting to MYR3.3 billion flowed out of Malaysia in July. This was more than offset in August with net capital inflows of MYR5.5 billion due to positive economic data in the US easing risk-off sentiments among global investors (**Figure 2**). In September, however, funds flowed out of Malaysia again, this time worth MYR0.6 billion due to the Federal Reserve's hawkish stance in hiking interest rates. For Q3 2022, Malaysia experienced net capital inflows of MYR1.6 billion, a reversal from the net outflows of MYR5.3 billion experienced in Q2 2022, due to the high volume of capital that entered the economy in August.

Foreign investors held a 23.4% share of Malaysian LCY government bonds outstanding at the end of July, which increased to 23.7% in August before falling back to 23.3% in September (**Figure 3**). The spread between the yields of the 10-year US Treasury and the 10-year Malaysian Government Security narrowed between the end of August and the end of September, making MYR-denominated bonds less attractive to foreign investors. At the end of Q3 2022, foreign investors held

**Figure 2: Capital Flows into the Malaysian Local Currency Government Bond Market**

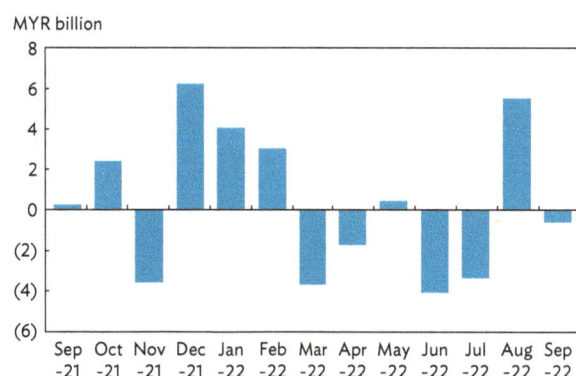

( ) = negative, MYR = Malaysian ringgit.
Notes:
1. Figures exclude foreign holdings of Bank Negara Malaysia bills.
2. Month-on-month changes in foreign holdings of local currency government bonds were used as a proxy for bond flows.
Source: Bank Negara Malaysia Monthly Statistical Bulletin.

MYR241.5 billion worth of LCY government bonds, which was less than the MYR239.9 billion held at the end of the previous quarter.

By the end of the first half of 2022, financial institutions and social security institutions were the largest investors in LCY government bonds, holding 35.2% and 27.4%,

respectively, of total bonds outstanding (**Figure 4**). Shares of financial and social security institutions increased from 34.7% and 27.2%, respectively, compared to the same period in 2021. On the other hand, the share of foreign holders declined to 24.0% at the end of Q3 2022 from 25.7% in the previous year. Insurance companies' holdings were the same at 4.8%, while the BNM's share rose from 1.9% to 2.7% between June 2021 and June 2022.

## Policy, Institutional, and Regulatory Developments

### Government of Malaysia Issues First Sustainability *Sukuk*

On 30 September, the Government of Malaysia raised funds through its inaugural Sustainability Government Investment Issues, worth MYR4.5 billion and with a tenor of 15 years. The issuance showed Malaysia's commitment to develop a sustainable economy. The sustainable bond served as a new benchmark bond in Malaysia's Islamic bond market. The proceeds will be used to fund the government's social and green projects under its Sustainable Development Goals Sukuk Framework.

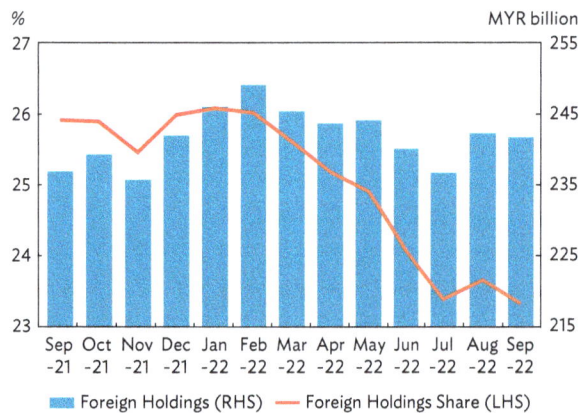

**Figure 3: Foreign Holdings of Malaysian Local Currency Government Bonds**

LHS = left-hand side, MYR = Malaysian ringgit, RHS = right-hand side.
Note: Figures exclude foreign holdings of Bank Negara Malaysia bills.
Source: Bank Negara Malaysia Monthly Statistical Bulletin.

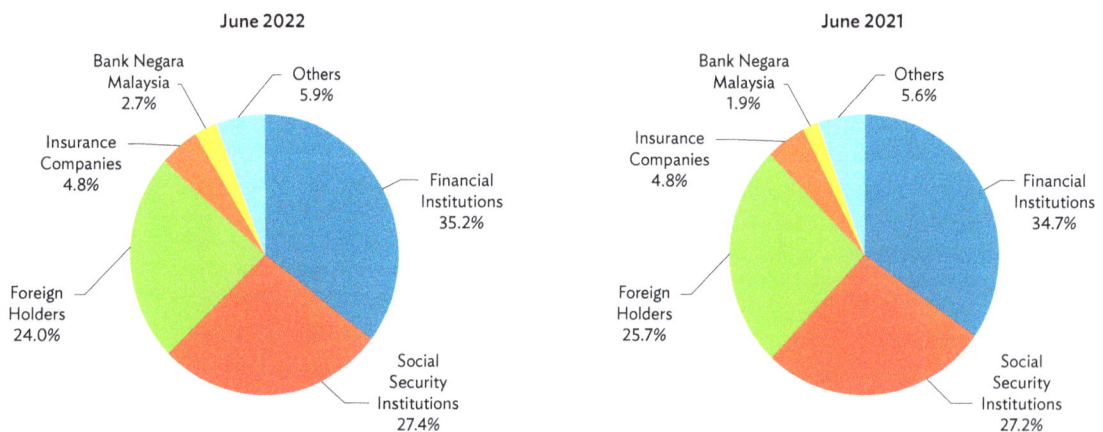

**Figure 4: Local Currency Government Bonds Investor Profile**

Note: "Others" include statutory bodies, nominees and trustee companies, and cooperatives and unclassified items.
Source: Bank Negara Malaysia.

# Philippines

## Yield Movements

The Philippines' local currency (LCY) government bond yields rose across all tenors between 31 August and 14 October, gaining an average of 86 basis points (bps) (**Figure 1**). Yields on the shorter end of the curve (from 1-month to 6-month tenors) inched up an average of 94 bps, with the largest increase seen in the 3-month tenor at 112 bps. Yields for the 2-year through 10-year tenors climbed an average of 101 bps, while yields at the longer-end of the curve (from 20-year to 25-year tenors) increased an average of 74 bps. The smallest increase in yields was seen for the 1-year tenor at only 1 bp. The spread between the 10-year and 2-year maturities widened from 145 bps on 31 August to 154 bps on 14 October.

The large uptick in bond yields across the curve was propelled by the Bangko Sentral ng Pilipinas' (BSP) aggressive monetary tightening stance to ease rising inflationary pressure. The BSP raised its policy rates consecutively each month from May through September, followed by the recent hike of 75 bps in November, for a total of 300 bps, lifting the overnight reverse repurchase facility rate to 5.00% starting 18 November. The BSP has become the most aggressive central bank in the region in terms of tightening monetary policy this year through 18 November.

Consumer price inflation accelerated to 7.7% year-on-year (y-o-y) in October, marking its fastest pace in nearly 14 years and the highest rate among major emerging East Asian peers that have released October inflation data thus far. October inflation also exceeded the BSP's target of 4.0% y-o-y for the year. Amid persistent domestic inflation and the United States (US) Federal Reserve maintaining its aggressive monetary stance, the market expects further BSP rate hikes before the year ends.

Meanwhile, the Philippines' seasonally adjusted gross domestic product (GDP) grew 2.9% quarter-on-quarter (q-o-q) in the third quarter (Q3) of 2022. On a y-o-y basis, GDP growth slightly crept up to 7.6% from 7.5% in the second quarter (Q2) of 2022. Soaring inflation, particularly in those sectors impacted by fuel and food prices, mainly contributed to the GDP slowdown in Q3 2022. The Philippine economy continued to be dragged down by headwinds and

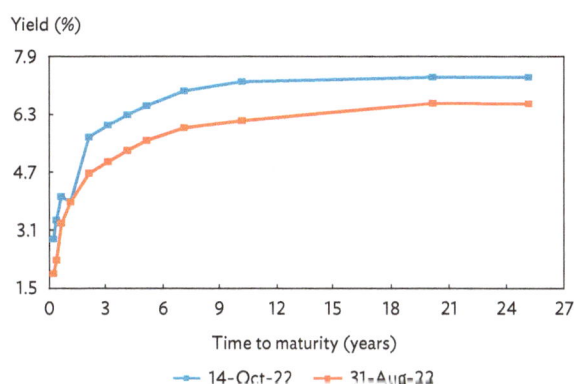

**Figure 1: The Philippines' Benchmark Yield Curve— Local Currency Government Bonds**

Source: Based on data from Bloomberg LP.

uncertainties in the global and regional outlook. From March through October, the equity market consistently posted monthly net foreign investor outflows, reflecting investors' negative sentiment toward the stock market. The bond market, on the other hand, faced marginal foreign capital inflows during Q3 2022. During the review period of 31 August and 14 October, the Philippine peso weakened 4.7% against the US dollar.

## Size and Composition

During Q3 2022, the Philippines' LCY bond market grew a modest 3.6% q-o-q, reaching a total size of PHP11,063.1 billion (USD188.6 billion) at the end of September and reflecting faster growth compared to the 2.4% q-o-q expansion in Q2 2022 (**Table 1**). The upswing in q-o-q growth was caused by a decent rise in Treasury bonds and slight growth in the corporate bond segment.

**Government bonds.** The outstanding amount of LCY government bonds inched up to PHP9,635.7 billion at the end of September, displaying growth of 3.9% q-o-q in Q3 2022 after a 4.1% q-o-q increase in the previous quarter. The marginal decline in the q-o-q growth was due to the declining stock of Treasury bills, central bank securities, and other government bonds. However, Treasury bonds continued to dominate the government bond segment and showed the largest growth during the quarter, offsetting the contraction of all three components of the government bond segment.

**Table 1: Size and Composition of the Local Currency Bond Market in the Philippines**

| | Outstanding Amount (billion) | | | | | | Growth Rate (%) | | | |
| | Q3 2021 | | Q2 2022 | | Q3 2022 | | Q3 2021 | | Q3 2022 | |
| | PHP | USD | PHP | USD | PHP | USD | q-o-q | y-o-y | q-o-q | y-o-y |
|---|---|---|---|---|---|---|---|---|---|---|
| Total | 9,762 | 191 | 10,680 | 194 | 11,063 | 189 | 4.4 | 20.0 | 3.6 | 13.3 |
| Government | 8,322 | 163 | 9,273 | 169 | 9,636 | 164 | 6.2 | 28.0 | 3.9 | 15.8 |
| Treasury Bills | 943 | 18 | 544 | 10 | 509 | 9 | (7.9) | 7.5 | (6.5) | (46.0) |
| Treasury Bonds | 6,880 | 135 | 8,108 | 147 | 8,669 | 148 | 8.3 | 24.3 | 6.9 | 26.0 |
| Central Bank Securities | 440 | 9 | 567 | 10 | 410 | 7 | 10.0 | 780.0 | (27.7) | (6.8) |
| Others | 60 | 1 | 54 | 1 | 48 | 0.8 | (0.01) | 50.2 | (10.5) | (19.7) |
| Corporate | 1,440 | 28 | 1,408 | 26 | 1,427 | 24 | (5.1) | (11.9) | 1.4 | (0.9) |

( ) = negative, PHP = Philippine peso, q-o-q = quarter-on-quarter, Q2 = second quarter, Q3 = third quarter, USD = United States dollar, y-o-y = year-on-year.
Notes:
1.  Bloomberg end-of-period local currency–USD rates are used.
2.  Growth rates are calculated from local currency base and do not include currency effects.
3.  "Others" comprise bonds issued by government agencies, entities, and corporations for which repayment is guaranteed by the Government of the Philippines. This includes bonds issued by Power Sector Assets and Liabilities Management and the National Food Authority, among others.
4.  Peso Global Bonds (PHP-denominated bonds payable in USD) are not included.
Sources: Bloomberg LP and Bureau of the Treasury.

At the end of September, the outstanding size of Treasury bills plunged to PHP509.1 billion, exhibiting a drop of 6.5% q-o-q and 46.0% y-o-y. Issuance of Treasury bills declined during the quarter as investors sought higher yields that the government was not willing to accept.

On the contrary, the outstanding amount of Treasury bonds rose to PHP8,668.6 billion at the end of September, posting a faster 6.9% q-o-q growth in Q3 2022 versus 3.9% q-o-q in Q2 2022. On a y-o-y basis, however, growth in outstanding Treasury bonds slipped to 26.0% in Q3 2022 from 27.7% in Q2 2022. Treasury bond issuance during the quarter rose 167.8% q-o-q, buoyed by the issuance of the 28th series of the Philippine government's Retail Treasury Bonds (RTB-28) on 7 September amounting to PHP420.4 billion. The issuance also included PHP108.5 billion from a bond exchange offer embedded in the issued RTB-28, where holders of the two retail bonds and two fixed-rate bonds that are set to mature later this year and early next year can switch to RTB-28, which bears a longer tenor of 5.5 years and a higher coupon rate of 5.75%. The exchange offer is intended to reduce the refinancing risk in the government's debt portfolio and the bond proceeds will be used to finance the government's infrastructure projects and development programs that aim to build an inclusive, broad-based, and sustainable economy.

Central bank securities, on the other hand, decreased by 27.7% q-o-q compared with 38.3% q-o-q growth in Q2 2022. Issuance of central bank bills totaled PHP1,670.2 in Q3 2022, down 4.1% q-o-q. The BSP opted to raise rates actively to help contain inflationary pressure.

**Corporate bonds.** In Q3 2022, the corporate bond segment's outstanding size grew to PHP1,427.4 billion, posting an increase of 1.4% q-o-q and a marginal decline of 0.9% y-o-y. Total corporate bond issuance during the quarter increased 37.7% q-o-q, reaching a total amount of PHP125.5 billion versus PHP91.2 billion in the previous quarter. Corporates rushed to sell bonds ahead of expected higher borrowing costs.

Banking and property institutions largely dominate the corporate bond market in the Philippines (**Figure 2**). Collectively, their outstanding bond stock accounted for 60.9% of the outstanding corporate total at the end of September. The banking sector remained the largest issuer of LCY corporate bonds with 31.9% of all outstanding debt in Q3 2022, reflecting a decline of 6.7 percentage points from Q3 2021, which was the most significant drop among all corporate bond sectors during the review period. On the other hand, property institutions' share in the corporate bond market increased to 29.0% from 25.1% in the previous year, while holding firms remained the third-largest issuer with outstanding debt slightly dipping to 16.8% at the end of September from 16.9% in the prior year.

## Figure 2: Local Currency Corporate Bonds Outstanding by Sector

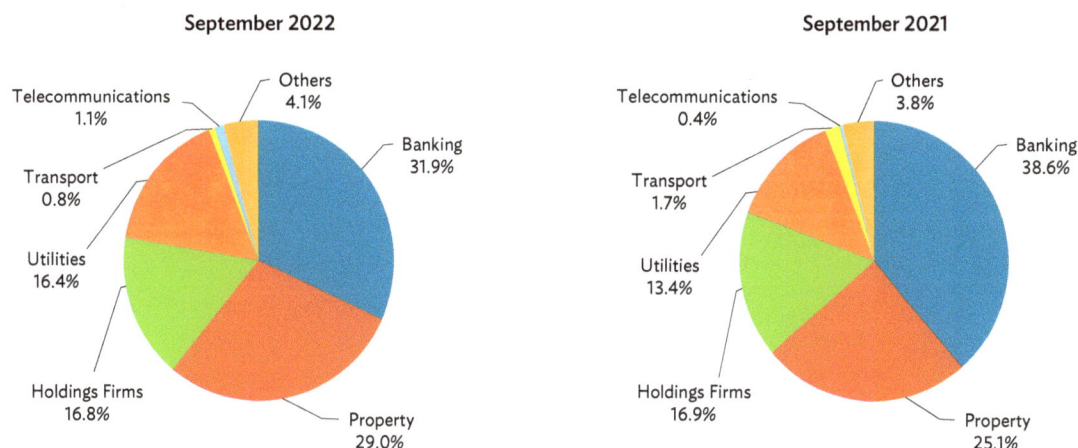

### September 2022

Telecommunications 1.1%
Others 4.1%
Transport 0.8%
Banking 31.9%
Utilities 16.4%
Holdings Firms 16.8%
Property 29.0%

### September 2021

Telecommunications 0.4%
Others 3.8%
Transport 1.7%
Banking 38.6%
Utilities 13.4%
Holdings Firms 16.9%
Property 25.1%

Source: Based on data from Bloomberg LP.

At the end of September, 80% of the top 30 corporate bond issuers in the Philippines comprised banks, holding firms, and property institutions. The top 30 firms had aggregate debt of PHP1,278.3 billion at the end of Q3 2022, which corresponded to 89.6% of the total corporate bond stock (**Table 2**). At the end of the quarter, the top issuer was a holding firm, SM Prime Holdings, with outstanding debt of PHP119.6 billion, or 8.4% of the total Philippine corporate bond stock. The second-largest corporate bond issuer was a property firm, Ayala Land, with bonds amounting to PHP118.3 billion, which corresponded to 8.3% of the total corporate bond stock at the end of September.

In Q3 2022, seven companies turned to the LCY corporate bond market for funding (**Table 3**). These companies were from the banking, property, and utility industries with total corporate bond issuance amounting to PHP125.5 billion and comprising 13 new bond series. During the quarter, SMC Global Power posted the largest aggregate issuance at PHP40.0 billion from the sale of its 3-, 5.8-, and 10-year bonds. The second-largest aggregate issuance came from Ayala Land, which raised a total of PHP33.0 billion from multiple tranches. Meanwhile, Security Bank issued the shortest-dated bond with a tenor of 1.5 years, and the longest-dated bond was issued by SMC Global Power with a tenor of 10 years.

## Investor Profile

A majority of LCY government bonds were still held by banks and investment houses, whose holdings moderately increased to 44.5% at the end of September 2022 from 39.4% in the previous year (**Figure 3**). Others' investment share also posted a marginal increase to 8.3% from 8.1% during the review period. Contractual savings institutions and tax-exempt institutions remained the second-largest investor in the government bond segment; however, their investment share decreased to 32.9% in September 2022 from 35.1% in September 2021. Government-owned or -controlled corporations and local government units' investment share remained constant, while all other investors' holdings showed a downward trend from their previous investment percentage shares a year earlier.

## Ratings Update

On 27 October, Fitch Ratings affirmed the Philippines' long-term foreign-currency debt rating at BBB with a negative outlook. The investment-grade credit rating reflects the sovereign's strong economic growth, sound external finances, and credible economic policy framework amid monetary tightening and domestic inflationary pressures. However, the rating agency maintained the negative outlook, citing risk from headwinds and uncertainties in the global economy—particularly higher interest rates, soaring commodity prices, and weaker external demand—that could affect the Philippines' medium-term growth prospects, fiscal adjustment path, and external buffers.

**Table 2: Top 30 Issuers of Local Currency Corporate Bonds in the Philippines**

| | Issuers | Outstanding Amount | | State-Owned | Listed Company | Type of Industry |
|---|---|---|---|---|---|---|
| | | LCY Bonds (PHP billion) | LCY Bonds (USD billion) | | | |
| 1. | SM Prime Holdings | 119.6 | 2.0 | No | Yes | Holding Firms |
| 2. | Ayala Land | 118.3 | 2.0 | No | Yes | Property |
| 3. | San Miguel | 103.3 | 1.8 | No | Yes | Holding Firms |
| 4. | SMC Global Power | 100.0 | 1.7 | No | No | Electricity, Energy, and Power |
| 5. | BDO Unibank | 86.5 | 1.5 | No | Yes | Banking |
| 6. | Metropolitan Bank | 76.3 | 1.3 | No | Yes | Banking |
| 7. | China Bank | 51.6 | 0.9 | No | Yes | Banking |
| 8. | Aboitiz Power | 51.0 | 0.9 | No | Yes | Electricity, Energy, and Power |
| 9. | Security Bank | 50.8 | 0.9 | No | Yes | Banking |
| 10. | Rizal Commercial Banking Corporation | 46.2 | 0.8 | No | Yes | Banking |
| 11. | Ayala Corporation | 45.0 | 0.8 | No | Yes | Holding Firms |
| 12. | Petron | 45.0 | 0.8 | No | Yes | Electricity, Energy, and Power |
| 13. | Vista Land | 42.7 | 0.7 | No | Yes | Property |
| 14. | Bank of the Philippine Islands | 42.4 | 0.7 | No | Yes | Banking |
| 15. | Filinvest Land | 35.4 | 0.6 | No | Yes | Property |
| 16. | Union Bank of the Philippines | 29.8 | 0.5 | No | Yes | Banking |
| 17. | Robinsons Land | 29.6 | 0.5 | No | Yes | Property |
| 18. | Aboitiz Equity Ventures | 27.6 | 0.5 | No | Yes | Holding Firms |
| 19. | SM Investments | 25.0 | 0.4 | No | Yes | Holding Firms |
| 20. | Philippine National Bank | 22.9 | 0.4 | No | Yes | Banking |
| 21. | Maynilad | 18.5 | 0.3 | No | No | Water |
| 22. | Doubledragon | 15.0 | 0.3 | No | Yes | Property |
| 23. | San Miguel Food and Beverage | 15.0 | 0.3 | No | Yes | Food and Beverage |
| 24. | Philippine Savings Bank | 12.7 | 0.2 | No | Yes | Banking |
| 25. | Bank of Commerce | 12.5 | 0.2 | No | Yes | Banking |
| 26. | Megaworld | 12.0 | 0.2 | No | Yes | Property |
| 27. | Puregold | 12.0 | 0.2 | No | Yes | Whole and Retail Trading |
| 28. | Metro Pacific Investments | 11.4 | 0.2 | No | Yes | Holding Firms |
| 29. | GT Capital | 10.1 | 0.2 | No | Yes | Holding Firms |
| 30. | ACEN Corp | 10.0 | 0.2 | No | Yes | Electric |
| | **Total Top 30 LCY Corporate Issuers** | **1,278.3** | **21.8** | | | |
| | **Total LCY Corporate Bonds** | **1,427.4** | **24.3** | | | |
| | **Top 30 as % of Total LCY Corporate Bonds** | **89.6%** | **89.6%** | | | |

LCY = local currency, PHP = Philippine peso, USD = United States dollar.
Notes:
1.   Data as of 30 September 2022.
2.   State-owned firms are defined as those in which the government has more than a 50% ownership stake.
Source: *AsianBondsOnline* calculations based on Bloomberg LP data.

## Table 3: Notable Local Currency Corporate Bond Issuances in the Third Quarter of 2022

| Corporate Issuers | Coupon Rate (%) | Issued Amount (PHP billion) |
|---|---|---|
| SMC Global Power | | |
| 3-year bond | 5.91 | 5.00 |
| 5.8-year bond | 7.11 | 25.00 |
| 10-year bond | 8.03 | 10.00 |
| Ayala Land Inc. | | |
| 2-year bond | 4.40 | 12.00 |
| 5-year bond | 6.21 | 7.00 |
| 7-year bond | 6.80 | 14.00 |
| Security Bank | | |
| 1.5-year bond | 3.74 | 16.00 |
| Robinsons Land | | |
| 3-year bond | 5.38 | 6.00 |
| 5-year bond | 5.94 | 9.00 |
| Bank of Commerce | | |
| 2-year bond | 5.03 | 7.50 |
| Megawide Construction | | |
| 3.5-year bond | 6.95 | 1.60 |
| 5-year bond | 7.97 | 2.40 |
| ACEN Corp | | |
| 5-year bond | 6.05 | 10.00 |

PHP = Philippine peso.
Source: Based on data from Bloomberg LP.

# Policy, Institutional, and Regulatory Developments

## Bureau of the Treasury Releases Borrowing Program for October 2022

The Bureau of the Treasury intends to borrow PHP200 billion from local creditors in October by offering PHP60 billion worth of Treasury bills and PHP140 billion worth of Treasury bonds with tenors of 3, 6, 10, and 13 years. The borrowing program for October is the same as September's planned borrowing, which the Bureau of the Treasury failed to meet due to investors' demand for higher yield in anticipation of a continued rise in interest rates. However, the government remains confident that funding requirements for its various programs remain adequate against current market circumstances.

## Government of the Philippines Taps the Global Bond Market a Third Time in 2022, Sells 25-Year Sustainable Bonds

In October, the Government of the Philippines tapped the global bond market for the third time this year, successfully raising a total of USD2 billion from a

## Figure 3: Local Currency Government Bonds Investor Profile

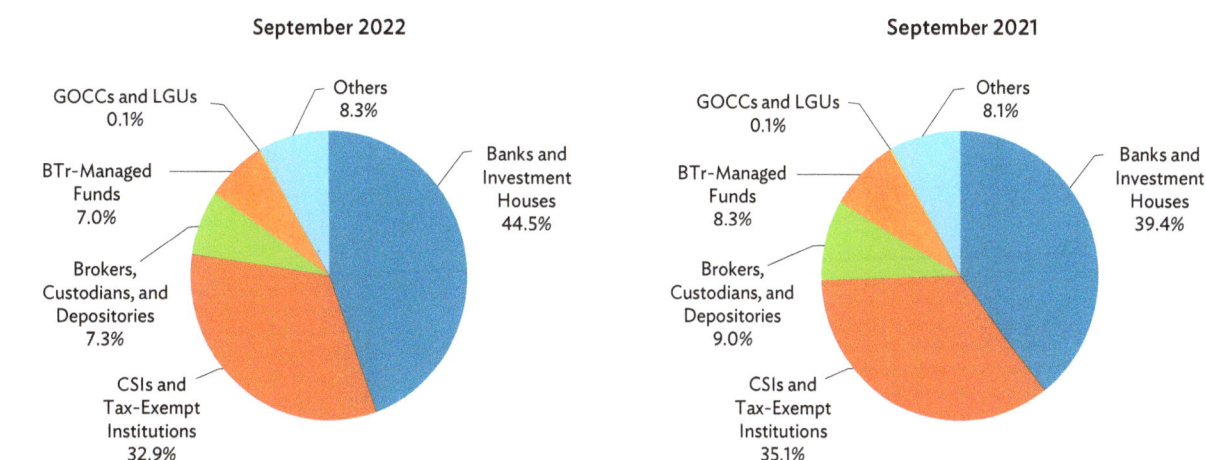

**September 2022**

- GOCCs and LGUs 0.1%
- Others 8.3%
- Banks and Investment Houses 44.5%
- BTr-Managed Funds 7.0%
- Brokers, Custodians, and Depositories 7.3%
- CSIs and Tax-Exempt Institutions 32.9%

**September 2021**

- GOCCs and LGUs 0.1%
- Others 8.1%
- Banks and Investment Houses 39.4%
- BTr-Managed Funds 8.3%
- Brokers, Custodians, and Depositories 9.0%
- CSIs and Tax-Exempt Institutions 35.1%

BTr = Bureau of the Treasury, CSI = contractual savings institution, GOCC = government-owned or -controlled corporation, LGU = local government unit.
Source: Bureau of the Treasury.

triple-tranche bond deal comprising a USD500 million 5-year bond, USD750 million 10.5-year bond, and USD750 million 25-year green bond. The total amount raised was a little less than the USD2.3 billion collected in the previous issuance in March, but the bonds carry higher interest rates. The new 5- and 10.5-year tranches were priced at 5.170% and 5.609%, respectively, and proceeds will be used for the government's budget financing. The 25-year tranche was priced at 6.10%, bearing a coupon of 5.95%, and was issued under the Sustainable Finance Framework of the Philippines, which marked the economy's third environmental, social, and governance G3 currency bond offering.

# Singapore

## Yield Movements

Between 31 August and 14 October, Singapore's local currency (LCY) government bond yield curve rose for all tenors (**Figure 1**). Government securities with short-term tenors (from 3 months to 1 year) soared 76 basis points (bps) on average. The belly of the curve (2 years to 15 years) increased 50 bps, while longer-term tenors (20 years and 30 years) jumped 18 bps. The yield spread between 10-year and 2-year government bonds marginally increased from 19.8 bps to 20.0 bps during the review period.

Yields increased as the Monetary Authority of Singapore (MAS) tightened its monetary policy in October to combat persistent inflationary pressure. The movement of the curve largely tracked the yield curve movements of United States (US) Treasuries, which rose for all tenors amid continued rate hikes by the US Federal Reserve.

On 14 October, the MAS decided to tighten its monetary policy for the fifth straight time since October 2021, moving the center of the Singapore dollar nominal effective exchange rate policy band to its prevailing level as the Singapore dollar had appreciated against the US dollar since July. The slope and width of the central bank's policy rate band was kept unchanged. This was the third time the center of the policy band was recentered following similar actions taken in April and July. The measure seeks to temper the impact of inflationary pressure in succeeding quarters.

Elevated prices for basic goods and services in Singapore were recorded in the third quarter (Q3) of 2022. Consumer price inflation in July was 7.0% year-on-year (y-o-y) before accelerating to 7.5% y-o-y in both August and September. In the first 9 months of 2022, the average inflation rate was 5.9% y-o-y, falling within the MAS full-year 2022 inflation forecast of around 6.0%.

Advance estimates showed that Singapore's gross domestic product jumped 4.4% y-o-y in Q3 2022, decelerating from the 4.5% y-o-y increase recorded in the previous quarter. The slower expansion was due to the lower growth logged in the manufacturing sector. Average economic growth in the first 3 quarters of 2022

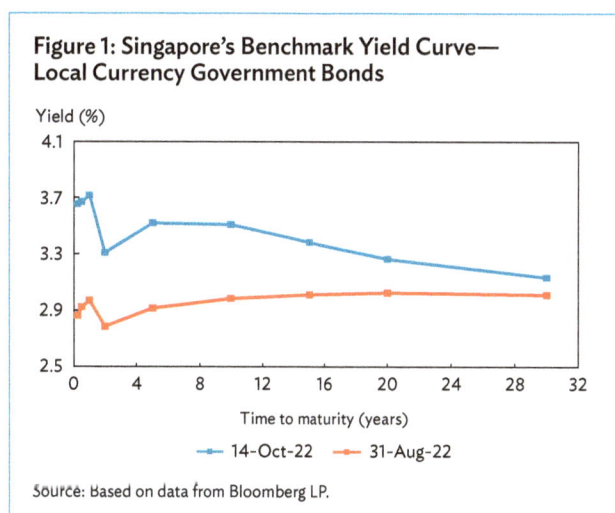

**Figure 1: Singapore's Benchmark Yield Curve—Local Currency Government Bonds**

Source: Based on data from Bloomberg LP.

was 4.2% y-o-y, which was above the Ministry of Trade and Industry's projection of 3.0%–4.0% for Singapore's 2022 annual economic growth. However, the MAS also projected the economy would grow at a slower pace in 2023.

## Size and Composition

The LCY bond market of Singapore expanded 3.5% quarter-on-quarter (q-o-q) in Q3 2022, totaling SGD666.4 billion (USD464.3 billion) at the end of Q3 2022 and slightly accelerating from the 3.0% q-o-q gain in the second quarter (Q2) of 2022 (**Table 1**). On an annual basis, Singapore's bonds outstanding rose 14.1% y-o-y at the end of September, decelerating from the 17.3% y-o-y surge logged in the previous quarter. Singapore's bond market expansion was driven by growth in the government bond segment, which comprised 70.4% of total outstanding LCY bonds at the end of Q3 2022.

LCY bonds issued in Q3 2022 climbed 14.4% q-o-q, spurred by increased issuance of government bonds and extending the 16.1% q-o-q uptick logged in Q2 2022.

**Government bonds.** Outstanding LCY government bonds grew 5.1% q-o-q in Q3 2022, accelerating from the 3.8% q-o-q growth registered in the prior quarter. Outstanding Treasury fixed-income securities, which comprised 48.9% of Singapore's total outstanding

**Table 1: Size and Composition of the Local Currency Bond Market in Singapore**

| | Outstanding Amount (billion) | | | | | | Growth Rate (%) | | | |
| | Q3 2021 | | Q2 2022 | | Q3 2022 | | Q3 2021 | | Q3 2022 | |
| | SGD | USD | SGD | USD | SGD | USD | q-o-q | y-o-y | q-o-q | y-o-y |
|---|---|---|---|---|---|---|---|---|---|---|
| Total | 584 | 430 | 644 | 463 | 666 | 464 | 6.4 | 21.6 | 3.5 | 14.1 |
| Government | 395 | 291 | 446 | 321 | 469 | 327 | 8.0 | 26.3 | 5.1 | 18.6 |
| SGS Bills and Bonds | 216 | 159 | 226 | 163 | 230 | 160 | 4.3 | 12.7 | 1.4 | 6.5 |
| MAS Bills | 180 | 132 | 220 | 158 | 240 | 167 | 12.9 | 47.7 | 8.8 | 33.2 |
| Corporate | 189 | 139 | 198 | 142 | 197 | 138 | 3.0 | 12.8 | (0.03) | 4.7 |

( ) = negative, MAS = Monetary Authority of Singapore, q-o-q = quarter-on-quarter, Q2 = second quarter, Q3 = third quarter, SGD = Singapore dollar, SGS = Singapore Government Securities, USD = United States dollar, y-o-y = year-on-year.
Notes:
1.  Corporate bonds are based on *AsianBondsOnline* estimates.
2.  SGS bills and bonds do not include the special issue of SGS held by the Singapore Central Provident Fund.
3.  Bloomberg LP end-of-period local currency–USD rates are used.
4.  Growth rates are calculated from local currency base and do not include currency effects.
Sources: Bloomberg LP, Monetary Authority of Singapore, and Singapore Government Securities.

government bonds at the end of the quarter, rose 1.4% q-o-q. Central bank bills, which comprised the other 51.1%, expanded 8.8% q-o-q.

Issuance of LCY government bonds expanded 15.0% q-o-q during Q3 2022, slower than the 15.2% q-o-q expansion registered in Q2 2022. The amount of MAS securities and Singapore Government Securities issued during the quarter grew 17.1% q-o-q and 0.5% q-o-q, respectively. In August, Singapore's first sovereign green bond worth SGD2.4 billion was issued. With a tenor of 50 years, the issuance also extended the LCY government bond yield curve of Singapore.

**Corporate bonds.** Outstanding LCY corporate bonds showed a marginal decline of 0.03% q-o-q at the end of September. This was a reversal from the expansion of 1.4% q-o-q logged at the end of June.

The 30 largest issuers of LCY corporate bonds in Singapore had aggregate outstanding bonds worth SGD107.4 billion, or 54.4% of the total LCY corporate bond market, at the end of September (**Table 2**). The Housing & Development Board, a state-owned corporation, continued to be the biggest issuer in Q3 2022 with SGD28.0 billion of corporate bonds outstanding. By sector, real estate companies (40.3%) had the largest share with SGD43.2 billion of the total at the end of the review period.

LCY corporate bonds issued in Q3 2022 dropped 25.2% q-o-q, a reversal from the 113.0% q-o-q expansion logged in the previous quarter. Many companies chose not to raise funds through a bond issuance due to the high-interest-rate environment brought about by the monetary policy tightening of Singapore's central bank, which was meant to combat inflationary pressure in the economy.

In Q3 2022, the state-owned Housing & Development Board raised a total of SGD2.1 billion from the issuance of 5-year and 7-year bonds with coupon rates of 2.940% and 3.437%, respectively (**Table 3**). The 5-year tenor was the largest LCY corporate issuance in Singapore in Q3 2022. It was also a green bond with proceeds to be used to fund the statutory board's green building projects. The state-owned Public Utilities Board issued a green bond with the longest nonperpetual tenor in Singapore: a 30-year bond worth SGD800.0 million. Proceeds from the bond will be used to finance projects under the company's Green Financing Framework. United Overseas Bank raised SGD400.0 million through a floating-rate perpetual bond. Funds raised will be considered as tier 1 capital of the bank, as required by the MAS. Toward the end of August, real estate company Perennial Holdings sold a 2-year bond worth SGD44.3 million and with a periodic distribution rate of 6.5%. This was the highest coupon rate of any LCY corporate bond issuance in Singapore during Q3 2022.

**Table 2: Top 30 Issuers of Local Currency Corporate Bonds in Singapore**

| | Issuers | Outstanding Amount | | State-Owned | Listed Company | Type of Industry |
|---|---|---|---|---|---|---|
| | | LCY Bonds (SGD billion) | LCY Bonds (USD billion) | | | |
| 1. | Housing & Development Board | 28.0 | 19.5 | Yes | No | Real Estate |
| 2. | Singapore Airlines | 14.7 | 10.3 | Yes | Yes | Transportation |
| 3. | Land Transport Authority | 8.9 | 6.2 | Yes | No | Transportation |
| 4. | Temasek Financial | 5.1 | 3.6 | Yes | No | Finance |
| 5. | CapitaLand | 4.6 | 3.2 | Yes | Yes | Real Estate |
| 6. | United Overseas Bank | 4.4 | 3.1 | No | Yes | Banking |
| 7. | Sembcorp Industries | 4.1 | 2.9 | No | Yes | Diversified |
| 8. | Frasers Property | 3.8 | 2.7 | No | Yes | Real Estate |
| 9. | Mapletree Treasury Services | 3.3 | 2.3 | No | No | Finance |
| 10. | DBS Bank | 2.9 | 2.0 | No | Yes | Banking |
| 11. | Oversea-Chinese Banking Corporation | 2.2 | 1.5 | No | Yes | Banking |
| 12. | Keppel Corporation | 2.2 | 1.5 | No | Yes | Diversified |
| 13. | CapitaLand Mall Trust | 2.0 | 1.4 | No | No | Finance |
| 14. | City Developments Limited | 2.0 | 1.4 | No | Yes | Real Estate |
| 15. | Singapore Technologies Telemedia | 1.7 | 1.2 | Yes | No | Utilities |
| 16. | National Environment Agency | 1.7 | 1.1 | Yes | No | Environmental Services |
| 17. | Shangri-La Hotel | 1.5 | 1.0 | No | Yes | Real Estate |
| 18. | Public Utilities Board | 1.4 | 1.0 | Yes | No | Utilities |
| 19. | Ascendas Real Estate Investment Trust | 1.3 | 0.9 | No | Yes | Finance |
| 20. | PSA Treasury | 1.3 | 0.9 | Yes | No | Transportation |
| 21. | Singtel Group Treasury | 1.3 | 0.9 | No | No | Finance |
| 22. | Ascott Residence | 1.2 | 0.8 | No | Yes | Real Estate |
| 23. | Suntec Real Estate Investment Trust | 1.1 | 0.8 | No | Yes | Real Estate |
| 24. | Olam International | 1.1 | 0.8 | No | Yes | Consumer Goods |
| 25. | GuocoLand Limited IHT | 1.1 | 0.7 | No | No | Real Estate |
| 26. | Keppel Infrastructure Trust | 1.1 | 0.7 | No | No | Diversified |
| 27. | Olam Group | 1.0 | 0.7 | No | Yes | Consumer Goods |
| 28. | Singapore Press Holdings | 1.0 | 0.7 | No | Yes | Communications |
| 29. | Singapore Post | 1.0 | 0.7 | No | Yes | Transportation |
| 30. | Hyflux | 0.9 | 0.6 | No | Yes | Utilities |
| | **Total Top 30 LCY Corporate Issuers** | **107.4** | **74.8** | | | |
| | **Total LCY Corporate Bonds** | **197.4** | **137.6** | | | |
| | **Top 30 as % of Total LCY Corporate Bonds** | **54.4%** | **54.4%** | | | |

LCY = local currency, SGD = Singapore dollar, USD = United States dollar.
Notes:
1. Data as of 30 September 2022.
2. State-owned firms are defined as those in which the government has more than a 50% ownership stake.
Source: *AsianBondsOnline* calculations based on Bloomberg LP data.

**Table 3: Notable Local Currency Corporate Bond Issuances in the Third Quarter of 2022**

| Corporate Issuers | Coupon Rate (%) | Issued Amount (SGD million) |
|---|---|---|
| Housing & Development Board | | |
| 5-year bond | 2.940 | 1,100.0 |
| 7-year bond | 3.437 | 1,000.0 |
| Public Utilities Board | | |
| 30-year bond | 3.433 | 800.0 |
| United Overseas Bank | | |
| Perpetual bond | Floating | 400.0 |
| Perennial Holdings | | |
| 2-year bond | 6.500 | 44.3 |

SGD = Singapore dollar.
Source: Bloomberg LP.

# Policy, Institutional, and Regulatory Developments

## Monetary Authority of Singapore Lays Out Vision for 2025

On 15 September, the MAS launched its Financial Services Industry Transformation Map 2025, which details Singapore's plans to be the chief financial center in the region. Under its key strategy of digitalizing financial infrastructure, the MAS aims to develop its bond market infrastructure by making the processes for listing, issuance, and settlement more efficient. This will allow investors to choose Singapore as their preferred destination for bond listing and issuance.

# Thailand

## Yield Movements

Between 31 August and 14 October, yields for Thailand's local currency (LCY) government bonds rose across all tenors, shifting the yield curve upward (**Figure 1**). The rise in yields was most pronounced along the belly of the curve, with yields for bonds with maturities from 3 years to 10 years posting an average gain of 64 basis points (bps). Meanwhile, yields for bonds with maturities of less than 3 years rose 27 bps on average, while bonds with maturities longer than 10 years registered an average yield increase of 49 bps. The 2-year yield rose 30 bps, while the 10-year yield jumped 73 bps. As a result, the spread between the 10-year and 2-year yields widened from 89 bps on 31 August to 132 bps on 14 October.

The rise in Thai LCY government bond yields followed a global trend of rising sovereign bond yields in response to aggressive monetary policy tightening by the United States (US) Federal Reserve. Domestic factors—particularly monetary policy normalization by the Bank of Thailand (BOT), elevated inflation, and a stable bond supply in the near-term—also contributed to the rise in Thai bond yields.

The BOT increased its benchmark policy rate by 25 bps to 0.75% on 10 August, and by another 25 bps to 1.00% on 28 September, noting that monetary policy normalization would be gradual to support sustainable economic recovery. The rise in the policy rate pushed up bond yields, as market participants priced in expected rate hikes in the future.

Thailand's consumer price inflation eased to 6.0% year-on-year (y-o-y) in October from 6.4% y-o-y in September and 7.9% y-o-y in August, but remained among the highest in emerging East Asia. The BOT expects inflation for full-year 2022 to reach 6.3% y-o-y before declining to 2.6% y-o-y in 2023 as global oil prices and supply chain bottlenecks ease.

On 27 September, the Thai government approved the public debt management plan for fiscal year 2023, which covers the period from October 2022 to September 2023. The borrowing plan included a maximum bond issuance amount of THB273.0 billion in October–December 2022 and a total of THB1.05 trillion of government debt

**Figure 1: Thailand's Benchmark Yield Curve— Local Currency Government Bonds**

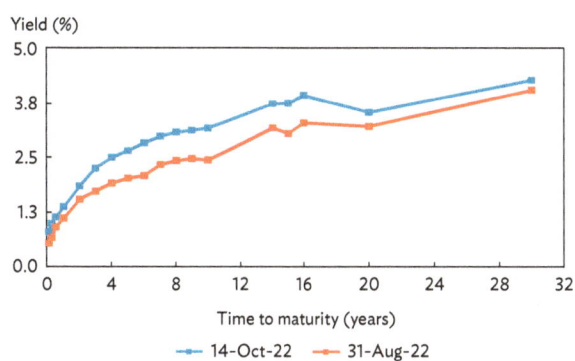

Sources: Based on data from Bloomberg LP.

issuance for fiscal year 2023. The announcement of the new borrowing plan assured an ample supply of LCY bonds in the near-term, which contributed to the decline in bond prices and the rise in yields.

The Thai economy continued to recover, with gross domestic product (GDP) growth accelerating to 4.5% y-o-y in the third quarter (Q3) of 2022 from 2.5% y-o-y in the second quarter (Q2) 2.2% y-o-y in the first quarter. The return of tourists amid the relaxation of travel restrictions continued to underpin Thailand's economic recovery. The National Economic and Social Development Council expects the Thai economy to expand at a rate of 3.2% in 2022 and within a range of 3.0% to 4.0% y-o-y in 2023 on the back of the continued tourism revival and private consumption growth.

The Thai baht depreciated 4.3% against the US dollar between 31 August and 14 October, trading at THB38.01 to USD1.0 on 14 October. From 1 January to 14 October, the Thai baht depreciated 12.3% against the US dollar, in line with the weakening of regional currencies against the US dollar amid continued monetary policy tightening by the US Federal Reserve.

## Size and Composition

The outstanding stock of LCY bonds in Thailand totaled THB15,494.7 billion (USD410.7 billion) at the end of September (**Table 1**). Quarterly growth accelerated

**Table 1: Size and Composition of the Local Currency Bond Market in Thailand**

| | Outstanding Amount (billion) | | | | | | Growth Rate (%) | | | |
| | Q3 2021 | | Q2 2022 | | Q3 2022 | | Q3 2021 | | Q3 2022 | |
| | THB | USD | THB | USD | THB | USD | q-o-q | y-o-y | q-o-q | y-o-y |
|---|---|---|---|---|---|---|---|---|---|---|
| Total | 14,563 | 430 | 15,108 | 427 | 15,495 | 411 | 2.5 | 3.9 | 2.6 | 6.4 |
| Government | 10,552 | 312 | 10,860 | 307 | 11,105 | 294 | 2.2 | 2.8 | 2.3 | 5.2 |
| Government Bonds and Treasury Bills | 6,683 | 198 | 7,327 | 207 | 7,603 | 201 | 3.1 | 16.5 | 3.8 | 13.8 |
| Central Bank Bonds | 2,926 | 86 | 2,571 | 73 | 2,522 | 67 | 0.3 | (21.0) | (1.9) | (13.8) |
| State-Owned Enterprise and Other Bonds | 943 | 28 | 962 | 27 | 980 | 26 | 2.4 | 14.5 | 1.9 | 4.0 |
| Corporate | 4,011 | 119 | 4,247 | 120 | 4,390 | 116 | 3.4 | 6.7 | 3.4 | 9.5 |

( ) = negative, q-o-q = quarter-on-quarter, Q2 = second quarter, Q3 = third quarter, THB = Thai baht, USD = United States dollar, y-o-y = year-on-year.
Notes:
1. Calculated using data from national sources.
2. Bloomberg LP end-of-period local currency–USD rates are used.
3. Growth rates are calculated from local currency base and do not include currency effects.
Source: Bank of Thailand.

to 2.6% in Q3 2022 from 0.7% in Q2 2022. The faster growth was driven by a rebound in the government bond segment, which outpaced the slowdown in the corporate bond segment. On an annual basis, Thailand's outstanding stock of LCY bonds rose 6.4% y-o-y in Q3 2022, the same rate of growth recorded in the prior quarter. Thailand's LCY bond market continued to be dominated by government bonds. At the end of September, government bonds accounted for 71.7% of the total LCY bond market, while corporate bonds comprised the remaining 28.3%.

**Government bonds.** The stock of outstanding LCY government bonds amounted to THB11,104.8 billion at the end of September. The government bond market expanded 2.3% q-o-q in Q3 2022, reversing the 0.7% q-o-q contraction in the previous quarter. Growth was driven by expansions in government bonds and Treasury bills (3.8% q-o-q) and state-owned enterprise and other bonds (1.9% q-o-q). Meanwhile, the stock of outstanding BOT bonds continued to decline, dropping 1.9% q-o-q in Q3 2022 after recording a contraction of 8.9% q-o-q in Q2 2022. On a y-o-y basis, Thailand's LCY government bonds outstanding rose 5.2% in Q3 2022, the same rate of expansion posted in the previous quarter.

Outstanding government bonds and Treasury bills reached THB7,602.6 billion at the end of September, accounting for 68.5% of the Thai LCY government bond market. Outstanding BOT bonds (THB2,521.9 billion) and state-owned enterprise and other bonds (THB980.3 billion) comprised 22.7% and 8.8%, respectively, of the total government bond stock at the end of September.

Issuance of new LCY government bonds totaled THB1,654.4 billion in Q3 2022. Issuance expanded 5.2% q-o-q, reversing the 5.9% q-o-q decline in Q2 2022. Growth in issuance was mainly driven by a rebound in BOT bond issuance. Meanwhile, issuance of government bonds and Treasury bills, as well as state-owned enterprise and other bonds, recorded contractions in Q3 2022, as the central government and state-owned agencies had already frontloaded borrowing during the first half of the year. On an annual basis, government bond issuance continued to decline, falling 11.3% y-o-y in Q3 2022 after a 9.1% y-o-y drop in the previous quarter. The government continued to ease coronavirus disease (COVID-19)-related borrowing as economic recovery gained ground with the revival of tourism.

The Thai government issued its second sustainability bond in Q3 2022—a 14-year and 9-month bond amounting to THB35.0 billion. The original target size for the sustainability bond was THB20.0 billion, but the government upsized the issuance in response to high demand. Proceeds from the bond will be used to fund the government's measures for COVID-19 relief as well as capital expenditures for agricultural water resources development and management.

**Corporate bonds.** Thailand's LCY corporate bond market expanded 3.4% q-o-q and 9.5% y-o-y in Q3 2022 to reach a size of THB4,389.8 billion at the end of September. Growth eased from 4.6% q-o-q and 9.5% y-o-y in the previous quarter due to maturities and a contraction in issuance.

At the end of September, the outstanding stock of LCY bonds of Thailand's top 30 issuers amounted to THB2,500.2 billion, comprising 57.0% of the Thai LCY corporate bond market (**Table 2**). CP ALL, True Corporation, and PTT remained the top three corporate issuers with an outstanding bond stock of THB241.1 billion, THB177.1 billion, and THB158.4 billion, respectively. The top 30 corporate issuers were predominantly firms in the energy and utilities, commerce, and communication sectors. The total outstanding

**Table 2: Top 30 Issuers of Local Currency Corporate Bonds in Thailand**

| | Issuers | Outstanding Amount | | State-Owned | Listed Company | Type of Industry |
|---|---|---|---|---|---|---|
| | | LCY Bonds (THB billion) | LCY Bonds (USD billion) | | | |
| 1. | CP ALL | 241.1 | 6.4 | No | Yes | Commerce |
| 2. | True Corporation | 177.1 | 4.7 | No | Yes | Communications |
| 3. | PTT | 158.4 | 4.2 | Yes | Yes | Energy and Utilities |
| 4. | Siam Cement | 135.0 | 3.6 | Yes | Yes | Construction Materials |
| 5. | Charoen Pokphand Foods | 131.5 | 3.5 | No | Yes | Food and Beverage |
| 6. | Thai Beverage | 129.2 | 3.4 | No | No | Food and Beverage |
| 7. | Berli Jucker | 107.4 | 2.8 | No | Yes | Commerce |
| 8. | Gulf Energy Development | 104.5 | 2.8 | No | Yes | Energy and Utilities |
| 9. | True Move H Universal Communication | 97.1 | 2.6 | No | No | Communications |
| 10. | CPF Thailand | 89.2 | 2.4 | No | No | Food and Beverage |
| 11. | PTT Global Chemical | 86.7 | 2.3 | No | Yes | Petrochemicals and Chemicals |
| 12. | Indorama Ventures | 80.6 | 2.1 | No | Yes | Petrochemicals and Chemicals |
| 13. | Banpu | 79.4 | 2.1 | No | Yes | Energy and Utilities |
| 14. | Bangkok Commercial Asset Management | 68.6 | 1.8 | No | Yes | Finance and Securities |
| 15. | Bank of Ayudhya | 68.4 | 1.8 | No | Yes | Banking |
| 16. | Minor International | 62.4 | 1.7 | No | Yes | Hospitality and Leisure |
| 17. | Krung Thai Bank | 62.1 | 1.6 | Yes | Yes | Banking |
| 18. | Muangthai Capital | 60.9 | 1.6 | No | Yes | Finance and Securities |
| 19. | Toyota Leasing Thailand | 56.7 | 1.5 | No | No | Finance and Securities |
| 20. | BTS Group Holdings | 54.8 | 1.5 | No | Yes | Transportation and Logistics |
| 21. | Global Power Synergy | 53.5 | 1.4 | No | Yes | Energy and Utilities |
| 22. | dtac TriNet | 50.4 | 1.3 | No | Yes | Communications |
| 23. | Bangchak | 46.5 | 1.2 | No | Yes | Energy and Utilities |
| 24. | Magnolia Quality Development | 45.6 | 1.2 | No | No | Property Development |
| 25. | Krungthai Card | 45.4 | 1.2 | No | Yes | Finance and Securities |
| 26. | Sansiri | 45.4 | 1.2 | No | Yes | Property Development |
| 27. | TPI Polene | 42.7 | 1.1 | No | Yes | Construction Materials |
| 28. | Bangkok Expressway & Metro | 41.6 | 1.1 | No | Yes | Transportation and Logistics |
| 29. | B Grimm Power | 40.7 | 1.1 | No | Yes | Energy and Utilities |
| 30. | Land & Houses | 37.8 | 1.0 | No | Yes | Property Development |
| | **Total Top 30 LCY Corporate Issuers** | **2,500.2** | **66.3** | | | |
| | **Total LCY Corporate Bonds** | **4,389.8** | **116.3** | | | |
| | **Top 30 as % of Total LCY Corporate Bonds** | **57.0%** | **57.0%** | | | |

LCY = local currency, THB = Thai baht, USD = United States dollar.
Notes:
1. Data as of 30 September 2022.
2. State-owned firms are defined as those in which the government has more than a 50% ownership stake.
Source: *AsianBondsOnline* calculations based on Bloomberg LP data.

bond stock of the energy and utilities firms among the top 30 list comprised 11.3% of the total LCY corporate bond market. A majority of the top 30 were listed on the Stock Exchange of Thailand, while only three were state-owned firms.

Issuance of new corporate debt totaled THB556.8 billion in Q3 2022. Corporate debt issuance declined 6.9% q-o-q amid rising borrowing costs as the Bank of Thailand raised its policy rate twice during the review period. To rein in record-high inflation, the BOT raised its benchmark rate by 25 bps in August and by another 25 bps in September.

A total of 83 companies tapped the LCY bond market for their financing needs in Q3 2022. Notable issuers in Q3 2022 are listed in **Table 3**. Gulf Energy was the top issuer during the review period, raising a total of THB35.0 billion from seven tranches, including the

single largest issue in Q3 2022—a 4-year bond worth THB15.9 billion. SCG Chemicals was the next largest issuer, with total issuance of THB30.0 billion from a quintuple-tranche bond with maturities ranging from 3 years to 12 years. True Corporation raised a total of THB17.0 billion from bonds with maturities ranging from 1 year to 5 years. Three companies issued perpetual bonds during the quarter. Minor International, Siam Piwat, and Dusit Thani issued perpetual bonds amounting to THB13.0 billion, THB4.0 billion, and THB1.5 billion, respectively.

## Investor Profiles

**Central government bonds.** Financial corporations, other depository corporations, the central government, and nonresidents were the primary holders of government bonds at the end of September 2022 (**Figure 2**). These four investor groups collectively held 86.9% of Thai government bonds outstanding at the end of the review period. Financial corporations held the highest share of government bonds at 36.1%, down from 38.1% a year earlier. The share of other depository corporations, which include commercial banks and finance companies, was little changed at 23.4% at the end of September from 23.2% a year prior. The central government, including state-owned nonprofit enterprises and the Social Security Office, had a 14.8% share at the end of September, while nonresidents' holdings of Thai government bonds slid to 12.7% from 13.4% a year earlier.

**Central bank bonds.** Other depository corporations and financial corporations remained the primary holders of BOT bonds, with combined holdings amounting to 78.2% of BOT bonds outstanding at the end of September (**Figure 3**). The share of other depository corporations increased to 45.9% at the end of September from 41.7% a year prior. Meanwhile, financial corporations' holdings rose to 32.3% at the end of September from 30.6% a year earlier. The BOT's holdings of its own bonds slipped to 10.3% from 13.6% during the same period. Nonresidents' holdings of BOT bonds remained negligible at 0.2% at the end of September, down from 0.3% at year earlier.

In Q3 2022, the Thai LCY bond market recorded net outflows of THB0.7 billion from foreign investors (**Figure 4**). Capital flows in the Thai bond market were highly influenced by the Federal Reserve's rate hikes during the review period. The Thai bond market

**Table 3: Notable Local Currency Corporate Bond Issuances in the Third Quarter of 2022**

| Corporate Issuers | Coupon Rate (%) | Issued Amount (THB billion) |
|---|---|---|
| Gulf Energy[a] | | |
| 3-year bond | 3.26 | 7.0 |
| 4-year bond | 3.50 | 15.9 |
| 4-year bond | 3.50 | 2.2 |
| 5-year bond | 3.57 | 1.0 |
| 7-year bond | 3.90 | 5.1 |
| 7-year bond | 3.90 | 0.8 |
| 10-year bond | 4.31 | 3.0 |
| SCG Chemicals | | |
| 3-year bond | 2.77 | 10.2 |
| 5-year bond | 3.25 | 11.8 |
| 6-year bond | 3.39 | 1.8 |
| 10-year bond | 4.00 | 4.1 |
| 12-year bond | 4.14 | 2.1 |
| True Corporation | | |
| 1-year bond | 3.00 | 3.7 |
| 2-year bond | 3.25 | 0.6 |
| 3.3-year bond | 4.00 | 4.0 |
| 4-year bond | 4.25 | 1.7 |
| 5-year bond | 4.90 | 7.0 |
| Minor International | | |
| Perpetual bond | 6.10 | 13.0 |
| Siam Piwat | | |
| Perpetual bond | 5.50 | 4.0 |
| Dusit Thani | | |
| Perpetual bond | 8.00 | 1.5 |

THB = Thai baht.
[a] Multiple issuance of the same tenor indicates issuance on different dates.
Source: Bloomberg LP.

## Figure 2: Local Currency Government Bonds Investor Profile

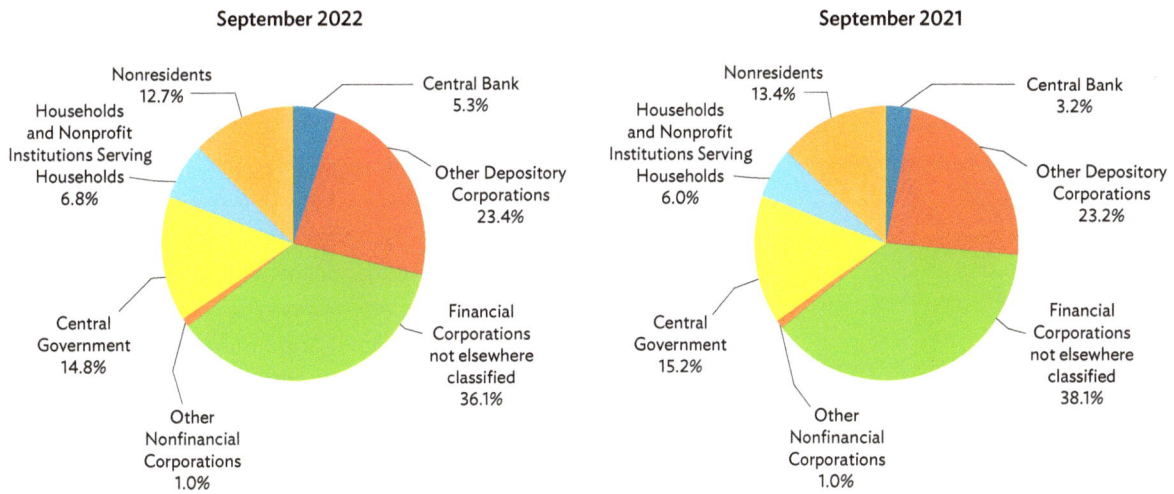

### September 2022

- Nonresidents 12.7%
- Households and Nonprofit Institutions Serving Households 6.8%
- Central Government 14.8%
- Other Nonfinancial Corporations 1.0%
- Financial Corporations not elsewhere classified 36.1%
- Other Depository Corporations 23.4%
- Central Bank 5.3%

### September 2021

- Nonresidents 13.4%
- Households and Nonprofit Institutions Serving Households 6.0%
- Central Government 15.2%
- Other Nonfinancial Corporations 1.0%
- Financial Corporations not elsewhere classified 38.1%
- Other Depository Corporations 23.2%
- Central Bank 3.2%

Note: Government bonds include Treasury bills and bonds.
Source: *AsianBondsOnline* and Bank of Thailand.

## Figure 3: Local Currency Central Bank Securities Investor Profile

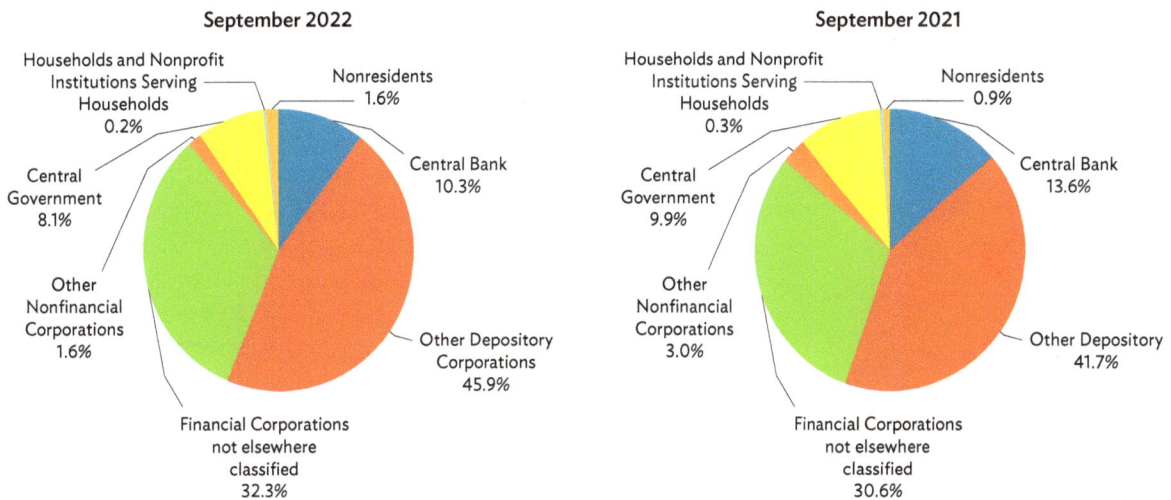

### September 2022

- Households and Nonprofit Institutions Serving Households 0.2%
- Nonresidents 1.6%
- Central Bank 10.3%
- Central Government 8.1%
- Other Nonfinancial Corporations 1.6%
- Financial Corporations not elsewhere classified 32.3%
- Other Depository Corporations 45.9%

### September 2021

- Households and Nonprofit Institutions Serving Households 0.3%
- Nonresidents 0.9%
- Central Bank 13.6%
- Central Government 9.9%
- Other Nonfinancial Corporations 3.0%
- Financial Corporations not elsewhere classified 30.6%
- Other Depository 41.7%

Source: Bank of Thailand.

**Figure 4: Foreign Investor Net Trading of Local Currency Bonds in Thailand**

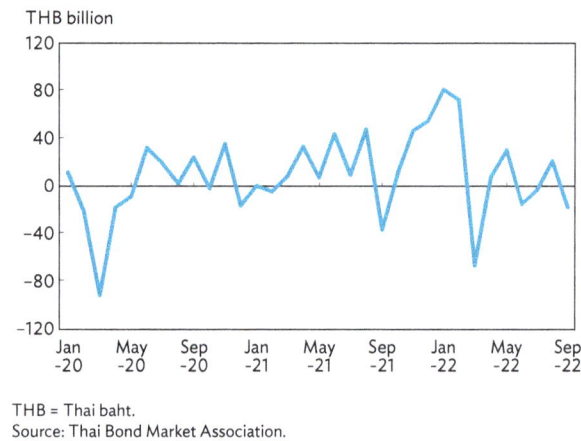

THB = Thai baht.
Source: Thai Bond Market Association.

recorded net outflows of THB3.6 billion in July, net inflows of THB20.8 billion in August, and net outflows of THB17.9 billion in September. The Federal Reserve's rate hikes in July and September increased the rate differential between Treasury and Thai sovereign bonds, resulting in net outflows from the Thai bond market.

# Policy and Regulatory Developments

## Thai Cabinet Approves Public Debt Management Plan for Fiscal Year 2023

On 27 September, the Thai cabinet approved the public debt management plan for fiscal year 2023, which started on 1 October. The plan puts the ceiling for government borrowing for fiscal year 2023 at THB1.05 trillion, of which THB820.0 billion was allotted for new central government debt to offset the annual budget deficit, manage liquidity in the Treasury, and invest in infrastructure projects. The remaining THB233.0 billion was allocated for new debt for state enterprises and other government agencies to finance investments in transport infrastructure, power transmission systems, and other general operations. Under the new plan, the ratio of public debt-to-GDP will reach 60.4% by the end of fiscal year 2023, which is within the public debt ceiling of 70.0% of GDP.

## Public Debt Management Offices Plans to Issue THB130.0 Billion of Government Savings Bonds in Fiscal Year 2023

On 12 October, the Public Debt Management Office (PDMO) announced that it plans to sell THB130.0 billion of government savings bonds in fiscal year 2023. The PDMO assessed that there is ample liquidity in the Thai bond market for government bond issuance. In fiscal year 2023, the PDMO will focus on issuing medium-term bonds with maturities of 10–20 years in response to high market demand for such tenors. The government plans to borrow up to THB30.0 billion from international lenders such as the Asian Development Bank and the Japan International Cooperation Agency, and it will not issue USD-denominated bonds unless necessary.

# Viet Nam

## Yield Movements

Between 31 August and 14 October, Viet Nam's local currency (LCY) government bond yields climbed across the curve, resulting in the yield curve shifting upward (**Figure 1**). Bond yields gained the most at the shorter-end, with the 1-year maturity rising 212 basis points (bps), and rose the least at the longer-end, with the 15-year bond gaining 132 bps. Yield upticks for the 2-year to 5-year maturities averaged 166 bps, while those for tenors of 7 years to 10 years climbed 143 bps on average. As yields rose more at the shorter-end than the longer-end, the yield curve flattened during the review period, leading the spread between the 10-year and 2-year bonds to narrow from 49 bps on 31 August to 20 bps on 14 October.

Viet Nam posted the largest upticks in both the 10-year and 2-year tenors among all emerging East Asian markets during the review period. Higher bond yields were largely driven by the surprise 100 bps rate hike by the State Bank of Vietnam (SBV) on 23 September. Subsequently, the SBV raised rates by another 100 bps on 25 October, lifting the refinancing rate to 6.0%. The rate hikes were taken to contain inflationary pressure and lead inflation below the government's target of 4.0% for 2022. Year-to-date consumer price inflation soared to 4.0% in September and climbed further to 4.2% in October. In addition, the rate hike also aimed to help stabilize the Vietnamese dong (VND) amid the broad strengthening of the United States (US) dollar due to the aggressive pace of monetary tightening by the Federal Reserve. Next to the Hong Kong dollar, the dong depreciated the least among regional currencies during the review period, weakening by only 2.8% against the US dollar.

Also contributing to the yield gains in Viet Nam was its strong economic performance thus far in 2022. Economic growth, as measured by real gross domestic product (GDP) accelerated to 13.7% year-on-year (y-o-y) in the third quarter (Q3) of 2022 after rising 7.7% y-o-y in the second quarter (Q2). GDP growth for Q3 2022 was buoyed by strong performances in manufacturing and exports, but was also due in part to a low-base effect from a year earlier. GDP growth in Q3 2022 was the second-fastest print among all regional markets that have released Q3 data at the time of writing. Since Q2 2022,

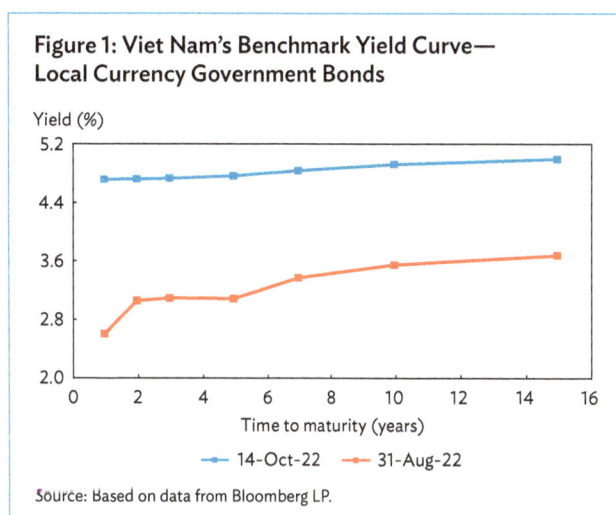

**Figure 1: Viet Nam's Benchmark Yield Curve—Local Currency Government Bonds**

Source: Based on data from Bloomberg LP.

Viet Nam's GDP growth has returned to pre-pandemic levels as economic activities rebounded. In the first 9 months of the year, GDP grew 8.8% y-o-y, the fastest pace since 2011, exceeding the revised 7.0% target by the Ministry of Planning and Investment for full-year 2022.

## Size and Composition

At the end of Q3 2022, Viet Nam's LCY bond market showed a marginal contraction of 0.2% quarter-on-quarter (q-o-q) to a size of VND2,323.5 trillion (USD97.4 billion), reversing the previous quarter's rapid growth of 8.0% q-o-q (**Table 1**). The decline was mainly due to a contraction in the government bond segment and a slowdown in the corporate bond segment. Compared with the same quarter in the previous year, Viet Nam's bond market grew 21.1% y-o-y in Q3 2022, slowing from the 31.4% y-o-y expansion in Q2 2022. At the end of September, government bonds remained prevalent in Viet Nam's LCY bond market, accounting for a 69.1% share of the total bond stock. The remaining 30.9% share was attributable to corporate bonds.

**Government bonds.** Viet Nam's LCY government bond market contracted 2.0% q-o-q to a size of VND1,604.9 trillion at the end of September. Much of the decline can be attributed to central bank bills, whose outstanding bond stock fell significantly by 70.3% q-o-q in Q3 2022. In contrast to the previous quarter's aggressive expansion, central bank bills displayed the largest decline

**Table 1: Size and Composition of the Local Currency Bond Market in Viet Nam**

| | Outstanding Amount (billion) | | | | | | Growth Rate (%) | | | |
| | Q3 2021 | | Q2 2022 | | Q3 2022 | | Q3 2021 | | Q3 2022 | |
| | VND | USD | VND | USD | VND | USD | q-o-q | y-o-y | q-o-q | y-o-y |
|---|---|---|---|---|---|---|---|---|---|---|
| Total | 1,919,434 | 84 | 2,327,764 | 100 | 2,323,523 | 97 | 8.3 | 23.7 | (0.2) | 21.1 |
| Government | 1,427,691 | 63 | 1,637,409 | 70 | 1,604,918 | 67 | 4.3 | 9.8 | (2.0) | 12.4 |
| Treasury Bonds | 1,284,678 | 56 | 1,392,934 | 60 | 1,434,693 | 60 | 4.5 | 11.0 | 3.0 | 11.7 |
| Central Bank Bills | 0 | 0 | 102,410 | 4 | 30,400 | 1 | – | – | (70.3) | – |
| Government-Guaranteed and Municipal Bonds | 143,014 | 6 | 142,066 | 6 | 139,826 | 6 | 2.3 | (0.3) | (1.6) | (2.2) |
| Corporate | 491,743 | 22 | 690,355 | 30 | 718,606 | 30 | 22.0 | 96.1 | 4.1 | 46.1 |

( ) = negative, – = not applicable, q-o-q = quarter-on-quarter, Q2 = second quarter, Q3 = third quarter, USD = United States dollar, VND = Vietnamese dong, y-o-y = year-on-year.
Notes:
1. Bloomberg LP end-of-period local currency–USD rates are used.
2. Growth rates are calculated from local currency base and do not include currency effects.
Sources: Bloomberg LP and Vietnam Bond Market Association.

among all bond segments during Q3 2022. At the end of September, the total stock of central bank bills slumped to VND30.4 trillion from VND102.4 trillion at the end of June. While issuance of central bank bills in Q3 2022 surged more than threefold, it had no significant impact on the outstanding stock due to the short-term nature of the bills' maturity profile.

At the end of September, Treasury bonds expanded to VND1,434.7 trillion in Q3 2022, continuing to dominate the government bond segment in Viet Nam. Growth picked up to 3.0% q-o-q in Q3 2022 from 0.8% q-o-q in Q2 2022 on increased issuance during the quarter. Treasury bond issuance rose 64.3% q-o-q to reach USD45.7 trillion in Q3 2022. Issuance of Treasury bonds was concentrated in long-term maturities, with 10-year bonds comprising 56.5% of the total issuance during the quarter. The remaining 43.5% share was accounted for by newly issued 15-year Treasury bonds.

In Q3 2022, the outstanding size of government-guaranteed and municipal bonds showed a slight drop of 1.6% q-o-q compared with the modest growth of 2.3% q-o-q in Q2 2022. The total size decreased to VND139.8 trillion at the end of September from VND142.1 trillion at the end of June, as issuance exceeded maturities. The sole issuance of government-guaranteed bonds during the quarter came from the Vietnam Bank for Social Policies' issuance of 3-year bonds amounting to VND500.0 billion.

**Corporate bonds.** Growth in the corporate bond segment moderated to 4.1% q-o-q in Q3 2022 from 9.5% q-o-q in Q2 2022. At the end of September, the total outstanding

corporate bond stock climbed to VND718.6 trillion and was mainly dominated by the banking and property industries, which collectively accounted for 75.3% of the aggregate corporate bond stock.

Viet Nam's top 30 corporate issuers largely comprised firms from the banking and property sectors, including a few finance and energy firms. The top 30 firms had an aggregate bond stock amounting to VND448.6 trillion at the end of September, which was equivalent to 62.4% of the total LCY corporate bond market (**Table 2**). The top corporate issuer remained the state-owned Bank for Investment and Development of Vietnam, with an outstanding bond stock of VND58.4 trillion at the end of Q3 2022, or the equivalent of 8.1% of the total corporate bond stock of Viet Nam.

In Q3 2022, bond issuance activities from the corporate segment slowed, with total debt sales amounting to VND48.5 trillion. This represented a contraction of 29.8% q-o-q in Q3 2022, reversing the strong 120.5% gain posted in the preceding quarter. Issuance was dragged down by the implementation of tighter regulations for the issuance and trading of private placement issues. The majority of corporate bonds in Viet Nam are issued via private placement.

The five largest corporate bond issuances in Q3 2022 are presented in **Table 3**, all of which were from banking institutions. Orient Commercial Joint Stock Bank was the top corporate issuer during the review period with aggregate issuance amounting to VND5.6 trillion in multiple tranches of 3-year bonds. The top issuer in the previous quarter, state-owned Bank for Investment and

**Table 2: Top 30 Issuers of Local Currency Corporate Bonds in Viet Nam**

| | Issuers | Outstanding Amount | | State-Owned | Listed Company | Type of Industry |
|---|---|---|---|---|---|---|
| | | LCY Bonds (VND billion) | LCY Bonds (USD billion) | | | |
| 1. | Bank for Investment and Development of Vietnam | 58,422 | 2.45 | Yes | Yes | Banking |
| 2. | Vietnam Prosperity Joint Stock Commercial Bank | 30,600 | 1.28 | No | Yes | Banking |
| 3. | Orient Commercial Joint Stock Bank | 29,535 | 1.24 | No | No | Banking |
| 4. | Vietnam International Joint Stock Commercial Bank | 28,950 | 1.21 | No | Yes | Banking |
| 5. | Asia Commercial Joint Stock Bank | 28,700 | 1.20 | No | Yes | Banking |
| 6. | Ho Chi Minh City Development Joint Stock Commercial Bank | 28,182 | 1.18 | No | Yes | Banking |
| 7. | Lien Viet Post Joint Stock Commercial Bank | 25,090 | 1.05 | No | Yes | Banking |
| 8. | Masan Group | 18,800 | 0.79 | No | Yes | Finance |
| 9. | Military Commercial Joint Stock Bank | 18,646 | 0.78 | No | Yes | Banking |
| 10. | Tien Phong Commercial Joint Stock Bank | 17,949 | 0.75 | No | Yes | Banking |
| 11. | Vietnam Joint Stock Commercial Bank for Industry and Trade | 17,509 | 0.74 | Yes | Yes | Banking |
| 12. | Vietnam Technological and Commercial Joint Stock Bank | 14,600 | 0.61 | No | Yes | Banking |
| 13. | An Binh Commercial Joint Stock Bank | 11,300 | 0.47 | No | No | Banking |
| 14. | NoVa Real Estate Investment Corporation JSC | 10,981 | 0.46 | No | Yes | Property |
| 15. | Saigon - Ha Noi Commercial Joint Stock Bank | 10,150 | 0.43 | No | Yes | Banking |
| 16. | Vinhomes JSC | 9,935 | 0.42 | No | Yes | Property |
| 17. | Vietnam Maritime Joint Stock Commercial Bank | 9,399 | 0.39 | No | Yes | Banking |
| 18. | Sovico Group Joint Stock Company | 8,550 | 0.36 | No | Yes | Property |
| 19. | Bank for Foreign Trade of Vietnam JSC | 8,240 | 0.35 | No | Yes | Banking |
| 20. | Saigon Glory Company Limited | 8,000 | 0.34 | No | No | Property |
| 21. | Southeast Asia Commercial Joint Stock Bank | 7,826 | 0.33 | No | Yes | Banking |
| 22 | Bac A Commercial Joint Stock Bank | 7,535 | 0.32 | No | Yes | Banking |
| 23. | Golden Hill Real Estate JSC | 5,701 | 0.24 | No | No | Property |
| 24. | Vietnam Bank for Agriculture and Rural Development | 5,688 | 0.24 | Yes | No | Banking |
| 25. | Vingroup | 5,425 | 0.23 | No | Yes | Property |
| 26. | Sai Gon Thuong Tin Commercial Joint Stock Bank | 4,800 | 0.20 | No | Yes | Banking |
| 27. | Thai Son - Long An JSC | 4,600 | 0.19 | No | No | Property |
| 28. | VPBank SMBC Finance Company Limited | 4,500 | 0.19 | No | No | Finance |
| 29. | Phu My Hung Corporation | 4,497 | 0.19 | No | No | Property |
| 30. | Trung Nam Dak Lak 1 Wind Power JSC | 4,440 | 0.19 | No | No | Energy |
| | **Total Top 30 LCY Corporate Issuers** | **448,629** | **18.80** | | | |
| | **Total LCY Corporate Bonds** | **718,606** | **30.12** | | | |
| | **Top 30 as % of Total LCY Corporate Bonds** | **62.4%** | **62.4%** | | | |

LCY = local currency, USD = United States dollar, VND = Vietnamese dong.
Notes:
1. Data as of 30 September 2022.
2. State-owned firms are defined as those in which the government has more than a 50% ownership stake.
Sources: *AsianBondsOnline* calculations based on Bloomberg LP and Vietnam Bond Market Association data.

**Table 3: Notable Local Currency Corporate Bond Issuances in the Third Quarter of 2022**

| Corporate Issuers | Coupon Rate (%) | Issued Amount (VND billion) | Corporate Issuers | Coupon Rate (%) | Issued Amount (VND billion) |
|---|---|---|---|---|---|
| Orient Commercial Joint Stock Bank[a] | | | Vietnam Joint Stock Commercial Bank for Industry and Trade[a] | | |
| 3-year bond | 4.50 | 1,000 | 8-year bond | 0.9% + average interest rate for 12-month deposit | 195 |
| 3-year bond | – | 1,000 | 15-year bond | 6.80 | 185 |
| 3-year bond | – | 1,000 | 8-year bond | 0.9% + reference rate | 50 |
| 3-year bond | – | 500 | | | |
| 3-year bond | – | 300 | 8-year bond | 0.9% + average interest rate for 12-month deposit | 50 |
| 3-year bond | – | 300 | | | |
| 3-year bond | – | 1,000 | 15-year bond | – | 100 |
| 3-year bond | – | 500 | 8-year bond | – | 230 |
| Bank for Investment and Development of Vietnam[a] | | | 10-year bond | – | 90 |
| 8-year bond | 0.9% + average interest rate for 12-month deposit | 1,000 | 8-year bond | 1.1% + interest rate for 12-month deposit | 3,000 |
| 1.75-year bond | 4.60 | 1,500 | Asia Commercial Joint Stock Bank[a] | | |
| 1.75-year bond | 4.60 | 1,500 | 1-year bond | 4.50 | 500 |
| 8-year bond | 0.9% + reference rate | 370 | 1-year bond | – | 150 |
| | | | 1-year bond | – | 150 |
| 7-year bond | 0.75% + reference rate | 124 | 1-year bond | – | 500 |
| | | | 1-year bond | – | 1,000 |
| 15-year bond | – | 60 | 2-year bond | – | 1,500 |
| 7-year bond | – | 500 | Military Commercial and Joint Stock Bank[a] | | |
| | | | 3-year bond | 4.80 | 3,000 |
| | | | 3-year bond | – | 500 |
| | | | 7-year bond | – | 100 |

– = not available, VND = Vietnamese dong.
[a] Multiple issuance of the same tenor indicates issuance on different dates.
Source: Vietnam Bond Market Association.

Development of Vietnam came in as the second-largest issuer in Q3 2022, with bonds totaling VND5.1 trillion in multiple issuances of varied tenors. In Q3 2022, 83 new corporate bonds issued by 34 companies were added to the corporate bond stock. Of the total issuance amount, 75.1% was from firms in the banking sector.

## Investor Profile

Viet Nam's LCY government bonds are largely held by insurance and banking institutions (**Figure 2**). At the end of September 2022, 60.5% of outstanding government bonds were held by insurance companies, up from a 56.8% holdings share in September 2021. During the same review period, banking institutions' holdings share in the LCY government bond market dropped to 38.9% from 42.3%. Offshore investors continued to account for a marginal share of less than 1.0% at the end of Q3 2022.

## Ratings Update

On 28 October, Fitch Ratings affirmed Viet Nam's long-term foreign currency credit rating at BB with a positive outlook. The rating affirmation was an indication of Viet Nam's strong medium-term growth prospects, favorable external debt profile, and lower government debt compared to its peers. The positive outlook was also retained in anticipation of continued medium-term growth in Viet Nam's exports stemming from its cost competitiveness, trade diversion from the People's Republic of China, and implementation of key trade agreements despite the vulnerability of Viet Nam's economy to external shocks due to the high degree of its trade openness.

## Figure 2: Local Currency Government Bonds Investor Profile

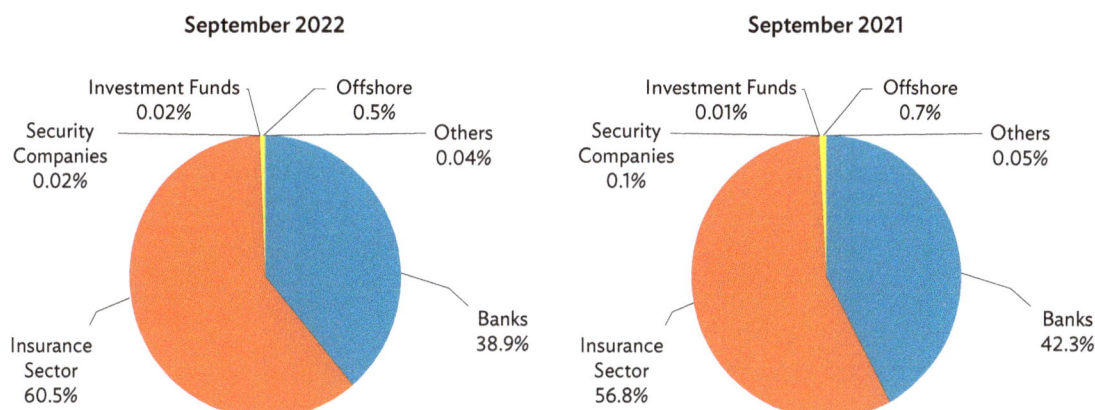

**September 2022**

- Investment Funds 0.02%
- Offshore 0.5%
- Security Companies 0.02%
- Others 0.04%
- Banks 38.9%
- Insurance Sector 60.5%

**September 2021**

- Investment Funds 0.01%
- Offshore 0.7%
- Security Companies 0.1%
- Others 0.05%
- Banks 42.3%
- Insurance Sector 56.8%

Source: Ministry of Finance, Government of Viet Nam.

# Policy, Institutional, and Regulatory Developments

## Government Releases Guidance on Offering and Trading Privately Issued Corporate Bonds

In September, the Government of Viet Nam promulgated Decree No. 65/2022/ND-CP (Decree 65) to amend the existing regulations on the offering and trading of privately issued bonds. Decree 65 aims to enhance transparency and sustainability in the bond market by tightening disclosure requirements and imposing more stringent conditions on bonds' private placements. It was developed to protect investors in several key areas, such as limiting the purpose of bond proceeds, implementing new requirements on the issuer's credit rating, and mandating additional disclosures by the issuers. Decree 65 also launches the centralized bond exchange system for bond registration and trading, which is expected to be operational by June 2023.

## State Bank of Vietnam Regulates Bank Guarantees

In September, the SBV issued Circular No. 11/2022/TT-NHNN regulating bank guarantees. The circular presents the legal framework and the practical requirements to ensure consistency with international practices and conformity with the applicable laws and regulations.

It also aims to resolve the current gaps in regulation while still ensuring the effectiveness, safety, and smooth operations of bank guarantees performed by local and foreign credit institutions. The new circular will take effect on 1 April 2023 and will replace previous circulars regulating bank guarantees that were issued in 2015 and 2017.

## State Bank of Vietnam Releases Guidance on Foreign Exchange Management for Foreign Borrowing and Foreign Debt Repayment

At the end of September, Circular No. 12/2022/TT-NHNN was issued by the SBV to provide guidelines on foreign exchange administration relating to institutions' foreign borrowings and foreign debt repayments, which are not guaranteed by the government. The new circular focuses on public administrative reform, supplementing related processes and procedures, and improving the reporting mechanism to sustain enterprises' practical needs to borrow and pay off foreign debts and meet the SBV's management objectives. The circular seeks to improve the legal framework for companies' borrowing and repayment of foreign loans, reflect the targets of public administrative reform through simplification and application of information technology in providing public services, and support companies to mobilize foreign financial resources for their business operations.

www.ingramcontent.com/pod-product-compliance
Lightning Source LLC
Chambersburg PA
CBHW042036220326
41599CB00045BA/7473